Prologue

As always, I find it best tilling
what went just before. Th
disappointment, and it cla   r
winning the league in suc.   er
Roberto Mancini was gon   ... ... ume, as the
season drew to a limp end, after the ignominy of an FA Cup final
defeat.

Mancini: The End

No one else could do it this way. No one. No other team would
dominate headlines on the eve of the biggest domestic cup final in
world football due to reports that their manager was about to be
sacked. Ah, Manchester City, it's good to have you back, just how
I remember you. You been well?

One disastrous game and a weekend of recriminations later, and he
was gone. Many commentators without a sentimental attachment
to City will not see Mancini's impending dismissal as harsh.
Supporters of other clubs have often derided his ability as a
manager, though they were probably clouded by the foolish notion
that with money at his disposal, a manager should win everything.
Now the few in the press pack that have pursued Mancini all this
time and doubted his ability can perform their traditional U-turns
and talk of City's lack of class, how hard done by Mancini is and
thus transform him into one of football's greatest martyrs. After
all, as many have already commented, City are no better than
Chelsea because they got rid of the country's 9th-longest serving
manager.

But Mancini has not been sacked for finishing second in the
Premier League. I'm not even sure he has been sacked for failing
in Europe. If he had been sacked on results alone, I'd agree it was a
disgrace, and City's official statement mentions his failure to meet
the goals set out for him. But he hasn't left just because of results,
and wailing that he has on Twitter, Facebook and message boards
doesn't change that. There are mitigating circumstances, but the

constant chatter is of a breakdown in relationships repeatedly, not only with internal staff, not only with those in the dressing room (you lose the players and you are always doomed), but also according to a friend of Mancini, his relationship with City's owner has broken down irrevocably. And if that last point is true, it makes everything else redundant. This is all speculation of course, with Stuart Brennan at the Manchester Evening News saying a lot more will come out that will show that his relationships at the club had broken down. He can't stay if this is so, though Mancini supporters will wonder how much propaganda is being fed to the media to paint a picture that suits them. Yes, the club are feeding a particular angle to the nation's journalists right now, but these stories have been around before, and there are too many of him. The sheikhs' 5-year contract for Mancini last summer showed they were not out to get him from the start, but during a truly disappointing season, Mancini has burnt his bridges.

It seems that Mancini does not help himself. You wonder if he will ever spend more than a few years at any club. He is not a people-person, he manages as he played – with fire, arguments and conflict. This is his way, and that is that. There is no right way to manage a football team, but when the results don't follow, his way starts to look flawed. He has publicly duelled with pretty much everyone at the club, and criticised players in the process, though this is a method that can bear fruit. Zabaleta and Lescott hardly rushed to his defence this weekend, whilst Joleon Lescott hardly masked his distrust of the man, but then it is not their job to fight his corner, and you can read too much into banal comments. Mancini does not manage by making friends and players can be precious souls of course. Managers can fall out with them and still succeed, it just depends which players (and how many) he falls out with. If the squad feels generally as one, then there can be no happy ending, and Mancini's many power struggles have a Machiavellian ring to them.

And let's be honest, the club has gone backwards this season. The list of truly poor performances outstrips the truly great ones. Key players appear to have gone backwards, and whilst Mancini did not get the players he wanted last summer, he still had a damn fine squad. No one season should kill off a manager at a club that once had a perpetual-motion revolving-door, but it hasn't helped when the owners want a Barcelona Mk II. And let's not get started on him not having a man upfront for opposition corners. His inability to suss out certain teams, his stubbornness, his failed 3-5-2 system (not flawed in itself, but a flop at City), his strange substitutions and his occasional inability to react during matches have all helped seal his fate. The reports that he never stepped foot in the academy could be the most damning story of all, but it's all speculation.

But he has still been let down. There is a palpable sense that he has been hung out to dry. It feels like Mancini has been a dead man walking since the day he was appointed. Rumours of his demise have followed him around like a loyal dog since the start. Questions about Mancini's future should have been banned from press conferences. No further discussion should have been allowed. This is the man that brought the club success, and is a legend to most fans. If he leaves, it feels all a bit tawdry that it is happening like this.

City's PR department is widely lauded as one of the best in the country by journalists, though you wonder how much of that is due to City being so accommodating. Either way, it is clear that this PR department was nowhere to be found on the two days before the Cup Final when journalists were keen to know if there was any truth in the Pellegrini rumours. But having said that, I'm not sure what else City could have done about the rumours, which were little more than irregular betting patterns. If, as seems the case, the rumours are true, they couldn't confirm it obviously. Nor could they lie and deny it. Perhaps a quick statement about a review at the end of the season and Mancini having their full support for the rest for the season may have helped? Whatever, the team was a disgrace at Wembley. Whatever is going on behind the scenes, no player should need encouragement to perform in an FA Cup final, especially against a depleted relegation-threatened opposition. Still, hysterical wailing on Twitter for news and a campaign to get Vicky Kloss sacked makes us all look like idiots. Classy. After all, I'm sure Vicky decides City's policy herself, and gets no guidance from above (#sarcasm). To think that Vicky is solely to blame for any PR gaffes is buffoonery of the highest order, unless you know something we mere mortals don't. Criticise City's PR all you want, but the perceived mistakes do not come from one person. And Mancini made spats public as part of his own agenda, so don't blame City's PR for not clearing up the mess every time.

As for making the announcement a year to the day after we won the title, I really couldn't care less. Nothing will ever diminish that day. Fans were wailing for days for City to make a statement, and when they did, they bemoaned the timing. Damned if you do, damned if you don't. Once the decision to remove Mancini had been made, and the news had leaked, his position was untenable. We all wanted to say goodbye next Sunday, but it wasn't a realistic wish.

But as the owners move on, the Pellegrini rewriting of history has begun, before he has arrived. I didn't want Mancini to be sacked, but I can still be excited at the possibilities of our new manager, a man who gets the most out of squads, who maximizes potential, a people-person who will fit into the ethos of the owners' vision and embrace the new academy. Quoting a lack of trophies won (whilst ignoring the trophies won outside Europe) is a very simplistic viewpoint considering that the likes of Mancini or Ferguson could not have done more with Pellegrini's Malaga and Villareal squads, and his single season at Real Madrid saw a 96-point haul and the sale of two key players against his wish. And if a single season of failure is an argument not to hire someone, presumably it's enough to dismiss Mancini too.

The owners are not interested in sentiment. They didn't go to Lincoln or Wycombe, or have 25 years of taunts from across the city (and beyond) rammed down their throats. They aren't swayed by a lovely video of Mancini with an emotional soundtrack on vimeo, nor obsessed at ripping THAT banner down. They are interested in making City one of the greatest clubs in the world, and will act accordingly to reach that aim. They are looking at the widest of pictures, and are planning long-term. And if you don't like it, well tough, because without them we wouldn't have any silverware, we wouldn't have our Aguerooooooo moment, and we'd be discussing on Bluemoon whether it was worth taking a punt on bringing Joey Barton back to the club whilst bemoaning finishing 8th in the Championship. Harsh I know, as we are all entitled to express our disquiet at anything that happens at the club we love, but the truth is harsh, and perhaps we can't handle it. I wanted stability and perseverance at this club, but it seems that will have to wait, for now.

But the vast majority of City fans are deeply upset at Mancini leaving. They don't care about internal rifts, PR (until now), or how much money we spend. All they know is that the last three years have been the best of our football-supporting lives. Roberto Mancini was the man who brought us our first trophy in 35 years. He was the man that brought us our first league title in 44 years. He brought us one of the greatest moments of our lives. He masterminded a 6-1 win at Old Trafford, and a Wembley win over United. He challenged Ferguson, he argued with him on the touchline, he brought success, and he punched the air in delight with the rest of us at the madness of it all. He had style, panache and a winning smile. He was, as Sam Wallace commented, a perfectionist at an imperfect club. All those memories he gave us will never be forgotten, in a wonderful period in this club's long history.
And I swear, we'll never see anything like it again.

The Summer of 2013

This is how it is supposed to be at City. A summer of uncertainty, speculation, rumours, and the appearance of a rudderless ship. It was a mirage really though.

The appointment of Manuel Pellegrini was a "done deal" for almost a month, with the odd story coming out of Real Madrid wanting him, Barcelona wanting him, PSG wanting him, then Porto wanting him. In the end it was said to be a small contract dispute that delayed the inevitable, but eventually the announcement of City's new manager was made, though it was not until the first days of July that Manuel Pellegrini actually got his feet behind an Etihad Stadium desk.

City fans raised £7000 to put an advert in La Gazzetta Dello Sport thanking Roberto Mancini, a nice touch, but I had better things to spend my money on, like PPI payments and salt and pepper spare ribs.

For the start of the post-Mancini era, there was PR work to be done with the bizarre spectacle of a post-season batch of friendlies versus Chelsea in New York, as the club sowed the seeds for the birth of a new "sister-club" in the Big Apple. The games themselves were actually highly entertaining.

The Summer Rumbles On

The bore of a close season in a year that ends with an odd number was clear for all to see this week as the newspapers continued to scramble around for non-stories to fill their pages. The Mirror discussed the possibility of Manchester City and United getting "Groups of Death" in the Champions League draw, by choosing the worst case scenario for a draw that was many, many weeks away. They may as well discuss the possibility of City and United drawing each other in the FA Cup next January, and their fears were not surprisingly unfounded.

Transfer gossip is the bread and butter of the football journalist during the summer months, and Manchester City have been linked with over 100 players, their situation akin to Jupiter aligning with Saturn during the winter equinox, or something. A new manager, a need to strengthen after poor dealings the previous summer, plus funds to spend. A football writer's dream. With Manchester United and Chelsea also under new management, there is enough conjecture to power a medium-sized African country.

Then there is the excitement of the announcement of the fixture lists, manna from heaven for the conspiracy theorists, most of whom happen to be football managers. Roy Hodgson complained, as some of his England squad may be required to run around for up to 90 minutes the week before an important qualifier.

And then there was Isco….. apparently a done deal, the player eventually plumped for Real Madrid and a whole fan-base cried. I wrote a sarcastic open letter, as a riposte to the ridiculous overreaction by a minority of our fans to missing out on one player and the usual avalanche of criticism the club received as a result.

An Open Letter To Txiki Begiristain & Ferran Soriano.

Hello Txiki, hello Ferran. I hope you follow my blog and read this.
You're probably too busy though. Why you'd claim to be busy
I've no idea.

You see, we're hurting Txiki, Ferran. (Can I call you that? Good.)
We're hurting bad. We thought a new hero was arriving on our
beachless shores. We were told it was nailed on by
tribalfootball.com and the Daily Mirror. It was 1/12 on Skybet. So
as a result we've bought the shirts, some have even got the tattoo,
and if those people don't like discos, then there's no going back.
We'd even written a song. It's been a painful few days.
An as we deal with this hurt, this raw pain inside us, we need
answers.

Smoke and mirrors.

I think it's necessary to give you a brief education on our proud
club. And there is a reason for this.
You see, the City of old wouldn't have stumbled around like a
blind, drunken tramp trapped in a badly-chosen metaphor. They'd
have acted decisively. They would have blown the competition out
of the water to get Lee Bradbury from Portsmouth. They'd have
put their money where their mouth is to complete the exciting
capture of Jon Macken from the illustrious Preston North End.
They'd pounce on any player who had a half-decent game against
them, be it a competitive match, a pre-season friendly or even a
testimonial, or snapped up anyone that had a nifty youtube
compilation online.
They'd have used the money set aside to repair a crumbling
Kippax stand to capture a player on their radar.
They knew how to deal in the transfer market. Sod the
consequences, they knew how to get their man, even if it meant
paying double the asking price and placing the club into
administration.
And the City of old would not be found scrambling around on
transfer deadline day for cheap cuts. Yes there was that Mido bloke
that we kept trying to get, and we did sign Benjani in September,
but those were the exceptions to the rule. With Swales, Lee or

Bernstein in charge, City acted quickly and decisively. We were no one's mugs.

But how times change. Yet again, City have been bullied out of a potential transfer by a lesser club. Real Madrid? Fake Madrid more like. Bayern Munich? Never heard of them. Manchester United? Don't make me laugh.

All it takes is some bloke called Zidane to waltz in and sign the player. It's embarrassing. Why wasn't one of our club legends on the phone to Isco to persuade him? Where's Ged Brannan? What's Buster Phillips up to? Why are we not utilising the pulling power of Adrian Heath?

I ask you this. What are we paying you for? PR campaigns in New York? Sound bites? Pointless academy campuses? It's a mystery to me, to be honest.

And why the lack of communication? I lost a whole weekend scrolling through a 3427* page thread on Bluemoon for updates on the Isco saga, before realising there wasn't a scrap of new news on there. Fans needed to know what was happening, it is their right to see a club respond to every piece of transfer speculation posted on social media sites by WUMS and your silence on the matter has been deafening and quite frankly disappointing.

Why did you not comment on the rumour that Isco had flown into Barton airfield at 5am on Sunday? Why did you not comment on the rumour that Isco was seen looking at maisonettes in Audenshaw last Wednesday? Why the radio silence once news broke that Adie Mike's private jet company had a plane chartered for Malaga? Why Txiki, why?!

A simple response to each incident and you could have knocked a good 3000 pages off that Isco thread in a heartbeat. For once think of the fans, especially the really needy ones.

Now I've never seen Isco play, but City should have moved heaven and earth to get him. With his signing, City would have dominated European football for 30 years, maybe more. Txiki (if that's really your name), you need to take a long, hard look at yourself. Preferably in a mirror. I once read on caughtoffside.com that Isco was available for just £7m two years ago, so why didn't you two go for him then? You purport to be professional high-level businessmen, yet some of your dealings are more akin to those of the Chuckle Brothers. To me, to you. Yet again, City are the laughing stock of world football. I'm beginning to wonder if you share our ambition for this club.

How many times must City be snubbed? Players used to queue up to play for us. Geoff Thomas would have crawled over broken glass to play for us (and still have passed the medical). George Weah had a picture of Neil McNab on his bedroom wall as a kid. Yes we have signed two players already, but no one else wanted them so it was hardly difficult. Even an Apprentice reject could have closed those deals. Maybe even Brian Marwood. I mean, who's heard of Fernandinho? Even Jo gets to play for Brazil ahead of him. Jesus Navas? How full of yourself do you have to be to call yourself that? I'll say it as it is - I don't like him.

I was under the impression that you two were hired to bridge the gap between City and the likes of Real Madrid and Barcelona. And yet over 6 months later, those two clubs still seem to be a bigger draw to players. Do you not consider yourself to have failed? Will you be resigning? I won't hold my breath. If I had such a catalogue of failure at the bank I work in, I'd have been out on my ear ages ago.

So this is a plea from all City fans, on whose behalf I speak. Get your act together, make us proud, and restores some superbia (pride) in our proelio (battle) to be the bestest team in the world. It's the least we deserve.

* Update: 6327 pages.

And then to make matters, worse, Carlos Tevez finally departed our shores, having polished off a fraction of his community service.

The Longest Goodbye

And so the class of 2012 loses another pupil. The one who wouldn't conform, was passionate about his beliefs, but a bit of a slow learner. The rebel and the truant. He stood up to the big boys across the road, but he was always just passing through. By the time he left, those boys didn't seem that big anymore anyway.

Carlos Tevez has moved on, signing for Juventus, the old lady, on a 3-year deal, whilst Wayne Rooney looks on in envy. Tevez's stay at City has seemed to run parallel with his old manager Roberto Mancini. Both seemed poised to leave as soon as they arrived (if you believed the press), both were successful but flawed, their baggage enough to incur a £10,000 surcharge with Ryanair.

Have no doubt though – Carlos Tevez was as important as any other player in the rise of Manchester City. Some City fans have proclaimed that Tevez is the best player they have seen in a City shirt. Not for me, and in ten years he certainly won't be, but for a short while he dragged the club kicking and screaming to the top level. In terms of influence on the club, maybe he was the best. He was a statement of intent signing for City, turning down United in the process, he riled them whenever he played against them thereafter, he battled and battled, he always wanted to win, an don the pitch he shirked no challenges.
He was adaptable, and worked the front line. He was too wild for me with his final shot much of the time, but he was always involved in play so it wasn't always going to come off. He could score out of nothing because he never gave up. Looking at his top twenty goals on City's official site and you realise that he won't be easy to replace. But it's easy to be swayed by a compilation video, especially if it's on youtube and the music's right.

There was always something with Tevez though. A desire to feel wanted. His desire to be closer to his family. The desire to play one day for his boyhood club. The lure of Argentinean golf courses. The boredom at Manchester's two restaurants. The inability to grasp the English language. The footballer's vanity that made him incapable of adhering to the Highway Code. The inability to comprehend the ramifications of a driving ban. The villain of an adviser. The ludicrous wages. The fall-out. The strike and exile. The teeth.

The events in Munich and beyond removed the possibility of Tevez ever becoming a club legend. His claim that he had simply refused to warm-up again, thus causing a misunderstanding with Mancini has some merit, but is undermined by the different account he gave immediately after the match. His subsequent strike and temporary emigration was indefensible.
His return to English shores was a driving force in City wrenching back the title from United in the 11/12 season, though the point must be made that if he hadn't buggered off in the first place then City might have already wrapped up the title. The fact is, in City's greatest season in a generation and more, Tevez wasn't actually there for most of it.

But his work rate will be hard to replace. City fans were slated for welcoming back the exiled Tevez, but apart from the fact that most fans are hypocrites with short memories who would sell their soul for success, the fact is that Tevez always gave 100% on the pitch, something fans always appreciate. On top of that, City needed him, he had been punished for his mistakes, financially and otherwise and it seemed he had patched up his differences with the manager. And if Roberto Mancini, a man who can make enemies over a misplaced pass could forgive him, then surely the fans could too. Talk of cancelling his contract and sacking him and thus making a moral stand was drivel - football clubs are businesses, and don't give away their greatest assets.
What's more, a little part of me always suspected the blame for the Munich madness was not totally one-sided. Mancini and Tevez are both fiery, passionate characters, and Mancini manages through

conflict. The manager was a willing conduit for the war that followed.

I wanted Tevez to stay, but I'm not devastated he is leaving. The club is at a level now that a player leaving does not throw them off course, and he will be replaced. Because Tevez the man has little to admire, there won't be many tears amongst the disappointment. Financially, City's decision to sell a player, thus saving £27m compared to him leaving for nothing next summer, makes perfect sense. Financial Fair Play is here and City will adhere to it, pathetic as it is. His contribution last season was not sufficient to take such a hit. Tevez hit a purple patch in the second half of the season, but also went over two months without a league goal. He had more assists than anyone however, but it was a low-key season for all of City's attacking players. Manuel Pellegrini will bring with him new systems, and it is hoped that contributions can be more evenly spread out across the pitch.

So goodbye Carlos, thanks, and good luck. A player to admire, not love, but who did his bit in getting his club to the top table of European football. He leaves England leaving a trail of controversy, but also a wave of appreciation from every club for whom he played. It's a loss to Manchester City and to the English Premier League as a whole, but Carlos Tevez was never one for setting down roots. He brought relative success to every team he represented, and now it's Juventus' turn to reap the benefits – though not for too long.

An unusual summer holiday location this year, namely St. Petersburg (the Russian one) and football geekery meant I had to take the metro (the world's deepest and most ornate, if you're remotely interested) so see Zenit St. Petersburg's stadium. It is a small stadium, holding a mere 20,000, but it was one to tick off the list, and soon (well, 2018) they will move to a much bigger ground further out of town. Still, it was nice to see a City scarf hanging up in the dusty window of the club shop. Nobody knows our name.

Transfer Speculation

With the Isco transfer saga still fresh in many a disappointed City fan's mind (alleviated slightly by a lively performance for Spain by Jesus Navas last week), the latest batch of transfer gossip in the national newspapers has caused wailing and gnashing of teeth aplenty by a minority of fans who expect us to be hovering up the world's best talent from this point onwards.

It's understandable – after all, the capture of Fred or Negredo might actually benefit Manchester City greatly in the future, but the signings wouldn't stir the loins like a Cavani/Falcao unveiling. However, it's rather arrogant to dismiss a striker available for £1.7m who will probably lead the favourites for next year's World Cup.

Certainly City have a good amount of money to splash, even within Financial Fair play restrictions. It is thought the City will save £30m a year now that certain high-earners such as Kolo Toure, Carlos Tevez and Wayne Bridge are off the wage bill (more on that later). Future signings won't be earning these levels of money, with wage structures linked to incentivised bonuses. Quite simply, win stuff and they'll earn more. Apart from the inflated fee Napoli are asking for Edison Cavani, the rumours of him wanting massive wages would alone kill any possible deal with City. They are not going to be paying any player £250,000 a week, however long the media and certain rival fans continue to portray the club as "moneybags City" who flash the cash around. Expect Chelsea to comfortably outspend City this summer, without a word of criticism.

The important thing to consider with Isco is that he was not a vital purchase when looking at how to strengthen the squad this summer. Without the appointment of Pellegrini, City probably wouldn't have even tried to sign him, but once it was clear that the Chilean was to take over from Roberto Mancini, then it is likely that his close relationship with the player was used to try and snatch him from Real Madrid's grasp. And for a while, it seemed like this approach would work. Now that it hasn't, there is no desperate need to sign a similar type of player. City have signed two good midfielders this summer, and as of yet not sold any.

What is needed now of course is a striker. Add to that a left-back, a centre-back and quite possibly competition for Joe Hart, and that is where attention will probably focus over the next two months. Pellegrini has often played with a single striker, so it's a bit early to be jumping off cliffs at the lack of striking options City possess right now, but the club will want to tie up deals as soon as possible.

Having said all that, I wouldn't dismiss just yet the scenario of City signing Edison Cavani, but Chelsea must surely be favourites at the moment (*how wrong was I?*).

In the long-term, the hope is that the new academy will bring players through to the first-team, though that point may be some time away. There is also the aspiration that a group of top-class English players will be included in this group, and looking at this summer's U21 & U20 tournaments, where England were quite simply abysmal, this could be the toughest task of all. Let's hope that the state-of-the-art academy can teach some of our youngsters the technical side of the game over physicality and old-fashioned notions of getting it into the mixer and substituting skill with effort and passion. A bit of everything would be perfect, but if English players are going to succeed in the future, then they have to be technically efficient and totally comfortable on the ball.

In the meantime. City are not going to be hunting down galacticos signings. Pellegrini is renowned for getting the most out of players, and that is where success will come – maximising what the club already has. With a couple of additions, there is little need for further strengthening, and then it is down to the players to justify their wages, and for the manager to mould a team that suits his philosophy. There is plenty to look forward to.

Away from City, and the summer had little sport to keep me busy, but having dipped into the Confederations Cup mostly out of desperation, it was far more entertaining than I had expected. A gap had been successfully bridged.

Back home, and there was little going on. So instead, here's the timeline of when football goes bad......

The Various Stages of a Football Outrage

A footballer does a BAD THING. To make matters worse, the referee doesn't punish him at the time of the incident.

Twitter goes into meltdown.

The offender's manager comments that he isn't that sort of player.

High profile player? The Sky Sports Trial begins.

This can last weeks, more than a real-life murder trial. It begins with a 24/7 looping replay of said incident. This incident will be slowed down to virtually a standstill and replayed from numerous angles.

An ex-player who can just about (on a good day) string a sentence together will be wheeled into the studio to give his views, which will include being horrified, may well contain a hint of xenophobia (if the offending player is from foreign parts), and will probably hark back to the good old days.

Ollie Holt will bemoan the lack of black managers in the game.

An ex-referee may also be called upon to give his expert opinion.

These opinions will then appear as news articles on Sky's (and many others') websites.

If this is a very high-profile club, there may be the need to interview a police commissioner.

"If he'd done that in the street, he'd be arrested," the commissioner will state with a straight face.

(Let's face it, we all know someone who has served " time" after going in knee-high on someone with a slide-tackle outside Greenhalgh's.)

Finally, Sky may merge in some "vox-pops" with members of the public, though only those that are disgusted and wish to repeat the line about him being-arrested-if-he-did-that-in-the-street.

Articles will now appear in newspapers. At least one football journalist will unfavourably compare football to rugby, or if the incident occurs during a certain year, the Olympics. Ollie Holt will bemoan the lack of black managers in the game.

Fans of the club of the offending player will point out that other players have done worse things before.

Fans of the club of the offending player will point out that the recipient of the tackle/punch/stream of saliva "made a meal out of it". Mental notes will be made to boo the fouled player vociferously the next eighteen times the two clubs meet.

Reports emerge that the police are investigating the incident after a member of the public made an official complaint.

The FA announce that there will be no further action against the player as the referee dealt with it at the time.

Twitter goes into meltdown again. It crashes for three hours, meaning posting a tweet takes a whole morning.

Two hundred and seventy articles are published slamming the FA. Various journalists comment on how they have now lost all credibility. Ollie Holt will bemoan the lack of black managers in the game.

Another footballer does a BAD THING…………

City's Media Presence

This week, the excellent Inside City video series continued with a clip following Manuel Pellegrini around as he spent his first day at City, beginning with the moment he left the airport.

Whilst very little of any note actually happened, it was still an interesting snippet into the inside machinations of the club. You do wonder however how happy our new manager was to be photographed and filmed during every moment of the day. I half expected a clip under a toilet door showing a pair of trousers around ankles. I'm not sure I could put up with that level of intrusion all the time, and Pellegrini had the look of a man wearing a forced smile.

After all, no doubt he is keen just to get on with his job. Arriving in a new country at a new club is a tiresome and stressful process, and the sooner he is settled the better. How nice of our owners though to provide him with over a week of beautiful weather. I hope Pellegrini doesn't think this is normal.

The big news however at City hasn't yet been announced and it is creating more anguish amongst the City faithful. You see, last week City made it clear (via yet another email) that City had a "big July Announcement". This was manna from heaven for those City fans that like to spend every waking minute speculating on future City-related occurrences, mostly transfer-linked.

Every possibility has been discussed. A stadium expansion. A huge transfer unveiling. Maybe even a new range of pies. Anger grew however when City failed to make this BIG JULY ANNOUNCEMENT by the close of play on July 1st (a.k.a. midnight). Yet again the club were treating their fans like scum. And now it's July 5th, and still not a word from the club, and there are only 25 days left in the month.

The announcement, when it comes, will be about something that I consider a lovely touch by the club, a GOOD THING. It's something no other club has done to the best of my knowledge, and is pretty exciting. Rest assured however, that after the announcement, a minority of vocal City fans will whinge and moan because the club had built up this BIG ANNOUNCEMENT and as it turned out it wasn't the unveiling of Lionel Messi, free season tickets for all for life, or heated, padded seats and free beer in the South Stand. Of course the fact that the impending announcement has only been built up due to idle speculation on message boards has escaped most of these fans, but never mind. Fans will just have to put up with transfers being announced the normal way, normal seats, and various other unique opportunities and privileges that no other City owner has ever offered. It's a hard life.

A New Manager Arrives

So on a seemingly random day in July, Manchester City's new manager Manuel Pellegrini held his first press conference, an opportunity for the new man to sit through thirty minutes of bone-headed pea-brained questions that brought no insight into anything City or Pellegrini-related. Needless to say that Manchester United were brought up on numerous occasions, allowing a certain United blogger to pen a whole article calling City obsessed. Good to see irony not only alive and well, but seemingly intent on taking over the world.

Press conferences are 99.8% of the time utterly tedious affairs, and I am led to believe that Pellegrini came across well, as expected, as did one of City's new signings, Fernandinho, a player clearly excited to be at the club if his online presence is anything to go by. Both also appear to be really nice chaps. I will never watch the press conference.

Of course the timing of the press conference may be more to do with the upcoming tour of South Africa, a tour that certain sections of the media reported last week may be abandoned if the gravely-ill Nelson Mandela was to die in the meantime, a period of mourning excluding the right to play football matches. As it stands, this does not appear to be an issue, and the tour goes ahead.

David Moyes' first press conference generated live coverage on Sky and five pages of coverage in the Manchester Evening News. Needless to say, Manuel Pellegrini didn't get such coverage, but had the honour of having his trophy-winning record questioned in print this morning, an honour David Moyes mysteriously avoided. Of course Moyes is the successor to Alex Ferguson, so the coverage makes more sense when factoring that in. Moyes may get more support from journalists by virtue of being both a familiar face and British, but I sense that Pellegrini's charm will win many over. After all, such a pleasant demeanour allowed Roberto Martinez an easy ride whilst taking his team to relegation.

Elsewhere, and the long-awaited big July announcement by Manchester City was finally made – CityLive. This is an event at Manchester Central on August 8th, kind of a pre-season party, including Jason Manford, music acts (to be confirmed, which may explain the delay in the announcement), player awards, the unveiling of the manager and new signings, a Q & A with Pellegrini, and a few surprises on top. The reaction was predictably cool from sections of City fans, who expect everything for nothing nowadays, or perhaps were put off by the likening of the event to the brash MTV music awards.

And then there was the price. £25 sounds steep, but when you look at the venue, it isn't really. A single comedian can cost that much to see (and more), so I fail to see why this event is considered extortionate considering the variety of what's on offer. Yes City could have made it slightly cheaper, and there are claims that this party is merely a money-making exercise, but like any other "product", no one is forced to purchase it, so if you don't like it, don't go, and let those that do want to enjoy it, without the constant background drone of whinging fans.

It's been said (by me) a million times already, but if you want a world-class team in a 60,000 seat stadium with brilliant facilities, a world-class media/online presence, a world-class academy and still some of the best-value season tickets in the Premier League, all under the umbrella of Financial Fair Play, then the owners of our club are going to try and generate revenue. You can choose when to spend. Having said that, City fans have been treated to free music in the past, from the rather ill-thought-out finale to the Maine Road era, to the Doves gig in the car park, an event naturally accompanied by tremendous amounts of rain water. Barring a leak in the roof, at least those that attend #citylive will be dry.

The Psychology Of A Transfer Saga

There was a good article by Nick Miller last week on football365.com about the fevered sense of hope/anticipation/expectation from Manchester United fans over the possible signing of Thiago Alcantara from Barcelona. A footballer with relatively little top-level experience and thus still a developing player, Thiago has been built up by many as the answer to all of United fans' prayers, the missing link in their troublesome midfield and a statement of intent for the coming seasons.

As Miller pointed out: "Thiago could be just what United need, and at the price mentioned it's potentially superb business, but it's tricky to escape the feeling that he is being built up far too much by a fan base who desperately need something to cling onto."

He does after all look to be an excellent player, who should only get better, but let's not compare him to Iniesta, Maradona and Pele just yet.

But this is a natural cycle for any football fan when linked to a well-regarded player, and more so when a subsequent transfer saga spreads out over many weeks.

We've all been here. Manchester City fans have been to this special place this summer, the place of clicking refresh every thirty seconds on a football message board eagerly awaiting the latest piece of idle speculation that may tip the balance in your club's favour. This was the summer of the 2000-page* thread on Isco on Bluemoon. Last year it was Hazard et al.
(* a rough estimate)

But the process of time and the process of waiting and waiting for a player to decide his future can have a strange effect on us all. When I first heard about City's alleged interest in Pepe, I was mortified. I even had to sit down to take in the news. However, as time has progressed, the rumours have persisted and the saga has rumbled on, I have warmed to the idea more and more with each passing day. Then I found out that he actually has an excellent disciplinary record over the past couple of years and suddenly in my world that youtube clip of him kicking Getafe captain

Francisco Casquero then stamping on him before trying to fight the whole of the opposition team and referee can now be dismissed in my mind as merely a "momentary loss of composure". I crave the positive reports on what he could bring to my club, whilst turning my nose up at anything remotely negative. The desire to snap him up grows with every passing day.

The Robbie Fowler transfer was another saga that towards its end I was offering limbs in exchange for the completion of his move to City. The move was a disastrous idea of course as David Bernstein foresaw quite clearly, resulting in his exit from the club, but it rumbled on for so long that I slowly became achingly desperate for it to go through, blinded to the folly of it all, and convinced that he could recreate past glories and drive City to a better place. In the end that place was almost administration.

A few years back, Benjani Mwaruwari had been banging them in for Portsmouth, so it seemed like a good purchase for City and their modest ambitions at that time as they swooped for the Zimbabwean hitman. I also liked his goal celebration, not that it made much sense. The fact that Harry Redknapp didn't seem too bothered in letting him go should have raised a few alarm bells, but never mind, he was probably getting a cut (that is of course sarcasm on my part – perish the thought). Further alarm bells should have given City's hierarchy tinnitus when said player managed to fall asleep in an airport and miss his flight (twice), but City ploughed on like a club who once made Paul Lake "run off" his cruciate ligament injury. When the transfer was eventually completed some days after the transfer window had slammed shut, I was ecstatic. What a coup. City had strengthened their squad at the last minute, and the future was bright once more.

It's the psychology of a transfer saga. City have long been linked with Osvaldo, Negredo, Jovetic, Pepe, Ronaldo, Di Maria, Rooney, Pizarro, Marquinhos, Falcao, Soldado, Higuain and many more, and I want City to sign them all. Thankfully, City's Spanish executive team like to think a little differently, and won't bung millions to an agent or father to get a deal done. And despite the fans' aching desire to get some big name signings completed, that's probably for the best. City could have had Hazard, Martinez and De Rossi, but they could also have broken the bank for Kaka, Terry and more. It all evens out in the end.

City's Transfer Dealings – A Summary

As Brad Pitt might say, it was "inevitable".

Manchester City have moved quickly (for once) and tied up the majority of their summer transfer business with six weeks of the window remaining, replacing two departed strikers with 2 new additions, whilst also bolstering the midfield with two other signings, all done in the nick of time as Manchester's once-in-a-decade hot-spell seems to be coming to an end. And as sure as night follows day, the accusations have begun about City trying to buy success, about them sticking up two fingers to the financial fair play regulations and to them once more killing football, because there seem to be no limits on how many times one football club can commit murderous acts.

And as usual, the accusations come from a position of such utter ignorance it is hard to get wound up. It's an ignorance that comes from just looking at transfer fees, and basing a club's expenditure on that alone. Of course there is also the small matter of wages, and it is wages that truly marks out the big teams, as naturally the top players have wages to suit, and over the course of a contract, the cost can be staggering.

City's new executive team, acutely aware of financial fair play regulations, and intent on meeting them, have been all too aware of City's wage bill as City offered big money to attract top players to join in their revolution. Thus, with the sort of wheeler-dealing that Derek Trotter would be proud of, City haven't really that much at all, compared to their previous costs.

As it turns out, City's net expenditure this summer so far has been estimated to have been around £25m. Looking at transfer fees alone, it is approaching £70m, but it is in wages that City are reaping the rewards. Not forgetting (as critics conveniently have) that City sold Mario Balotelli for a fee approaching £20m in the January transfer window, and did not replace him, thus saving millions in wages over the remainder of the season, City have also offloaded many of their biggest earners whilst signing players on much lower wages with incentivised extras. Carlos Tevez was the biggest earner of all, thought to be on a cool £250,000 a week, and thus by replacing him with someone like Negredo, who is reported to be on under a third of that amount, City recoup £35m over a four-year contract. It is thus cheaper in theory to give away the likes of Tevez and Balotelli and buy replacements for £20m+ on lower wages.

When you factor in City getting rid of the likes of other huge earners like Kolo Toure, Wayne Bridge, Maicon and Roque Santa Cruz, then their new recruitment drive is actually costing very little indeed in the long-term, if you compare it to sticking with the squad of old instead. City's hierarchy do not intend to pay silly wages in future. Incentives will be built into contracts that rewards success. As success brings monetary reward, it will be the case that players will only earn extra when City do likewise. City's owners are not stupid, and have been fully observant of financial fair play rules, even hosting meetings with UEFA in the past. Those critics thinking City will be punished for ignoring such rules are going to be sorely disappointed.

All the while, large swathes of Manchester United fans are hoping for signs that the rumours of Ronaldo's return for £80m or the £60m bid for Gareth Bale or the £30m (plus bonuses) swoop for Cesc Fabregas are true, and if in some parallel universe United did sign them all, you can guarantee there wouldn't be a single comment in the media about the extent of their spending, what with it being part of their organic growth of course. This is not a dig at United per se, more the way City's spending is still perceived. City or United could sign Ronaldo for £80m and theoretically it wouldn't cost them a penny as he is a cash-cow for any team he represents - Real Madrid's Ronaldo shirt sales alone are thought to have paid for his move to Madrid from Manchester United.

Now that City have been consistently linked with Pepe, and also a Benfica winger costing close to £30m, signings that would really get rival fans frothing at the mouth. Never mind that some players may leave at some point (taking their wages with them) for considerable fees, and let's ignore the money paid for Tevez and Maicon, modest as it may have been.

City haven't disregarded financial fair play. If they had, they'd have paid for Cavani and Falcao if possible, and the City of 2009 may well have done that. But times have changed, and the criticisms of old were tiresome two years ago, let alone now. One day, everyone will realise that. Don't hold your breath just yet though.

CityLive Review

So the much-ridiculed and derided CityLive event came around last night, an event I felt like a social pariah for daring to attend. I mean, how dare City put on an event and charge admission whilst not forcing people to go! How dare they! The insatiable need for revenue means we can all expect more events like this, which seems to have offended many, but this is modern football. As a fan you're perfectly entitled to stay at home and whine about it on message boards instead.

To be fair, I wasn't sure what to expect myself. There was always a nagging doubt that it would be a disaster, that it was an idea that just wouldn't work. Thankfully that wasn't the case.

The event was billed as a sell-out. Or as City put it, "a sell-out to capacity". This led to further criticisms that City's initial ambitions had been rather-scaled down, reducing the capacity to 4,000 and being forced to sell cheaper standing tickets to get numbers in, whilst giving away plenty of freebies. The initial blurb seemed to mention 10,000 fans being there, a number that was never mentioned again. Manchester Central holds just under 13,000 standing spectators, but the event last night appeared to be full, with seats to the back. There was an extra area at the entrance for drink and food stands, but that is always there, for any gig. There was space down the sides too, but anyway, the place looked packed to the rafters bar the occasional empty seat, which was good to see. Perhaps everything was squeezed in to give the impression of a full house, including bringing the stage forward. So if City made one mistake above all it was to overestimate the demand for the event, and to perhaps overcharge. £25 is a fair amount for what was on offer, but cheaper tickets would naturally have led to greater sales, and thus charging more may well be something of a false economy. If the primary function of the night was to earn revenue, I think it's fair to say it wasn't a resounding success.

Anyway, here are my thoughts on the event itself:

The show was professional. This shouldn't be a surprise any more, this was not organised by Peter Swales.

Jake Humphrey was a good, professional host. In addition, being a Norwich City supporter allowed him to compliment City without a bitter edge to his words.

The opening montage and the Bert Trautmann section were very enjoyable – my only gripe is that both sections weren't long enough – I wanted more. Still, however many times I have watched THAT goal (and it's over 200 times by now), it was nice to watch it with thousands of fellow City fans.

The interviews with manager and players were ok, nothing more. I expected the advertised "Q & A" with Pellegrini to be somewhat more substantial.

And likewise, the player awards were unspectacular but enjoyable.

The only bit that failed for me was the quiz. It didn't bore me, and there was entertainment to be had from guessing the answers, but I felt it disrupted the rhythm of the night, as proceedings had been rattling along prior to that.

Jason Manford was excellent. I'd heard some of the stuff before, which was to be expected as I have seen him live four times before, but he didn't disappoint and it raised the night onto a higher level by having him there, by adding extra variety to proceedings. I've seen hundreds of live comedy gigs but this was unique in that it was football-orientated and playing to a like-minded crowd.

As for Miles Kane, he was fine. It's all a matter of taste of course, and it was disappointing that Primal Scream pulled out, but his replacement put on an energetic set. It's just a shame most people left before he came on stage.

I think the players will be impressed at the show that was put on for them. It was nice that for once there was no cynicism, and every player got a cheer, be it Nastastic, Aguero, Sinclair or Kolarov.

Overall, the night was a success. And judging by the survey being sent out to non-attendees, it will be a regular fixture. It appeals to a certain demographic, and clearly isn't for everyone. But there's something for everyone at the club nowadays – including some rather nice football.

But £4.50 for a plastic bottle of Heineken? Unbelievable.

And come on Sergio, at least learn a bit of English. If Wayne Rooney can manage it, anyone can.

Adnan Januzaj – Believe The Hype

Please note this entire article is fabricated, a parody of the fawning articles United's latest academy product was the subject of.

It was the final game of the 2012/13 season. It was the end of the Alex Ferguson era, an era that finished predictably with silverware, glory and with the rest trailing in their wake. As the West Brom game came to an end, a grey cloud moved ominously over the Hawthorns and a single drop of rain fell upon the turf. We could be forgiven for believing that Matt Busby had shed a solitary tear as he watched from above, content that the legacy of Manchester United had lived on.

Sitting on the bench, next to the imperious Ryan Giggs and the legendary Paul Scholes, two players who seem to have defeated time itself, sat a young man with a young face, who did not look out of place amongst his peers. Soon the world will hear a lot more about Adnan Januzaj.

On United's popular message boards, there has been an orgasmic explosion of moist anticipation at the latest prodigy to roll off United's over-worked conveyor belt. United have carefully nurtured Januzaj since kindly taking him off Anderlecht's hands two years ago. Janujaz is special. With feet so quick he can create a sonic boom, he will mesmerize opposing players, twist their blood and leave them forlorn on the floor for decades to come. He is the link between past and present, he is United's north, their south, their east their west. He is their working week and perhaps may be their Super Sunday best.

Over at the Etihad, where oil money rules and excessive splurges on fashionable players is the norm, Manchester City's own prodigal son, Denis Suarez, a man with Archimedial levels of precision and a Socratereal reading of the game, will be quietly shuffled off to Barcelona having been blocked from the first team by Mancini's under-achievers. No one will blink an eyelid in Abu

Dhabi, where PR and short-term gains are the priority. They know nothing of the prodigious talents of a young David Brightwell.

Across the borough, as David Moyes settled into his new role, sat behind his mahogany desk, surveying his new empire built on toil, sweat and dreams set amongst the stars, he will have felt a quiet satisfaction that his fruitless pursuit of players was done with the knowledge that the answer to his problems was already at the club. This may explain why United walked away from targets with a dignified silence. The future of the club is in safe hands. With Sir Alex Ferguson's guiding hand planted gently on his shoulder, metaphorically and perhaps literally, Moyes knows that he has what he needs already. And United, unlike others, know when to walk away, head held high, dignity intact.

United are not an ordinary club of course. Are they even a club at all? No, more of a concept, a state of mind, a freedom of expression woven into every seat and blade of grass in England's premier club ground. Edvard Munch, Francis Gruber and Ramón Castellano de Torres would be at home on the banks of the Bridgewater Canal.

And as the ground-staff finished off clearing the pitch after Rio Ferdinand's emotive testimonial on Friday night, a solitary dove swept down from the heavens and settled near one of the goals. A cynic might suggest that it was looking for food. The more romantic of us, those that have experienced this club's rich history woven onto the tapestry that is our heart or something, might speculate that it had sensed something special on that hallowed turf. Tales of glory, of fulfilled dreams, the roar of the Stretford end as they swayed as one, roaring on another young hero. Now it is Adnan Januzaj's turn. He steps into shoes that have ruled the world, organically. And like those before him, he is ready, as Moyes' Marvels begin a new chapter in a glorious history.

"As soon as Manchester United showed an interest, I knew where my destiny lay," said Adnan yesterday. "You do not say no to such an opportunity."

The man spookily born precisely 1000 days after United's first trophy win under Alex Ferguson says all the right things off the pitch, but is letting his feet do the talking on it. The future, as always, is bright.

Adnan Januzaj was speaking as a Nike ambassador, part of a Mahee promotional day.
Mahee - proud to be Manchester United's official noodle partner in Asia and Oceania.

A pithy 300-word Season Preview for AskMen.com (whoever they are)

A new manager, new players and a fresh start. You could forgive Roberto Mancini for sporting a heavy frown for much of the summer as Manchester City embarked on the player recruitment drive that he had pleaded for last summer, but his dismissal as last season drew to a close was not just about results but about relationships, and now City's owners have hired a man that they feel fits the new "holistic" approach of the club. Manuel Pellegrini is a coach more than a manager, but as a manager of men, Pellegrini is seen as a significant step up on his predecessor. It is also hoped he is a step up in Europe too, as his record suggests. And so the new season brings with it fresh hope. One of the main problems with Mancini's City was a lack of width and pace, and in Jesus Navas, that problem has been solved. Stevan Jovetic is a real talent that will further freshen up City's attacking options, whilst Alvaro Negredo is there to score goals, and Fernandinho will add extra dynamism in midfield.

Little can be deduced from pre-season, but goals have been leaked regularly, and Pellegrini will be keen to add an extra defender before the transfer window closes, especially since the release of Kolo Toure, Pepe being at the top of his shopping list. The added dimensions added to the attack were necessary to replace the departed Carlos Tevez and Mario Balotelli. This is a squad which should produce a bucketful of goals, which was the major problem of last season. If City can boast the tightest defence for the fourth season in a row, they stand a good chance of regaining the Premier League title.

City's chief executive joked that Pellegrini needs to win five trophies over the next five years, but for now the aim will be to simply compete for every trophy. With the three favourites for the title all under new management, an intriguing season lies ahead.

On 19th July 2013, news reached us that Bert Trautmann had passed away in Spain at the age of 89. The man we had thought to be indestructible had lost his final battle.

The club has numerous tributes planned for the Newcastle match on Monday night. A wreath will be laid pre-match, there is an extensive tribute in the match programme, including a replication of the 1956 Cup final programme, a minutes' applause will be carried out before kick-off and the players will wear black armbands, whilst Trautmann family members will be in attendance. Prior to that, an annual award in his memory was announced at City Live.

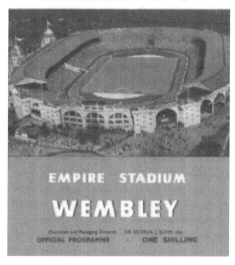

There have been calls for a permanent tribute to Bert over the summer by many fans, and the club have said that they will announce something in due time. I am normally loathed to agree with claims for renaming stands and bars and statues when ex-players die, but I cannot disagree this time. I don't know what the rules are on naming stands and having statues outside the ground and the like, what with the ground not being fully owned by City, but I think it would help with the identity of the place, and better than having stands named after geographical positions. And Bert Trautmann above all is deserving of such an accolade in my opinion.

If you want to read about his amazing life, there are two highly-recommended biographies available: Trautmann: The Biography by Alan Rowlands and Trautmann's Journey: From Hitler Youth to FA Cup legend by Catrine Clay, whilst occasionally an excellent documentary pops up on the Yesterday channel.

The 2013/14 Season

Manchester City 4 Newcastle United 0

Wasn't Monday nice? The sun was out, City were imperious, the team were professional and did their job, the manager stayed in the background and said the right things, the team briefly topped a table that has no importance at such an early stage, there were new pies and chips and burgers and everyone went home happy. This is how it should be, even if it was slightly boring without a midweek scrap on the training ground, a grumpy Mancini on the touchline distributing fruit pastilles like they were going out of fashion and without the other mercurial Italian moodily slouching round the pitch on the brink of a red card.

That mercurial Italian was instead playing for AC Milan this week in a Champions League qualifying tie at PSV, and he was back to his old, snarling self, throwing himself to the ground with every gust of wind, arguing with officials and players, sulking and generally making a nuisance of himself. Balotelli was booked and spent much of the remaining minutes remonstrating with the referee. He was booked six times in 13 Serie A appearances for AC Milan last season, missing one game through an automatic suspension and a further one for insulting an assistant referee. As a result, AC Milan coach Massimiliano Allegri has told him to accept refereeing decisions and stop answering back to officials in future.

I am often told that football needs characters. They make the game what it is – after all, imagine the boredom of eleven Michael Owens in every team. Football might well need characters, but my football team does not. Let other teams have them and City can get on with winning games.

I spent two years defending Balotelli against the ridiculous press coverage he received in this country, but in the end even I gave up. Even Roberto Mancini did. He didn't deserve much of that coverage, but he didn't help himself. A brilliant player he most certainly is, and his move back to Italy probably suited all sides as he may reach his potential back in his homeland, eventually. He certainly wasn't going to at City.

You can't see City's new manager making the back pages of the newspapers for any off-the-field antics, nor most of the players, driving discretions apart, obeying the speed limit being a skill that many a modern footballer hasn't yet mastered. This naturally helps the team in their title challenge, as it is always a bonus not to have your best player out for the first six games of a season, or not have some other controversy hanging over the club for months on end. So I'm sorry, but give me twenty-five boring professionals every day of the week.

Cardiff City 3 Manchester City 2: Some Thoughts

Sigh. New manager, some new players, same old story. These things happen in football, but the glass-half-empty part of me (which is basically all of me) would argue that United would never go to a promoted side, play that bad, and lose. In reality they've probably done it plenty of times, but it doesn't make it any less annoying.

But if you are going to put in a stinker of a performance like this, then early in the season is the time to do it. There's plenty of time to put right the wrongs. City have two fixtures coming up that they should win, so if they respond in the correct manner, as they surely must, then the damage can be limited for now.

Maybe stinker is a slight overreaction. City were not THAT bad – this was not reminiscent of Southampton last season. Hopefully no match will ever be reminiscent of Southampton last season. But City certainly under-performed, and key players didn't play to their full ability. Yes Cardiff were excellent, but there is no excuse for the City players not being either. If City's players play to the full extent of their ability, then they win, and unless they do this consistently, then it will be another frustrating season. The match was lost to individual mistakes, as once again a domination of possession was not converted into goals.

One journalist commented that Pellegriini's halo had slipped, because it seems keeping a low profile and acting like a gentleman is now a crime. This is all a learning curve for him of course, and he should have the team beside him to learn quickly, but like any match, it's down to the players once the whistle blows. Pellegrini could be criticised for playing Silva out of position or starting with Dzeko but he can't help the sloppiness of some of the players, unless the preparation was not up to scratch.

Dzeko's apparent wonder-goal seemed to justify his inclusion once more, but the fact is it may have gone wide if it hadn't taken a handy deflection – Dzeko still deserves credit as deflections are part of the game and it was still a hard, direct shot after finding space and at least he was prepared to shoot, unlike others who still persist in trying to walk the ball in sometimes. But I do wonder why Negredo has been overlooked, and personally I'd prefer him in the team. He'll miss chances but I think he gets involved more and will score as many goals.

It's too early to be panicking. A new manager means new ideas, such as a change from zonal-marking, and it may take time for players to adapt. For all the mocking of United's managerial appointment and their buffoonery in the transfer market, it could work in their favour in the coming months, as Moyes can carry on where Ferguson left off with a settled team playing in a similar way to before. City's need to adapt could cost more points down the line. Chelsea too struggled against Aston Villa last week with their new-but-not-so-new manager, but they got away with it.

Another s**tstorm will have descended on Hart today, and it is clear "Itchy & Scratchy" has had rocky moments over the past year, but he was not City's worst performer against Cardiff, and saved City twice in the first half and then saved superbly prior to their equalizer. Greater criticism should be directed at Pablo Zabaleta and to a lesser extent David Silva and Sergio Aguero, but some players are pretty immune from criticism at City. Silva's passing was shocking at times, Aguero offered little, and others failed to shine. I doubt the truth in the old adage that the players thought they only had to turn up to win, as I cannot comprehend any player thinking that against a fellow league team at their ground.

So in a season of many acts, City have messed up Act I. With the gentlest of starts to the season, coupled with United's tricky fixture list, this was an opportunity to steal a march on our neighbours. Now we face the possibility of United coming through their tricky fixtures ahead of City in the table, or at least level. They have two tricky games of course, so only time will tell, and I will be forced to support Chelsea on Monday night because I could never support United, even if Chelsea were the bigger threat, and also because the thought of losing to the title to Chelsea is more palatable. A draw would do I guess.

I was camping over the weekend so thankfully missed what I imagine was a pretty suicidal Twitter timeline, especially when you factor in the taunts of "money not buying you success" from rival fans. Still, I can state categorically that the Yorkshire Dales are very beautiful indeed. Alcohol continues to dull the pain of a City horror-show.

Cardiff City's chairman looks like a complete ****.

The Sham of the Champions League Draw (Parody)

In an EXCLUSIVE, I reveal how the Champions League draw,
held over 7 days in Monaco was nothing more than a farce, a pre-
ordained process that allowed nothing to chance in its eventual
outcome. The headlines may have been made by BALLGATE,
which left Billy McNeill in tears, Michael Owen with a dislocated
shoulder and ended with Luis Figo brawling with Michel Platini in
a hotel lobby at 4am (due to the new Adidas Excelsior balls, which
the manufacturers claim are more aerodynamic than any previous
cup draw balls), but it was in the draw itself where the real scandal
lay.

The draw has a number of caveats and rules that shapes who plays
who. There are two coloured halves of the draw, and rules on
teams from the same country, plus 74 other directives not known to
the general public – until now.

Arsenal came out of the Pot Bowls first, and were drawn into
Group F. So far so good. Then Chelsea came out of the pot and
were placed into Pot C. The rest of the top seeds were drawn, and
everything was fine. The draw for the second seeds began.
Marseille were drawn into Group F, but this caused a problem, as
their third kit clashes with Arsenal's European 2nd away kit, so
they had to be moved to pot D. AC Milan were drawn into Group
H, then CSKA Moscow were drawn into Group D, but Marseille
were already there, so they had to be moved into pot F. PSG went
into Pot C, and the other second seeds were drawn without any
problems, apart from when a drop of gel fell into Luis Figo's eye
and, temporarily blinded, he went down clutching his knee. The
10-minute delay was filled with a montage of previous draw
highlights, including the infamous 1997 draw which descended
into farce when one of the delegates did not have a pen and paper
to write the draw down on.

The draw for the third set of seeds though was a scandal.
Manchester City and Manchester United were both drawn in the
blue half of the draw, which isn't allowed as two teams from the
same city cannot play at home on the same night. So United were
moved to Group B due to their superior coefficient. Unfortunately
this meant City had to move from Group C as they can't be in a pot
that is only 1 letter away from a team from the same city as this

would compromise TV deals. So City were moved to Group D. Next out of the pot were Basel. They were immediately excluded from Pots A,B,D & E as past Champions League winners cannot be drawn in the group stage against a team that sounds like a herb. This left only Pots C ,G and H, as they couldn't go into G either due to possible clashes with Viktoria Plzen, and UEFA rules stress that any team named after a girl must not be paired either with a herb, a Portuguese team (the Portuguese secretly lobbied for this rule prior to the 2006/7 draw, having previously gone out of Europe to the little known Romanian club Lily Plovdiv), or a team that won the European Cup in the 1960's. As Basel had to be in the blue half of the draw due to a TV deal with a Czech TV station specifying they would play on a separate night as Viktoria Plzen (the station pandering to the huge Swiss population in the Prague ghettos), Basel were drawn into Group H, but had to be moved to C anyway because AC Milan were already in H and Basel can't be drawn against a team from Milan in a group stage due to sub clause c(ii), section 14 in the UEFA Champions League draw guideline document.

Then it emerged that Arsenal couldn't play in Group F as this would mean playing a home game that clashed with the National Cheese Festival at Olympia, whilst PSG requested no games on Tuesdays as they didn't want supporters to miss out on a re-run on Canal+ of the 3rd season of Luther (with subtitles). Then someone pointed out that Chelsea couldn't be drawn in the same half of the draw as Arsenal so were placed in Pot A, but this left to a fixture clash with United, so this was fixed by Borussia Dortmund swapping Groups with Bayern Munich, Shakhtar Donetsk outbid every club for the right to be drawn in Pot E, and CSKA Moscow had to have their home games moved to pre-December due to weather concerns. This meant Manchester City would be playing at home to CSKA on the same night as both Sarah Millican and Sean Lock were in town, so the kick-off had to be put back to midday, which thankfully suited the Asian markets. City agreed to play that game in their new third kit in return for a promise not to draw Barcelona at any point in the competition.

As Real Madrid's pitch was to be used for a Nickelback concert on 26th November they had to be away that night, meaning a further swap of fixtures. This swap though would leave Manchester

United & City once more playing on the same night, so for no reason Real Sociedad were moved to Group F to avoid fixture clashes. This left Chelsea in limbo so they were moved to Group G, City were temporarily placed in two groups, bringing a $15,000 fine from UEFA, before switching back to Group C. Austria Vienna played their joker card to be moved from Group H, and were moved to G, leaving Celtic in the Group of Death (H), causing Neil Lennon to go on a 2-hour rampage around Parkhead (leading to the despatch of a police helicopter). Anderlecht were placed into Pot C so that their fixtures did not clash with Yom Kippur. Ajax requested special dispensation for Match Day 3 as their players fasted every 4th Tuesday, and Zenit St Petersburg delegates stormed out of the conference hall complaining about the standard of borsch.

With one final demand from the Manchester United delegation, who requested no home matches on Matchdays 2 & 4, as "the trams will probably break down those days", the draw was finally completed shortly after midnight. But the shocking details of that draw show that it is little more than an exercise in maintaining the status quo and assuring that the "big boys" get exactly what they want. For the cheeky upstarts like Manchester City, there was the desire to put them in their place once more. Only a sold-out Sean Lock tour and a kit clash with Borussia Dortmund's home kit and City's 1999 play-off final kit prevented them from being in an even harder group.

Manchester City 2 Hull City 0: Some Thoughts

Skill, guile, ruthless attacking, fluid movement and devastating interplay, imperious defending and sublime ball control. All characteristics not displayed by Manchester City against Hull City.

Despite last week's defeat, I fully expected a return to normal service and a comfortable home victory, the type that has become the norm in recent seasons. This was a rude awakening.

If last week's defeat signalled the end of Pellegrini's honeymoon, then this week was akin to him getting back off the holiday to find he had left the iron on, a burst water pipe and that his cat had deposited a huge poo on the lounge rug.

The line-up provided one surprise, with Clichy dropped for Kolarov. I am amazed that Kolarov is still at the club especially after the Norwich game that closed out last season, and to see him in the starting line-up raised a few eyebrows. Clichy may have been punished for Cardiff's first goal last week, and perhaps Pellegrini has decided he needs a wake-up call, and that it was safe to make the change at home to a promoted club. And as it turned out, Kolarov played OK and made one crucial tackle.

Clichy is a player I find hard to assess. He hasn't made many mistakes and has undoubtedly been a top-value buy, but he seems to perform fine without excelling, and has been treading water for some time. Could City do better?

Does David Silva have a role in this formation? He is less effective out wide, but he has no place in this 4-4-2 of sorts. Pellegrini may have to consider changing the formation to fully utilise some of his players. I doubt the likes of Silva and Aguero are out of form at the moment, more likely that they are struggling to prosper under a new system.

Likewise, the Fernandinho and Toure axis continues to underwhelm. But they need time to develop an understanding.

The change at half-time, introducing Negredo paid dividends. It is ridiculous to suggest that I know 1/100th of what Pellegrini does about football or picking teams, and I don't see players in training every day, but it mystifies me that Dzeko is being picked ahead of Negredo. Neither did much wrong pre-season and Dzeko has not been playing badly but Negredo seems to offer more and he is a goal-machine. He has come off the bench three times and scored three legitimate goals, and is stronger and links play better. Hopefully he will start against Stoke – he should relish that challenge.

Where is Stevan Jovetic? It seems he may have been injured, and thus isn't fully fit, but I have read very little about him. I wouldn't expect him to start away at Stoke, so it could be some time before we see him in a City shirt.

It seems we have finally found a free-kick taker, at least for kicks to the left of centre. Now all we need is a corner-kick taker.

The uncomfortable start to the season has led to the inevitable reopening of the debate about the decision to sack Roberto Mancini. To repeat myself for the 50th time, Mancini was not sacked for results alone, and there were numerous games last season that were just as bad as the Hull match, but they tended to be away from home. There's no time in modern football for players to find their feet or managers to implement new ideas. Fans and the media expect immediate returns and a seamless transition, but it doesn't work like that.

As I left the ground I heard a tirade from an elderly Hull fan about the evils of money buying success. If only our club could be run with the class and decorum of the Hull Tigers.

Off the pitch....

Martin Demichelis – An Oveview

In news that had been brewing for over a week, it came as little surprise as Manchester City announced their fifth and final signing of the summer transfer window as Martin Demichelis posed at the ground for the traditional photo holding a club shirt. The 32 year old has signed a two-year contract on a reported wage of £18,000 a week.

As someone who spends far too much time on message boards and social media sites, it is readily apparent that it's the signing of the summer that has left vast swathes of City fans rather underwhelmed. Signings nowadays have to be marquee, exciting, big-money and definitely not cheap, short-term deals for players that can "do a job". They have to be young too, it seems.

Well the reality is far from that. Ambitious clubs can sign older players and make the deal work. Jose Mourinho would happily play John Terry for the next two years, so there is no problem in City doing likewise with Demichelis, who is a couple of weeks younger than Terry.

Part of the attraction for Pellegrini will be that this is a player he knows well, and who has performed for him and recently too. He has managed him at River Plate and Malaga and the player responded well, being picked in the La Liga team of the season for 2012-13 (though rather surprisingly, so did Carlos Vela). He has enjoyed success throughout his career, firstly in Argentina and then at Bayern Munich, the Champions League being the one trophy that eluded him whilst there. He helped Malaga to an offside-goal away from last season's Champions League semi-final, and youtube clips of him (which are of course always reliable) show him as a committed defender who is comfortable on the ball and will help guide the defence if selected.

The other complaints being bandied about are that he is slow and that he could have been bought for nothing just a couple of months ago, which is precisely what Atletico Madrid did before selling him on for a quick buck. The latter point is neither here nor there to be honest, unless City's owners invent time travel. Their interest has been rather recent, and they can only assess the deal as it stands now. He has been bought cheaply and on low wages. There's little secret that Pepe was the primary target, but a deal could not be brokered. City have looked elsewhere and made their choice. Those that complain about a lack of pace at the same time decry the possible exit of Gareth Barry. Pace is less important if a player can show anticipation and read the game well. Too many defenders use their pace to try and rectify an initial mistake.

You can look around Europe and suggest better deals that were available, but there is some logic to this move, apart from the aforementioned fact that Pellegrini knows and trusts the player. This is a player that adds depth to the squad (you could see him as a direct plug for the hole left by the departed Kolo Toure), who adds experience for City's European and domestic campaigns (let's not forget 37 caps for Argentina), but at his age will not block the development of any youth players with potential, such as Karim Rekik, currently on loan at PSV, or the already-entrenched Nastastic. You can't just have two first-choice central defenders nowadays, especially in teams playing in Europe and Joleon Lescott has hardly started the season on fire, but there is a pecking order as always and signing another top-class central defender in his prime could be problematic.

But here is a man who will earn under a quarter of what Joleon Lescott currently does, about a sixth of what Gareth Barry earns, so you can see in the signing the new methods and policies of City's owners, namely lower wages with incentivised add-ons. As a sidenote, you can never have too many Argentinean defenders at a club.

On deadline day, while logic suggests that City should be happy not to be involved in a last-day scramble for reinforcements at inflated prices, there is that little pang of envy not to be part of the madness, as United swoop for Herrera and Fellaini and Arsenal sign Ozil. But just because City's last signing was rather low-key as huge amounts of money are thrown around elsewhere, this does not mean Martin Demichelis cannot be a success at Manchester

City. He has spoken of a desire to continue to improve even as he reaches the twilight of his career, and under Manuel Pellegrini there is no reason why that can't happen. As always, only time will tell.

Gareth Barry – A Sad Goodbye

It had been rumoured for days, but time was running out - maybe he was staying after all? And then, at an hour so late that even the pea-brained idiots behind the reporter had decided to call it a day, Sky Sports News announced that Gareth Barry had arrived at Everton's training ground. It seemed he was going after all, and some time after Big Ben bonged eleven times, the news came through that Barry had moved on a season-long loan to the Toffees.
A loan deal it may be, but this is the end of Gareth Barry's Manchester City career, with a mere year left on his contract.

So I hope I can safely say from everyone at Manchester City football club – thank you.
Thank you for being the rock in our title-winning side. Thank you for never appearing on the front or back pages of a newspaper, thank you for being a consummate professional who simply did his job. Thank you for never moaning, even when not picked. Thank you for choosing us over Liverpool – it was the right decision in the end.

Barry joined City in 2009 from Aston Villa and made 175 appearances for City, scoring eight goals, and picking up two major trophies along the way.
He was the engine room during City's most successful period in a generation. He controlled the area in front of the defence, kept the team ticking over, linked defence to attack, and as David Silva commented "let me do my job". No wonder he was Silva's player of the year in the title-winning season. He was the ultimate team-player, not chipping in with goals, not top of the assists chart, not making eye-catching last-gasp tackles. He didn't need to. He

anticipated and read the game as well as any of the more illustrious players that surrounded him. He wasn't fast, and that didn't matter either.

It's an oft-mentioned point, but Barry was the acid test of what a fan knew about football. If you thought Barry was a rubbish footballer, then you knew little. Many footballers are immortalised because of one solitary moment, and Barry's misfortune was to be remembered for being outpaced by Mesut Ozil as England capitulated to a 4-1 defeat to Germany in the 2010 World Cup. Never mind that he wasn't fully fit, never mind the poor performances of many of his team mates. For many, this is how he will be remembered. Like many around him, Barry never excelled at international level, but like many around him he was never properly utilised. But if you saw him week-in, week-out, you soon realised what he brought to the table.

Barry could still have done a job this season, and many fans are desperately disappointed at him leaving. But this is the new holistic Manchester City and this is the consequence. Barry would not have been a first-team regular, and it seems the City hierarchy were not prepared to have a player sitting on the bench drawing £6m wages a year. Barry earns more than Jovetic, more than Navas, more than Negredo. In a world where breaking even is now a necessity, in the eyes of those that run our club, he had to go. What's more, it's rather optimistic to expect the performance levels of the Gareth Barry of two years ago. His performances tailed off last season, and now another year closer to retirement, he is in the twilight of his career.

Unfortunately Barry will now be the new Nigel De Jong, a handy reference point every time City perform poorly. But what's done is done, and he has moved on to pastures new, the desire for regular football understandable. After all, this is not just about what is good for City, but what is good for the player. Like any footballer not called Winston Bogarde, Gareth Barry needs to be playing. It's a World Cup year, and his chances of adding to his 53 England caps may be slimmer than Kolo Toure locked in a diet-pill factory, but if he sits on City's bench he will never know.

So like Mario Balotelli, Kolo Toure and Carlos Tevez before him, he goes with our best wishes and our deep gratitude for his contribution to a wonderful few years. When this period of City's rich history is looked back on then Gareth Barry might not feature on the cover of the brochure, his picture might not dominate the museum wall – but he has earned his place in history, and he was a gentleman throughout. All the best Gareth and thank you.

Colin Murray in **Metro**: 'Instead of investing the £85.3million gained from flogging Gareth Bale on new players, I wonder would Spurs consider buying new kits for every semi-professional and amateur team in the UK?'

(I think he was being serious)

Fans' Forum

Last night I attended a Fans' Forum in the Commonwealth Suite at Manchester City football club, which was organised over the summer by the 1894 Supporters Group, and was attended by City employees Danny Wilson (Director of Sales, Service & Operations), Nick Becker (Head of Events) and Lisa Eaton (Service & Fulfilment Manager). Kevin Parker made his debut as compère, and performed solidly.

The meeting was initially arranged to discuss one issue – atmosphere. Over time though, as the date moved closer, it began to encompass other issues such as stadium expansion, and both were discussed at the meeting, though the atmosphere at matches remained the main focus of debate.

This is not an issue peculiar to City of course. The atmosphere at most Premier League grounds has faded over the years, and I have no doubt that the main solution would be a return to restricted terracing, an issue Wilson said the club are open to, but of course the club's hands are tied somewhat on this issue. The big games take care of themselves most of the time, but it is the smaller games, the likes of the 12:45pm kick off v Hull where the real problems lie.

Like all forums, a wide range of ideas were suggested by those present, some excellent, the occasional point utterly ridiculous. Banning fans for not taking up their seats seemed a tad draconian though not awarding loyalty points for the same offence could stop those buying tickets just to stockpile those loyalty points.

Other suggestions mooted included utilising the vocal City support at away games and using videos of them in pre-match videos around the ground and in the concourse. The issue of flags and banners and choreographed cards was also mentioned, plus previous efforts to whip up an atmosphere such as the blue moon on the scoreboard and the "dimming" of the lights. Blue Moon should be performed just prior to kick off and not earlier, and perhaps be a fan rendition. Supplying free scarves once more gives the ground colour, but only for that match. The general gist was that City's immense social media presence could be utilised more to help generate atmosphere and fan interaction.

The issue of relocating away fans was discussed in some detail, there being a strong support in the room for grouping the vocal fans together in one group rather than having them separated by the away fans. Danny Wilson put forward the counter-argument that it could be just as beneficial as it stands by having vocal fans on both sides of the away fans. Either way, they cannot in my opinion be moved to the gods, as this would kill the atmosphere stone dead. Consultation is still ongoing regarding this, another option being thinning the away block to three tiers after the expansion has taken place.
But linked to that, there is no doubt also that many still feel strongly about being forced to move seats. The issue of the Family Stand reared its head, not only because it forced people out of seats, but because it is an area that supplies little atmosphere.

Other points worth mentioning include the role of players in the atmosphere in a ground. One person wanted them geeing up the crowd at corners, but the simple acknowledgement of the fans by the team as a collective at a match-end is something that would certainly go down well. The acoustics of the stadium was also mentioned, and the simple fact that if the club could get the fans in earlier, to drink in the ground rather than elsewhere, then this would improve the atmosphere immensely. This isn't going to happen though whilst prices remain as they are, or whilst the choice of beverages is so narrow.

Throughout the meeting, the Premier League was compared with the tremendous atmospheres found in many other European Leagues, and whilst some inspiration could be taken from their methods, the fact remains that the English culture prevents the type of synchronised displays that you may see in the Bundesliga.

Regarding the stadium expansion, it seems that it is as yet undecided on the extent of the plans. The south stand alone may be expanded, or perhaps the North Stand too. There can be little doubt that any applications for expansion will be waved through by the council, and any expansion would be in place for the 2015/16 season, with little impact on existing seats, though some areas of the ground away from the seats would have to be closed for a season (e.g. the Legends Lounge) as the ground expanded outwards.

As for the creeping premium seating in the stadium, it was made clear that such seating would only expand when the stadium had expanded and thus the £299 season tickets had been introduced. Danny Wilson intonated that previous fan surveys had shown a strong demand for premium seats, which raised a few hundred eyebrows in the room, and I said to him afterwards that if he wants the stadium to sell out, the annual price increases must stop, as breaking points are being reached for many. Wilson seemed to suggest that the new £299 seats would cover this problem, but it doesn't as it still leaves the vast majority of fans paying more. After all, we can't all sit in the cheap seats.

But in many respects the club are damned if they do and damned if they don't. Not many clubs would hold such a forum with fans, but after the meeting there were already disparaging remarks about the forum on social media sites suggesting that the club won't act on ideas put forward, something that many would argue has happened before. Only time will tell, but those representing City last night do not run the club, and can only do so much. Danny Wilson & Nick Becker answered the questions put to them honestly and seemed open to suggestions.

A quick raffle continued my run of having never won anything, ever, and the meeting was wrapped up and the expensive Amstel drained.

Further meetings are planned, including with safety officers regarding the use of wooden flag sticks (which of course in the modern world are now deemed offensive weapons), and time will tell what improvements will be made.

Modern Football

Along with this week's announcement about ticket prices for the Bayern Munich match came some not-so-little caveats on the official site that beautifully sum up the modern game.

I'm referring to the matter of compulsory seat relocations for a select few City fans due to UEFA regulations. The unlucky fans include those in East, South and Family Stands Level 1 – Rows A and B. Row C of block 105 of the East Stand, East Stand Level 1 – Block 105, Rows S, T and U Colin Bell Stand Level 1 – Block 126.Colin Bell Stand Level 2 – Block 223……. and on and on and on.

But of course, there's no need to get angry, as further inspection shows that such moves are necessary. After all, we can't be having a football match on prime-time television with a global audience without those essential raised-height perimeter advertising boards. And it's only fair that long-suffering City fans are shuffled elsewhere to accommodate the UEFA Champions Club in the Commonwealth Suite. And I think we can all agree there is an urgent need in Champions League games (but no other games) for an expanded technical area around the home and away dugouts.

It's also common courtesy for City to provide an allocation of 'First Class' seating to the Visiting Club, located between the 16m lines. We wouldn't want visitors feeling uncomfortable during the match, and I would hope that any supporters forced to move would agree it is for the best. And if you are going to supply padded seats for away team visitors, then you can't overlook the lovely UEFA family, thus requiring an allocation of 'First Class' seats to UEFA and UEFA Champions League Partners.

And what's more, the global audience demand the best spectacle possible, hence the UEFA requirement for an expanded television and media commentary area and the inconvenient positioning of the reverse-angle television camera.

You can almost imagine Platini and his group of bodyguards turning up at a game and Showsec security turfing people out of seats before dusting down the seats and placing a fluffy pillow down before assisting the UEFA chief to his seat. Well I can anyway. God bless the UEFA family. They care about the game just as much as you and me, but they really do need the comfiest seats, the best food, 1st class travel, and a man at hand to mop their brow at any time should the temperature be more than a couple of degrees past the optimum.

But perhaps I'm being harsh. After all, UEFA themselves have stated: *"We have a clear vision: a united European football family working together to improve enjoyment of the game"*

UEFA's core objectives are, amongst other things to:
• *ensure that sporting values always prevail over commercial interests*

And the first of their "Eleven values"?
Football first

In everything that we do, football must always be the first and most important element that we take into consideration. Football is a game before being a product, a sport before being a market, a show before being a business.

So there you go. Give them a break. And enjoy your new views at the Bayern Munich match.

Stoke City 0 Manchester City 0

I don't go to Stoke matches anymore as it has always been a miserable, dour experience. And so it proved again.

The result is no disaster, as it is par for the course for any season with City (in the league at least), but the performance was another matter. Injuries abounded but the team City put out was easily good enough to win comfortably. Stoke had Jon Walters upfront and brought on Peter Crouch. We had the choice of Negredo or Dzeko with Aguero coming off the bench. No excuses.

The team selection raised a few eyebrows once more but whilst many changes were enforced, there seemed to be a desire to fight fire with fire. Fernandinho's relegation to the bench is not a good sign for one of City's costliest signings. Presumably Aguero's late exit was due to a small injury, as he still made it onto the pitch eventually.

You could easily single out individuals after such a performance, but it may be better to look at the formation and system set up by Pellegrini, which once more left the team looking utterly disjointed. There are many players that look totally out of place over recent weeks. Yaya Toure looked lost, Rodwell ineffectual, Nasri anonymous, along with everyone else. To not muster a good chance all match is staggering.

We need to talk about Gareth Barry. I think all City fans wish him the best, even if it is for Everton, and his excellent debut in darker blue will surprise few, but it will once more open the debate over why we let him go (the answer – money). But I don't think he would have made any difference against Stoke. He links defence and midfield, but City's problems lie across the park, and he's not the answer to all our prayers, just like Nigel De Jong wasn't after he left. Move on.

Still, Joe Hart doesn't have questions to answer for once, and that's four clean sheets on the row for club and country. Not bad for a player seemingly suffering the worst form of his career.

Alan Hansen actually did some meaningful analysis on Match of the Day, pointing out City's defensive frailties, though why he had to use an example from last season's derby I have no idea. Hansen commented on City paying a fortune on forwards whilst neglecting the defence, but then the defence that has conceded the fewest goals for the past three seasons is intact bar the exit of a squad player in Kolo Toure, whilst the forward line lost Balotelli and Tevez this year. It's hardly a surprise this is where the focus of our transfer spending lay.

Pellegrini out? The first pathetic whispers have begun. A small number of City fans need to take a good look at themselves and stop acting like spoilt brats. We should be thankful for what we have, even during the rough spells. It's fine to criticise, obviously, but be realistic.

You could argue City have missed opportunities or you could argue they have received a get out of jail free card, but either way there is no one team who has come out flying this season. Arsenal top the pile but lost at home to Aston Villa, United have of course lost at Liverpool, and Chelsea lost at Everton. It's just unfortunate that City's fixture list was probably the easiest of all the contenders.

Finally, a hypothetical question: what if City are trying to build a whole new ethos from the management through to the youth team to all aspects of the club including a set playing style and approach to the beautiful game that set the club up for a generation **but** necessitated two or three years of upheaval and limited success. Would you take that? Or is instant success more important? Of course it's possible to transform the club's methods and remain successful in the meantime. But every year the club goes through a huge transformation, and we must accept that it may at times be a bumpy ride, but the final destination is worth the odd bruise or two.

So with 4 games gone, City find themselves in 4th place, with 7 points. Liverpool lead the pack with 10 points, but then it's always "their year" isn't it? Onwards and eastwards, to Europe and the hype of the Champions League.

Viktoria Plzen 0 Manchester City 3: Some Thoughts

Huzzah. City's first ever victory in the Champions League, apart from those other two that didn't really count. #sarcasm #lolz

That was, quite simply, a good professional European performance. There was a system in place that seemed to suit the players far better than in previous games and as a result there was a raft of improved performances. Aguero was back to his best up front, Nasri filled the hole left by Silva superbly (more on him later), and the defence as a whole coped admirably with a skilful opposition team. Merit is also deserved for Fernandinho, who did his job quietly and efficiently, allowing Yaya Toure the freedom to get forward and thus delayed further pining for Gareth Barry for a few days at least.

And that's what happens when Yaya Toure ventures forward. Now let him do that every game please.

You don't just go to European aways and expect to wipe the floor with the opposition, it rarely happens (we'll ignore Real Madrid last night, ahem). I have watched endless Champions League games down the years, I have seen United at their peak churn out dour 1-0 away wins at average teams (I know, I know I shouldn't ever watch them, please forgive me), I've seen them lose plenty too, and I've seen Barcelona at their peak in recent years play poorly away from home time after time after time. It was a good result and a good performance, simple as that. And it could easily have been at least 5-0.

You can argue that the opposition are poor, but then you've probably also seen some of Plzen's recent results in Europe bandied about. A 5-0 aggregate win over Napoli stands out, plus a victory over Atletico Madrid. And they're double Czech champions. You can only beat what's in front of you, etc etc.

So that's five clean sheets on the row for crisis keeper Joe Hart, and City's "shambolic" defence have only conceded in one game this season. I know there are problems to be addressed in that area, but sometimes a bit of perspective goes a long way.

Which brings us to the main man. Welcome back Vincent, we've missed you. Probably best to cut out the sliding tackles in innocuous areas of the pitch in future though. His form last season wasn't the best (along with all his team-mates), but he showed last night his immense influence on the team, that spreads well beyond making the odd tackle or headed clearance. He also made 51 passes and was successful with all of them.

Time for the paranoia section. Funny how the City goals and chances were met with not only indifference but at times complete silence from the commentators, yet if Viktoria Plzen ventured within 40 yards of the City goal then the anticipation in the voice of Martin Tyler was tangible. I've watched countless Champions League games of other English clubs over the past decade and more (including United – I know, I know) and there has never been such a lack of support from the commentary team. Nor have I ever heard the cost of United's team compared to the cost of the opposition's.
Told you I was paranoid. They're all out to get us.

On the other hand, Graeme Souness is a superb pundit.

The new kit might look like a cigarette packet, but it's damn nice. I would have preferred however for it to have been unveiled at 3:32am in Singapore.

And finally, a note on priorities. Will the Champions League be Pellegrini's priority over the Premier League? He has basically said as much, backed up by the team picked for Stoke, which is a shame as City have a much better chance of winning the league than the Champions League (the bookies odds show that) but let's be honest, either would be magnificent. But here's a thought – why not just treat both competitions equally seriously?

After the Plzen game, he changed his tune considerably, claiming the Champions League was not the priority. He probably realised how the fans would take such a situation, and back-tracked.

There was no time to rest though, as it was that time of the year again, the gut-wrenching nail-biting experience that is derby day. We needn't have worried.

Manchester City 4 Manchester United 1

Mick Hucknall, Terry Christian, Eamonn Holmes, James Nesbitt, Mumford and (bloody) Sons, Terry Christian again, Zoe Ball, Paddy Crerand, Lou Macari, Clayton Blackmore, Terry Christian again, Mark Ogden, Usain Bolt, Gary Neville, Howard Webb, some bloke who used to present Play School, Terry Christian again. Your boys took one hell of a beating.

I hate derby day. Anyone who enjoys it needs medical help. It really doesn't get any easier with time….. but hey, at least the sun was out. A beautiful day as it turned out.

The line-up was exactly as I'd hoped, Negredo replacing Dzeko, the pace of Navas to exploit United's defence and keep Evra pinned back, the omission of Clichy and Silva unavoidable after recent injuries. It shows our strength in depth that they weren't needed, along with Jovetic, Richards, Demichelis, Milner et al. As for United, there was no doubt that the late withdrawal of Van Persie was a huge boost.

And as for the match itself…..

That was, without doubt, the perfect performance, at least for an hour. No criticisms, no weaknesses, utterly dominant, every player doing their job and the team (eventually) ruthless. Only after victory was assured did the team ease off and let United back into the game.

City still could have had six or seven if truth be told. But easing off in the last third of the game was utterly unacceptable (City completed just 75 passes in the 2nd half to United's 255).

That last point was a joke.

Well, partly.

But history tells me never to relax, and even at four goals to the good, I was clock-watching. It was only as the board was held up to show three minutes' injury time that I could finally relax.

But you know a performance is good, really really good, when you feel guilty for singling out a star performer. I'd struggle to be honest. Throughout the team, from Fernandinho's week-long arrival as a player of substance, through to the magnificent front-two, the in-form Nasri, the rampaging Toure and the defensive wall erected by City, featuring at its heart one of Vincent Kompany's best games.

Having said all that, what do I know about player performances? After all, Fernandinho was 'hardly noticed as he was outshone by Toure' according to The Sun. Ian Ladyman thought Kompany put in a 7/10 performance.

(In truth, Fernandinho made more interceptions (five) than Carrick, Fellaini and Valencia combined, and set up three scoring opportunities. Kompany made 2 interceptions, 12 clearances (highest on pitch), had an 81% pass accuracy, and made 9 ball recoveries (also the highest on the pitch). Elsewhere, Zabaleta made almost as many tackles as the entire United team.)

Perhaps if I am to single out individuals it is best to mention the two players most often the target of flak from City fans. Samir Nasri made the absence of David Silva an irrelevance, and he continued his good form. Long may it continue. The Frenchman has always appeared to be a fragile soul, and just maybe City's executive team's desire for a holistic approach, including a manager who coaches and encourages players, is having an effect in this regard.
And then there's Aleksander Kolarov. We've all thrown the odd expletive his way over recent years, but he deserves credit when he plays well, and he contributed as much as many yesterday. Like Nasri, perhaps it is time to cut him some slack and see if he can flourish under the guiding hand of Pellegrini. And he clearly has his uses. I very much doubt that Gael Clichy would have made the lung-bursting run that led to the first goal.

Was this better than the 6-1 at Old Trafford? A strange assertion, but it was a more dominant performance, against 11 men throughout, and remember City scored three late on at THE THEATRE OF DREAMS as United's heads went, but to destroy your rivals like that away from home does give the 1-6 the slightest of edges for me.

Across the divide, it was not surprising that Wayne Rooney was United's best player, the only player to cause City problems. Still, as usual it seems that the usual rules do not apply to Mr Rooney, the only surprise being his eventual booking. Or maybe I'm being prejudiced. Either way, his goal though made him the top derby scorer of all time, and he continues to turn up against City, unlike some of his colleagues.

Ryan Giggs engaged in a half-time "tirade" at the fourth official, no doubt exasperated at not being on the pitch, thus missing the chance to spend 90 minutes surrounding the referee and trying to get opposition players dismissed - so you can understand his frustration on this occasion. The only thing more woeful was David Moyes once more bemoaning the random fixture list.

Rooney took up the mantle of referee-baiter, especially after a pathetic attempt by United to win a penalty. I imagine Howard Webb said to him, "sorry Wayne, even I can't do anything about this".

Still, United fans can look on the bright side. Alex Ferguson lost his first derby 5-1 – therefore Moyes > Ferguson.

There must be something to criticise City for though? Well you could write an article that clutches at straws so tightly they turn to dust, claiming that at least your fans were the noisiest, but the award must go elsewhere on this occasion.
Step forward Neil Ashton. A quite pathetic piece in the Daily Mail bemoaned City's foreign outfield 10 in the derby and what bad news it was for the England team. "Could be the day football died," tweeted Ashton, no doubt with a straight face.

It's a quite idiotic assertion that one team selection has somehow affected the future of the England team, when you consider that Milner and Lescott have had match-time this season, and that Richards wasn't match fit. It's also very convenient to omit City's goalkeeper from his argument. Nothing changed because of the team played yesterday, and we all know there is a good reason for playing foreign players – they are usually better than their English counterparts. But if Ashton had bothered to even do a quick Google search he'd be reminded of the academy plans, and its intention to bring through English talent, as is already being shown by the crop of 13 and 14-year-olds enjoying national success. It's not news anyway, as it has happened before (away from City), but then most articles on the Daily Mail website aren't news, so I guess it's par for the course.

Apropos of nothing, Ashton claimed United's selection of six Englishmen was part of their core values, which probably helps explain why they got their arses spanked.

God I love derby day……

Manchester City 5 Wigan 0

A second-string League Cup line-up often ends in disaster for City, but not on this occasion as they strolled to victory over Wigan. Inevitably it wasn't long before someone opined that this was revenge for the FA Cup Final defeat. Hardly.

Still, at least we got proof that Stevan Jovetic exists and he looked very promising indeed.

Aston Villa 3 Manchester City 2: Some Thoughts

Oh for f**k's sake.

I said after Sunday that the derby counted for little if we didn't follow it up with a victory at Villa Park. And so it proved – the Manchester derby thrashing is a distant memory.

And the woeful away form continues, but how on earth did City lose this one? You could write it off as a freak result, a one-off, if it didn't happen with depressing regularity. 67% possession, 21 attempts on goal, 13 corners and a defeat.

But in a way it was a freak result. An offside goal, a wonderful free-kick (was it even a free-kick? Probably not), and horrendous defending from a goal-kick. At no point in the match were City on the back foot, yet they conceded three goals against a mid-table team missing their two 1st choice strikers. It is baffling that City could concede three goals in this match.
This was different from Cardiff and Stoke though in as much as City created, and they created chance after chance after chance. But as has happened before, wasteful finishing and that killer pass did for us once more. Pellegrini said as much, but his comment that "we played well" is somewhat undermined by the three goals conceded. But as he said – you must concentrate for the full 90 minutes, and City have this nasty habit, whoever the personnel, of turning off and paying for it. But at least over the past couple of weeks there has been a noticeable upturn in overall performances.

Nastastic is on slippery ground, and not performing to his full ability. Two fouls have led to free-kick goals for the opposition in the past six days, and he could easily have been sent off in both matches, though as mentioned, the free-kick conceded yesterday was a case of the referee being conned into a decision. It's at times like this that you understand why Pellegrini wanted reinforcements. But hey, let's not forget that Pepe is not very nice and Demichelis is way too slow, or so I've been told. On days like this, we could do with them.
But Nastastic is young, with his best years ahead of him.

Though to be fair, regarding Pepe – if you watched the Madrid derby last night you'd not want him at City either – an Oscar-winning portrayal of a spoilt, petulant child from beginning to end.

Hart will predictably come in for stick, but Kompany was as more to blame for the third (but is untouchable), and the free-kick for the 2nd equalizer top-notch, even if he didn't move. For that 3rd goal however he would surely have been better served staying close to his line, but it should never have got to that point anyway.

What is it with the disparity in home and away form? There have been studies on the topic, and still no one has really nailed the reason. City have of course improved from the old days when they could go a whole season without experiencing the thrill of victory, but they have never truly shaken off the ability to under-perform away from home. I wish I had the answers but I don't. Half of it must be in the head for managers and players alike, then there's the crowd factor, the lack of familiarity in the routine for the away team, but it is not logical. There is no reason really for City or anyone else to play differently away from home, but it happens around the world, and has done since the dawn of the game (1992).

Having said all that, Arsenal have won their last 8 away league games.

And City show another anomaly when you look at the stats for the year. This is a team that racks up the clean sheets, hence Joe Hart's repeated golden gloves awards, but when they concede, the floodgates tend to open, on average conceding 2.2 goals per game. This suggests to me a problem with mentality. The City of recent times do not cope well with conceding a goal and it makes an incorrect offside call all the more important.
It's also a 2nd half problem – City barely concede in the first half in recent times, and haven't yet this season. Only Norwich have bucked the trend since mid-March.

Thankfully City have been helped by the fact this could be a tight league, and points are being dropped all over the place. Having said that, they are being dropped by other teams in tough encounters, whilst City have dropped 8 points in 3 very winnable away games, with all the tough away games to come.

So the small matter of the European Champions coming to town. The team will look somewhat different of course, but the aforementioned necessity to concentrate for 90 minutes will never be more apt than in midweek. Yet again, a response is needed.

The A to Z of City Legends

Aguerooooooooooo. A good place to start, and no further explanation is required really. What's more, he is always smiling, which is both endearing and also annoying as it's a constant reminder of just how much better his life is than mine (and yours). (Apologies Malcolm Allison. It's a stupid way to devise a list)

Bell, Colin. Nijinsky. Not because he is hung like a grand-national winner (thanks for that Lord Flashard, Edmund Blackadder's wife-stealer), but because of his tremendous stamina, and the king because of his sublime, supreme elegance on a football pitch. To many, he will always be City's greatest player, and the fact that he alone has a stand at the Etihad named in his honour says it all. Not surprising that a nasty tackle from a United player ended his career.

Coton, Tony. Really?! Yes, really, he was a bloody good keeper, and he had a bushy moustache. Then he spoiled it all by going to United. But I'm keeping him in because I'm not quite convinced enough by Gerry Creaney's credentials.
(Oh ok, it should be Joe Corrigan really)

Dickov, Paul. Scored an important goal once. Said goal resulted in me catapulting four rows down Wembley's west stand and picking up significant bruising, not that I cared. The rest, as they say, is history.

Eric Brook. No, me neither. City's all-time record goal-scorer from the inside-left position. From 1928-1939 he made 450 appearances for City, scoring 158 goals. He also scored 10 goals in 18 appearances for England. Brook scored a 'wonder goal' in front of a record crowd of 84,569 against Stoke City in the sixth round of the FA Cup. According to Gary James, 'many fans from the 1930s claimed it was the greatest City goal ever scored at Maine Road'. A fractured skull from a car crash ended his career, not that a world war particularly helped either.

F

Goater, Shaun. Feed the goat and he will score. The most recognisable of chants, even if it makes no sense whatsoever. Perhaps said goat gets horny on a full stomach? Anyway, leaving aside the early scepticism from many a city fan at Goater's prowess on a football field, he soon won everyone over, and was a true goal-scorer with a winning smile and all the attributes to attain cult status. A god back in Bermuda, he even has his own day (21st June). I bet Dwight Yorke doesn't.

Horlock, Kevin. If you shower eternal gratitude on Paul Dickov, then you must acknowledge the player that made THAT moment possible, in the same way that there would have been no league title without Edin Dzeko. So all hail the All-England Aggressive Walker Champion, the Twitter United-fan-baiter and all round good guy, with a left foot so cultured team-mates were known to kiss it after he scored.

Ireland, Stephen. The man with 16 grand-parents. Oh to spend 10 minutes inside his head. Oh to have his fish tank (he can keep the pink car though). A wonderfully-talented player, but not the first of his type to never reach his full potential, his stock having fallen so far he now plays for StokeCity.

Jimmy Grimble. I'd love to honestly say that this was a wonderful film. I really would.

Kinkladze, Georgi. "Better than David Silva," said one blue on a City message board last month. He wasn't, because being a great footballer is about a lot more than skill alone, and a player superior to David Silva would not have moved on to Derby County. But let's not quibble over one of the most naturally talented players to put on a sky/laser/all the other shades of blue shirt. It's just a shame he was at the club at completely the wrong time.

Lee, Franny. His legacy may be somewhat tainted, but without his chairmanship we'd never have experienced the Shirehorses' Ballad of Franny Lee, so every cloud and that.

Maine Road. God bless its misshaped stands, outside toilets, massive floodlights, surrounding terraces, cantilever roof, Gene Kelly stand, the plastic bird hanging down from the Kippax roof. But most of all, god bless its memories.
1923-2003.
(Tough luck Andy Morrison, Billy Meredith and the colour maroon)

Negouai, Christian. A City career that summed up the club of old. Blighted by Cityitis throughout his brief stay, the man for whom Kevin Keegan predicted superstardom stumbled from disaster to disaster. Keegan said he was the most exciting player he had seen, and exciting is certainly one way of describing his time at City. An appalling home debut capped with a goal palmed into Rotherham's net set the tone nicely. A red card at Blackburn capped off his first spell nicely (he was rather harshly sent-off, I might add), before severe injury derailed the inevitable meteoric rise, but there was still time for a quick return to action and a goal in the UEFA Cup, a missed drugs-test, a loan spell in Austria, a revelation as a reserve striker, another injury, and a further red card after 3 minutes on the pitch, before his eventual disappearance. A cult hero was born.

Oakes, Alan. City's record appearance holder, with 680 appearances between 1959 and 1976. In his time at Maine Road, Oakes became part of more trophy winning sides than any other Manchester City player in history. In 2005 he was inducted into City's Hall of Fame.

Paul Lake. Wonderfully-talented, a diamond in the rough, but cruelly blighted by injury, and woefully treated by many at the club. Thankfully he had the strength to fight back, and move on, and still love the club like we do. Also the (co-) author of the best football autobiography I have ever read.

Quinn, Niall. Oh Niall, why did you have to ruin it all by pursuing a media career and being absolutely rubbish? By virtue of his surname he was always making the list, a disastrous 10-minute substitute appearance would have sufficed, but he was a great servant to City, and had "surprisingly good feet for a big man". He played 244 games for City, scoring 77 goals. He also once said hello to me in JD Sports.

Roberto Mancini. First trophy in 35 years. First title in 44. 6-1 at Old Trafford. Boosted scarf sales. Didn't give a f**k what people thought. Nuff said.

Sheikhs. Thanks for everything. But when are you going to serve real ale inside the ground? And where's the WIFI? Oh, and…..

Terry Christian. Yes, that's right. It's people like Terry that remind me, even when times are tough, why I am glad I am a ManchesterCity fan. Terry Christian is a modern-day martyr. I salute you Terry (but I've had to un-follow you on Twitter).
(Oh ok, not really – it's got to be Trautmann, Bert – – no further text really required. If you haven't already, do check out one of his biographies, it's one hell of a story.)

Uwe Rosler. Grandson of a Luftwaffe pilot (*Editor: Can you check this please*), 177 appearance, 64 goals. All round good guy, has made me want Brentford to do well.

Vincent Kompany. Michel Vonk cruelly overlooked, but we can't have this list without City's inspirational captain.

Wright-Phillips, Shaun. He feels like one of us. He was great, but not the greatest and he played with a smile on his face, he terrorized many a defence, scored many stunning goals and for a while was our only shining light. Times have changed since then, but I won't forget the pride of him pulling on an England shirt for the first time and scoring too.

X Erm, well, err – Xavi? Bear with me. <fires up google>. Just one minute. Almost there. Right, here we go:
Xavi helped Barcelona win the 2009 Champions League Final versus Manchester United, which ended 2–0, assisting the second goal by passing the ball to Lionel Messi after 69 minutes. Legend.

Yaya, yaya yaya, yaya yaya, yaya yaya toure. Kolo, kolo kolo, kolo kolo, kolo kolo toure. Yaya, yaya yaya, yaya yaya, yaya yaya toure. Kolo, kolo kolo, kolo kolo, kolo kolo toure.
For THAT goal alone at Newcastle, he is a legend, let alone the FA Cup winning contribution, but of course there is far more to him than that. The man dubbed a Barcelona reserve by Brian Reade ("seduced by the whores of world football"), he is now considered by many to be one of the finest midfielders in the world.

Zabaleta, Pablo. Last week's revelation that he doesn't eat fish and chips after all has severely weakened his reputation at City, but I have decided to keep him on the list. Everything you want from a player, and more.

Manchester City 1 Bayern Munich 3: Some Thoughts

City's EDS team got the day off to a superb start with a 6-0 shellacking of their Bayern Munich counterparts - could the senior side complete the job?

No, no they couldn't.

But even before the game began, the formation and player picks raised eyebrows once more - Micah Richards was chosen ahead of Pablo Zabaleta, presumably for his pace and power that would hopefully pin back their left-sided attacking players and help with the threat of Ribery. But along with Clichy, Pellegrini picked two full backs returning from injury, against the best side in Europe. It was a strange decision. And as for picking Dzeko over Negredo, I've given up trying to work that one out, not that Dzeko was THAT bad, or the cause of all of City's ills.

To put it bluntly - City were outclassed in every department by the best club side in the world, a settled team at the peak of its powers. A new manager has not affected this team, which is not surprising as that manager is Pep Guardiola. With summer signing Thiago injured, it was very similar to the Bayern of last season that destroyed everything in front of it, including the oft-quoted Barcelona masterclass. Only Javi Martinez was injured from the old guard and that doesn't really matter when you have Lahm to protect the back four.

Bayern pretty much did to City what City did to United the other week. They pressed hard and harried, the City players were shellshocked and were unable to find the time to get a passing rhythm going. The most impressive things about Bayern was the speed of the passing, their energy levels and the movement. But City's heads seem to drop by their goals coming at key times, bright starts on both halves undone by a single moment. Joe Hart couldn't even find space to pass out from goal – resulting in endless punts almost inevitably leading to Bayern possession. Bayern however seemed to get into dangerous positions almost at will.

But then Bayern are basically just a better side. Better than City, better than Barcelona, better than everyone. Something to aspire to.

This was a match though that raised many questions - two stood out more then others

The main one is the sobering acknowledgement that Manuel Pellegrini got the formation and set up of the team completely wrong. It was clear from the start that City were being overrun in midfield. Michah Richards commented afterwards that it felt like they had an extra man, and that's because they did, in the middle of the pitch, out wide, almost everywhere. By the time Pellegrini reacted it was too late - to not make any substitutions at half - time was baffling. I have said repeatedly - a new manager has the right to be given time – but last's night line-up was nothing to do with settling in, or getting to know new players. Managers often get things wrong tactically, even the best. The disappointing thing was Pellegrini's failure to react to what was in front of him. He should surely have seen from the start the need to stifle Bayern in midfield, and thus put an extra man in there. When Nasri was dragged inside, he helped little and left a gaping hole out wide. 4-4-2 could only work if the strikers dropped back to assist the midfield, which they didn't.

When City did add strength and numbers to the midfield, the response was immediate, with a goal, a red card for Bayern, the crossbar rattled, and a free header going wide. But then Bayern may have been easing off, and had taken off Ribery, Robben and Schweinsteiger. It is telling that David Silva created more chances than any other City player (2) and got an assist despite only being on the pitch for 20 minutes.

Maybe he thought that City weren't doing that bad at the break - for all Bayern's domination of the ball in the first half, Joe Hart had little to do. But at times it felt like Bayern were toying with city. On the flip-side, for all the Bayern domination, all three goals were essentially down to individual errors.

But it's hard to say the players were terrible, even though that's how it looked to the naked eye, when the set-up left them chasing shadows.

The stats tell the story though. Bayern made 597 passes, with an 88% accuracy. City made 254, with an accuracy of 77%. Bayern had 59% possession, though it felt like more. Bastian Schweinsteiger made 69 passes, with 95% accuracy, 3 key passes and had a 100% tackle success. Toni Kroos completed 97% of his passes. Yaya Toure, who averages 41 passes in the Premier League, made just 12 in the first half.

A note on the atmosphere - conceding early does doesn't help of course, but against the champions of Europe it was flat one more. I'm not vocal so am not one to criticise others, but it does seem that the Champions league is still falling to captivate the fans - maybe a modicum of success in the competition will change that. But let's stop talk of trying to match what the Bayern fans do, or the Porto fans or the Napoli fans – we're (mostly) English, we don't do things like that. The odd swear word and kicking the seat in front of me in frustration is the limit of my match-day exertion.

So to Joe Hart (as usual). There is no denying he was poor (though made good saves in the second half) - and such flaky goalkeeping so early on deflated the team and left them up against it against a team that do not tend to throw away leads. He was also partly to blame for the third, and despite me defending him in the past, as not all the criticism had been fair, you get the feeling that he could be one bad performance away from being dropped.
Doing so though would be a huge decision to make for Pellegrini, and may be one he will want to avoid. It may help him, it may make matters worse for his fragile confidence, and is the back-up any better? It should be pointed out also that once more he wasn't helped by his team mates.

And predictably the Pellegrini backlash is back in full force - and with it the tiresome Mancini pining and once more last season is whitewashed from history. I've heard it said numerous times that Mancini "wouldn't have let that happen" even though he did against Borussia Dortmund (the only difference being a goalie in form), and oversaw other appalling European displays. He might have reacted to the midfield issue last night, but history doesn't suggest we'd be doing any better in the group with him still at the helm. Still, Pellegrini's head is already on the chopping block for some, but I'll wait a couple of months before judging him properly.

And in the same way that Pellegrini has now been labelled a "dinosaur" for his 4-4-2 system, the players are now all rubbish. Nastastic has been downgraded to "little better than Savic" by the same people hailing him as a revelation last season, Yaya is lazy, Fernadinho worse than Gareth Barry and Nigel De Jong, Clichy a waste of space.

But despite the downbeat mood today, this was never the crucial match of the campaign. Yes, a victory would have made qualification a near-certainty, but it was always unlikely as Bayern rarely lose. No, the two matches against CSKA Moscow will decide who qualifies with Bayern, and City must be looking to get at least four points. A draw in Moscow wound be no disaster, if the job can be finished off in the return match - what may go in City's favour is that once more the final match will be a dead-rubber for Bayern. Ten points should be enough this time around if four of the points come off City's main competitor for that second qualifying place.

You know the opposition are good if the City fans applaud them and individual players off the pitch.

More moronic reporting from The Mirror's Martin Lipton, suggesting Mancini was ditched for similar Euro failures. Except that he wasn't Martin, the fact he had fallen out with everyone, which was very widely publicised at the time, may have had more to do with it.

It should be noted City are still 2nd in the group.

So the Everton match becomes vital now. A response is needed in the competition City fans want more than any, against a bogey team unbeaten this season. They've also got a new club crest, so they're bound to be on a high. Now we'll see what they are made of.

Do City Lack The Mental Toughness When Conceding Goals?

There are two narratives to Manchester City's defence. There is the narrative about the league's meanest defence, an accolade earned over the past three seasons. This is the mean defence that keeps more clean sheets than anyone else, the defence that thus wins Joe Hart repeated "Golden Gloves" awards.
Then there is the other narrative. The leaky defence, that wobbles and occasionally falls over. And this is the defence found mostly away from home that every now and then loses its grip on reality. And it's in this second narrative that we see an interesting anomaly – when City concede a goal, the floodgates often open.

It is no surprise that the Champions League holders added further goals to Franck Ribery's early strike this week, but it is more surprising to see Aston Villa score 3 in fairly quick succession, for Cardiff to do the same (all 6 goals coming in the second half, against a side yet to concede in the first half in the league this season). City finished last season by conceding three at home to Norwich. They conceded three quick goals at Spurs prior to that, three at Southampton, two at home to Liverpool, three at Norwich, three at home to United. They also conceded twice in the first three games of the 12/13 season.

There are caveats to this general rule. If the opposition scores their first goal late, then further goals are naturally unlikely to follow - for example, Wigan's FA Cup Final winner or West Ham's consolation goal at the Etihad last season. In the recent Manchester derby, Rooney scored fairly late, and too late for City to capitulate.

This rule is not always the case of course - it is not an exclusive occurrence, but the stats show that over the past year, in games where City have conceded, they have on average conceded over 2 goals per game. This doesn't mean that when conceding a goal a second follows the majority of the time, as City's propensity to concede three goals skews the figures somewhat. But there clearly seems an inbuilt inability to "shut up shop" after a first goal is conceded.

It's hard to explain why the team with the tightest defence often concedes goals in clumps. The only explanation I can offer is that it is purely a case of mentality. Perhaps there is a lack of mental toughness that rears its ugly head when a goal is conceded - heads drop and the team fails to recover, conceding further. Recent goals conceded can mostly be attributed to individual errors and a momentary drop in concentration. Roberto Mancini's first job at City was to tighten a defence that leaked regularly under Mark Hughes, yet even under his stewardship there were random games where the defence malfunctioned (some of which are mentioned above). With Manuel Pellgrini's desire for "beautiful football" and an under-fire goalkeeper under intense scrutiny, this is a trend that looks likely to continue.

Manchester City 3 Everton 1

Now that was better.

As I was on my way to Turkey, I had the "pleasure" of watching the match on BT Sport. Good lord. An appalling set of pundits have been put together, who combined to produce the effect similar to watching Everton's in-house TV channel.

Mark Halsey has made his own headlines elsewhere, shamelessly sticking the knife in, in the pursuit of money and fame, the latter something a referee should never have, and he distinguished himself with a master-class of talking out of his anus during this match.

Apart from the contentious penalty decisions and the desperate portrayal of a cheated Everton side, the fact is that City were the better side for the final 75 minutes, and fully deserved the win. Once Everton took the lead, the season was already tottering over a precipice, but the response from City was excellent, and it could have been a bigger margin of victory if Sergio Aguero has been more clinical.

And despite the desperate need by some to somehow implicate Joe Hart in Everton's goal, he was not at fault for the goal, and with many of his supposed mistakes, they were preceded by other mistake from team-mates. On this occasion, he had a fairly comfortable day.

Job done, and off the pitch, the club signalled its intentions in taking the club onto the next level and beyond…

The Expansion Of The Etihad That's Literally Splitting The Fans

The natives are revolting once more. With another batch of literature from Manchester City dropping through letterboxes across Stockport postcodes this week, the creeping realisation of the effects of financial fair play and the club's insatiable desire for extra revenue (that this week led Tom Glick to declare City would soon be in the top five club revenues) has meant that with the proposed stadium expansion comes the inevitable extension of the corporate areas spreading out away from the halfway line and the subsequent exodus of many of the East and West stand 's current inhabitants, priced out of their seats.

Whatever the rights or wrongs of this reorganization there can be no excuse for being surprised at the developments. It has been coming for years, and previous club literature has mentioned the possible expansion, so there has been fair warning, however wronged people may feel.

I attended a fans forum in the Commonwealth Suite a few weeks ago and at the meeting, Danny Wilson (Director of Sales, Service & Operations) said that the trade-off for the expansion of the corporate areas is the introduction of cheaper seats – so the club presumably see it as like for like, with no detriment to the fans. As was seen with the conversion of the North Stand into a family area, they clearly see the situation whereby fans have to move as an acceptable by-product of the club's development and expansion. You may not, and that's fair enough. It's not for me to preach to you whether it's acceptable to have to move. It's not nice, and you have the right to complain. Either way, it's happening though, so start planning now.

There is an obvious consequence to enlarging corporate areas, and that is enlarging the swathe of empty seats after half-time and perhaps before it too. We've all seen the inability of some "corporates" to return from the bar after the break, and a 4-0 lead in a Champions League final wouldn't be enough to lure some of them back from their Asti Spumante* and prawns with vanilla foam (they're to die for). It also seems unlikely to me that the market is out there to sell these seats week-in, week-out, but City have done plenty of research on this and are clearly confident they can. At the aforementioned Fans' Forum, Danny Wilson commented that fan surveys had shown a strong interest in premium seating, which not only raised my eyebrows, but caused them to levitate out of the room.

But there is another section of fans that is forgotten in this scenario, the silent majority. They don't sit in padded seats, they won't be squeezed out by the corporate expansion and they won't be sat in the cheapest seats also. It's the fans who will remain exactly where they are, and presumably put up with the constant, creeping increases in prices, year on year. This separate problem of pricing out the majority of the stadium not affected by the expansion is the biggest problem of all, because once swathes of various blocks around the ground say enough is enough, then that is the beginning of the end of the match-day experience, an experience already tarnished across the land by modern consumerism and the reluctance to talk about a return to terraces. The introduction of cheap season tickets by the club is a great move (just like the introduction of direct-debit options), but it won't house everyone that wants to move there, it won't satisfy everyone feeling the pinch as modern football becomes more and more expensive with each passing season.

The situation hasn't been helped by the scurrilous rumours that have abounded over the future plans of the club and the usual jumping-of-the-gun and doom-mongering amongst a minority of fans. The best I heard was that the whole of the 2nd tier was to become a corporate section, just like Wembley, an idea so ridiculous I've only just stopped laughing. At least the club have been open with us fans and had a full consultation, including the opportunity to see the plans at the ground.

The owners have given us so much, we almost have lost the right to complain, but a wonderful team in a wonderful stadium is not as impressive or fulfilling when experienced through a television screen, a scenario many are already resigned to and a scenario that creeps ever closer for me personally, as I already spend money on football way beyond my means. We cannot however allow our perception of modern football to be clouded by a warped sense of nostalgia, as things are better now, but there is, as always, a price to pay. We'll never know if the owners are increasing match-day revenue solely to meet financial fair play criteria, or whether they always intended to break-even come-what-may. But it is a false economy increasing prices if it results in reduced attendances. It is a fine balancing act getting it right, and at this moment many fans are wobbling.

*that's what posh people drink, right?

West Ham 1 Manchester City 3

The away-day hoodoo put to bed and like the previous 3-1 victory, the win was thoroughly deserved by a City side who were the better side for the vast majority of the game. 63% possession told the story, along with nine shots on target compared to West Ham's two.

As is often the case, the team line-up raised an eyebrow or two, with the inclusion of Javi Garcia in defence, ahead of Joleon Lescott. Thus the traditional slating of him commenced long before a ball was kicked in anger, but thankfully in the end he did just fine. Micah Richards also got the nod ahead of Pablo Zabaleta, showing that Manuel Pellegrini has faith in using him (unlike others) and we can expect plenty of team changes whilst City fight for trophies on multiple fronts.

Another poor United result buoyed spirits prior to kick off. You can never write them off, even without Ferguson in charge, but we are getting close to the point of taking more notice of Arsenal's results than United's. Strange days.

With every good result, it is hard and probably not necessary to single out individuals. Great performances were scattered across the park. There must be a mention for Sergio Aguero though, who was imperious, and is back to full-fitness and thus is back to his best. Likewise David Silva.

Like the manager who is gradually imposing his brand on the club and slowly reaping the rewards, Fernandinho continues to improve, and thus as Gareth Barry hacked his way round Goodison Park, we are spared, at least for a few days, more pining for players since departed.

It's a shame you don't get an assist for ignoring the ball, but Alvaro Negredo deserves one in the lead up to City's opener. His knowledge of Aguero's positioning suggests that their partnership is moving onto a new level.

Even with Andy Carroll absent, it was feared that City could suffer from an aerial threat, not an uncommon feature of a Sam Allardyce team, especially as the defence had already shown vulnerability in this area in previous matches. In the end, City coped admirably, and this helped nullify the home team's threat. City players won 21 of their 29 aerial duels, with Garcia winning the most headers – 5 – along with Fernandinho.

You could argue that the West Ham keeper could have done slightly better with Aguero's header, but I won't dwell on the matter as I struggle to spell his name.

Better substitutions from Pellegrini this time too, as he seems to have learned some lessons from recent weeks – the changes helped tighten up the midfield and nullify the moderate West Ham threat.

There's no need for negativity right now, but I still wonder about Gael Clichy. I never thought I'd say these words, but you can see an argument for Kolrov's inclusion in the team for some games – mostly due to the fact Clichy just will not cross. Every time he gets near the opposition penalty area, a check back inevitably follows. Kolrov, for all his faults, can put in a mean cross, though his team mates seem to have a problem anticipating them.

Thankfully there were no presents from City for Sam Allardyce on his 59th birthday. Devoid of any controversies to blame West Ham's defeat on, Allardyce used the trusted excuse of City's wealth. I imagine he will do the same when next they lose to United. That might be some time away though.

Everyone seems to love cheeky Kevin Nolan, but is there a bigger gobs**te on the pitch outside Old Trafford than him? Bred the Ryan Giggs way, namely to get in the referee's face at any opportunity, he is never to blame for anything, happy to try and get opposition players booked and always the victim when any decision goes against him, even if the decision to book him followed the decapitation of David Silva.

For his goal celebration ALONE, Nolan should be the most reviled footballer in Britain, if not globally. What could have possessed him to think one day: "How should I celebrate if I score? A salute to the crowd? Run the length of the pitch waving my shirt above my head? Perhaps some TOP
BANTZ with team-mates, or a complicated dance routine? Nah, I think I'll impersonate poultry."
The worst goal celebration since Robert Earnshaw last machine-gunned the crowd, let's all pray that he never scores again.

And whilst we're at it, thank god Gareth Bale has buggered off to foreign climes so that we are not subjected to his appalling (trademarked!) heart celebration.

So two tricky league matches successfully navigated. And so onto Russia. CSKA Moscow are out of form, and lost to Zenit St Petersburg this week, but no game on the other side of the continent is ever anything less than difficult. I was in Russia in June and it never went dark, but if you believe stereotypes the game will be played in bitterly cold, dark conditions, and it will probably be snowing too.

Actually, I've just checked the forecast and it is going to be cold. Fancy that. Anyway, City enter a vital winner-takes-all section of the Champions League campaign now, the two legs against CSKA probably deciding who joins Bayern Munich in the knock-out stage of the competition. A draw would be no disaster, especially if City can finish the job off in the return game, which would then require CSKA to turn over Bayern. And even then, with Bayern's last game probably a dead-rubber for them (again), there are further opportunities for City. Let's hope the quick dash home for the early kick-off is rewarded with a professional performance.

No Surprises In Alex Ferguson's Myopic Memoirs

The 2pm unveiling was greeted by journalists like the fall of the Berlin Wall, man landing on the moon and the JFK assassination all rolled into one. One small step backwards for Man United, but a giant leap forward for mankind. By 4pm I had read most of the book simply by scrolling through my Twitter feed. Journalist Mike Calvin commented at his surprise at the blanket coverage of a man who despised Calvin's profession so much, not that the journalists had much option.

Touching Cloth

Alex Ferguson's autobiography launch was always going to be big news, but it was notable for what it didn't say as much as for what it did. Ferguson's ire, strong opinions and ideology did not extend to dissecting the Glazer's influence on the club, his fall out with the previous owners that led to the American takeover or his son's role as an agent. He even forgot to mention his speeding ticket and bowel evacuation caused by a dicky stomach. If you've ever had a session on Holts bitter, you'll understand his predicament.

Moustaches

But what of City? Unsurprisingly they don't make much of an appearance until recently. You see, nobody knew their name.

Even less surprisingly, Ferguson's miserly myopic musings tend to bare little basis in fact or reality. His most laughable claim regarded the 6-1 victory at Old Trafford.

"There was never a point where City looked superior to us."
"We battered them."

That is without doubt the most ridiculous thing I've ever read, and I've seen excerpts from Harry Redknapp's autobiography. The truth is, it should have been ten.

Or at least it WAS the most ridiculous thing I've read, and it kept that record for a good 5 days until Ferguson embarked on the first of his Q & A sessions at the Lowry as part of his SELL-OUT tour.

Ferguson, 71, said: "We had bad starts to the season many times. We are the only club in that league that can come from behind to win the league because of our history."

Let that sink in for a moment.

Fergie, Sign Him Up

There was further drivel reserved for Carlos Tevez, who Ferguson considered an impact player, which is strange considering United paid £18m to loan him for two years and then announced on the that they had tried to sign him on a permanent deal, which would have made him the highest-paid player at the club. The club announcement still sits sullenly in the depths of the official site to this day. And they call us liars.

As for Mancini allowing Tevez to return post-strike, Ferguson commented: *"Showed desperation…..as a manager, he let himself down."* He added that Mancini lost some prestige over the affair.

Haunted

Thus says the man who welcomed back a player that karate-kicked a supporter, the man who was so desperate he dragged Paul Scholes out of retirement (that's the Paul Scholes that once refused to play for United) and let Wayne Rooney hold his club to ransom. I doubt Mancini was too bothered about the loss of prestige when the title was won soon after. I'm guessing that helped his prestige a wee bit.

The Tevez poster obviously rankled with him, as was the intention, but if you have an approved banner in the ground counting the years since City won a trophy (and I don't have a problem with that, it's TOP BANTER), then you lose the moral high ground.

The only surprise is he didn't mention our 20,000 empty seats every week. Perhaps the Welcome to Manchester posters would have been more dignified if they had the club's sponsors mentioned in the corner, as AIG were happy to do for the Munich tragedy anniversary posters.

Knocked Off His Perch

Even from snippets it's clear the book is full of contradictions. Ferguson doesn't rate Gerrard as a top, top player yet once said he was the best midfielder that Liverpool had ever had (along with Souness) and commented in 2004 that he was the one player who could replace Roy Keane.

"He is physically and technically precocious. He's got a good engine and remarkable energy. He reads the game and he passes quickly. I would hate to think Liverpool have someone as good as Roy Keane."
"He has become the most influential player in England, bar none. More than Vieira. Not that Vieira lacks anything, but I think he does more for his team than Vieira does and has way more to his game. I've watched him quite a lot. Anyone would love to have him in their team.'

His words, not mine.

One Mirror reporter estimates that he tried to sign him on at least three occasions. He talks of the Newcastle job as the one that should excite any manager, a missed opportunity, yet last year called them a "wee club in the north-east".

The snidest digs appear not to be towards City but Liverpool, his sparring with them well-documented in the past. To score extra points he lowers himself to criticising some of their current squad. As Daniel Taylor tweeted – imagine if another manager had done something similar with one of his players – how do you think he'd take that?

Thankfully Jon Snow was prepared to break ranks and question Ferguson about his past. "I don't hold grudges," stuttered the man who banned the BBC for seven years. Roy Keane also fired back, but taking sides over a Keane/Ferguson fall-out is akin to supporting Piers Morgan when he's arguing with Alan Sugar.

Kryptoknight

The problem Ferguson now has is that the day he retired, his powers waned. He can't ban Channel 4 now they've dared question his socialist ideals, unless he removes the channel off his TV at home. And a book deal means schmoozing the very people he's shown utter disdain for over the years – to the point of disliking younger journalists for the casual way they often dressed.

Ferguson said he wrote the book for the fans, as they had a right to know what happened on various issues, apart of course most of the major issues that he completely avoided, and I think we can all agree that United fans were keen to have Ferguson dissect various Liverpool players, diss Owen Hargreaves or reveal secrets from the dressing room.

But Keane got one thing right. Alex Ferguson is not one to talk about loyalty when he releases a book that unsettles the club he managed for 27 years, timed to make maximum impact and income, and which naturally discusses and criticises many of the players that made him the success he is. A knight of the realm hawking his book round Stretford's Tesco Extra? I'm not sure that Robbie Savage has got a point with that particular criticism, not that Ferguson cares what people think. He'll make more money out of this book than he ever could from horse spunk. At least for us bitter blues there's comfort in the knowledge that Aguero's goal will haunt him forever.

The Bumper Bundle of City Slurs

The sheikhs will get bored. This was the default setting for the anti-City brigade in the early months and years of the new regime, but you may still see the odd straggler pop up every now and then with the same claim, their desperation tangible. The construction of one of the world's premier academies has rather scuppered this argument, as has the announcement this week of the club-backed plan to build 7000 homes on wasteland near the ground.

How can City spend so much money during a recession? My personal favourite this one. Never mind that every second, City players' wages are making the government money, every ticket sold makes the government VAT, never mind that owners from Abu Dhabi aren't responsible for the British economy, never mind that they are regenerating a swathe of east Manchester, the bulls**t mountain peaked soon after the takeover when Mark Lawrenson commented that City's money could be used to build hospitals, whilst Mike Calvin opined that the Sheikh should take over FCUM.

Spent a billion pounds on the team. Textbook figure-spinning here, as repeated by prize buffoon Brian Reade this week. You will have read 100 times about City's billion pound team. It is nothing of the sort of course, as a billion pounds is the total investment in the club by the owners, including huge building projects and naturally the figure ignores income from sales and suchlike. But it's such a nice, big, round figure for the world's dimwits to quote.

City are the Sheikh's "plaything". As a kid I had a lego fire station and Subbuteo. Sheikh Mansour clearly moves on different levels. To be fair, I do recall that the rich kids at my school all owned football clubs.

The oil will run out. When it does City will be royally screwed, goes the argument. When City's owner makes a couple of billion pounds in one afternoon from selling his shares in Barclays, the argument falls down somewhat.

City have bought success. Remember football before City came along and killed it? I particularly remember United's band of plucky part-timers, loanees and free transfers that swept all before them in the 1990s. Simpler times. We will all be reminded of City's buying power should Liverpool win this season's Premier League, whilst their spending, good and bad, will be consigned to history's dustbin.

You can't buy success. Some argue the opposite of the above point. Yes, yes you can, as demonstrated by United and Chelsea over the past 20 years. Repeatedly breaking the transfer record suggests otherwise doesn't it United? Paying a player £300,000 a week might not be quite successful however. Now that United have had a bad season, what will they do? Spend of course, and spend BIG.

Emptyhad. TOP BANTER KLAXON. Yep, City never sell out, apart from all those games that they have sold out, and woe betide if anyone goes to the toilet during a match as the watching nation will seize upon your naked seat in an instant. This is an argument that has transcended social media and is parroted by MEN, Guardian journalists and beyond. As news filters through that City's ground expansion will start imminently, prepare to be bored senseless by witty comments on not selling out.

City fans are bitters and liars. As shown by the previous point, the rest of this article and the season as a whole for the team across the city, I think we can now all say with some conviction who the bitters and liars are.

Most City fans used to support Chelsea. Back to the playground we go, for a claim so puerile and stupid it's hard to dissect. The sad thing is that the people who come out with this think they are actually being funny. Think about that for a moment. #Megalolz.

You can't buy class. Well indeed. Can't really argue with this. You can't buy class such as Vincent Kompany, Fernandinho, David Silva and Sergio Aguero, players who ooze class and humility on and off the pitch, but you can buy a striker banned for racist remarks, a defender banned for racist remarks, a compulsory cup scheme, owners leeching hundreds of millions out of the club, owners who change the colour of the home kit or the name of the team and you can buy £1000+ season tickets or Marione Fellaini. So yeah, spot on. If only City fans could demonstrate such vast reservoirs of class to fly a plane over the ground during a match calling for our manager to be sacked because we couldn't cope with six months without success.

All City fans have moustaches. A ridiculous claim. I know at least two City fans who don't have moustaches (hello Karen and Clara).

All City fans live in Stockport. Yet somehow we are all glory-hunters, supported Chelsea until 5 years ago and the ground is full of day-trippers, because as we all know…

Where were we when we were s**t? Nothing to say on this. Embarrassing.

City players are all mercenaries. Unlike Wayne Rooney.

City fans will ruin the minute's silence for the 50th anniversary of the Munich tragedy.
One journalist demanded one policeman on the touchline for each City fan in the ground. Every other journalist demanded severe sanctions before the inevitable had even happened.
As the minutes' silence was played out impeccably, Sky turned the volume up to 11, so that you could hear a tramp shouting at a pigeon in the city centre. All to no avail. The City fans refused to play ball and give the media the story they desperately wanted and then the team made things worse by winning.

With the money they've spent….
A favourite refrain of Barry Glendenning on the Guardian podcast, after which another guest usually posts a more balanced view after which Glendenning gets tongue-tied by his own flawed arguments. Anyway, with the money City have spent, they should:
1) Have the league sewn up by Christmas

(subsection point: "If Ferguson or Mourinho were in charge of this team", etc)
2) Win every trophy
3) Be a match for Barcelona et al
4) Be nurturing the future England team
5) Be able to sell out the occasional match
6) Not be playing Martin Demichelis, ever.

Ok, I'll give them that last one*.

*not really.

CSKA Moscow 1 Manchester City 2: Some Thoughts

Another tricky match navigated, another victory. No injuries reported either, and those two facts alone are the only things that matter. Because of the pitch, it is hard to analyse player performances when the whole game was turned into a near-lottery. Some have mentioned that the venue problems doesn't bode well for the World Cup of 2018, but apart from the fact that 2018 is five years way, I think it's fair to say that money will be thrown at that particular spectacle. As we will see, there is a far bigger elephant in the room for 2018.

It is embarrassing for Russian football though that prior to a Champions League match a club was painting its pitch green, and not even the same shade as the grass that had survived on the pitch. It also doesn't paint (sorry) UEFA in a good light that they passed the pitch as fit for use, considering how anal they usually are (see their ridiculous set of rules of the Champions League final venue, where it is forbidden to as much as sneeze near the pitch for up to a fortnight prior to the blue riband event).

There was the traditional raising of the eyebrows as the team news filtered out. The full-backs were rotated once more, showing not only that City have some strength in depth in that area, but also that no full-back is having a sensational season so far. They are all interchangeable.

GARCIA KLAXON. Yes, once again, Javi Garcia got the nod at centre-back. I can only presume that Pellegrini does not want to play with two left-footed central defenders, but surely that is a better option than Garcia? Anyway, those bemoaning the Demichelis signing are probably counting down the days until he is match-fit. Garcia wasn't quite as bad as some proclaimed, but it's fair to say he wasn't good. As slow as ever, ponderous, barely bothering to jump prior to their goal and so susceptible to any ball over the top. Time is running out for him to "come good". Having said that, along with Zabaleta he made the most interceptions (3). It still felt like Nastastic was bailing him out for much of the time though.

Yet again though City have won deservedly, but are painted (sorry once more) as somehow being fortunate to come away with 3 points. It makes a change I guess from a string of undeserved defeats. Maybe the high-foot decision before CSKA's disallowed goal was touch-and-go, but it should be mentioned that the players, most notably Garcia, stopped playing on hearing the whistle. It may have made no difference, but we will never know. What I do know is that City were the better side, but almost paid once more for their profligacy by retreating in the last 20 minutes. CSKA's penalty appeals were weak, and whilst Negredo did appear to hand ball for City's disallowed goal, a yellow card was ludicrously harsh considering he didn't know what was going on.

And so onto the paranoia section (part 1). City were portrayed by many as nailed-on victors prior to the match, against an out-of-form CSKA. You'd think they only had to turn up to defeat the Russian champions. Funny though that no other English team is expected to travel across Europe and win easily. Have these people never watched Champions League football? Did Barcelona go to Celtic and turn them over? Have United regularly thrashed teams away, as they played middling team after middling team, and ground out repeated 1-0 victories? No of course not. Yet a City victory on a cabbage-patch pitch in a freezing Moscow is somehow portrayed as a fortunate victory.

Time for Part Deux of the weekly paranoia section. Except it isn't paranoia anymore. On Tuesday I watched Arsenal fall at home to Borussia Dortmund, and you could almost picture Clive Tydesley and Andy Townsend sat in the press box in full Arsenal kit, clutching Aaron Ramsey hot water bottles, vigorously swinging their Emirates rattles. They were so pro-Arsenal it started to affect their judgement, and at one point Townsend even proclaimed "come on Arsenal!" When Aaron Ramsey made a mistake that cost a goal, if you listened carefully you could hear Clive Tyldesley's tears dropping gently onto his microphone. All well and good you may say, it is fine for commentators to favour the English side. Fast forward 21 hours. Aguero slices the ball wide when he should have scored – near-silence from Martin Tyler. A CSKA player breaks in midfield – Tyler shrieks like a 15-year-old girl meeting

One Direction. Repeat on a loop for 90 minutes. And then there was.....

Niall Quinn – dear oh dear oh dear.

Joe Hart has a propensity to come out to onrushing attackers and do a "nothing" type of jump as he is lobbed. I wonder if he should stay closer to his line in such circumstances. Anyway, that's the ultra-cynical bit out of the way, he coped admirably on a pitch that must give goalkeepers sleepless nights, and he has responded to the avalanche of criticism of previous months in the perfect way. His save at the end didn't require him to move to be honest, but he still has to be in the right place and that one moment has greatly increased City's chances of qualifying for the knock-out stage.

Fernandinho was excellent once more. Who knew that a player could improve after having a bit of time to settle in a new country? He made six successful tackles, twice as many as any of his team-mates. Whilst Yaya made the most passes as usual (83, with 88% accuracy), Fernandinho was second with 70 passes with an 89% accuracy.

There was one penalty that should have been awarded last night. You won't have read about it in any match reports, and you won't have heard a single word on the matter from the commentators. For one of Dzeko's first misses, he got to the ball before the CSKA keeper and prodded wide. Groans all round, but after he got to the ball, the keeper took him out. It was a penalty, and yet they never seem to be given, and no one seems to care one jot. Strange.

That chip from Negredo for Aguero's 2nd goal. Oh my. And what a brave and intelligent header too. Aguero had actually been rather wasteful before his brace, but thankfully made up for it. It is saying something about City's European history that he is now City's leading European scorer of all time with 10 goals (passing Francis Lee)

Graeme Souness. Now we're talking. I have admired Souness as a pundit for a while now, and last night he did not disappoint once more. He actually says it as it is, uses common sense, and seems to know his football. Fancy that! He also got the Dzeko/Negredo analysis spot-on. And he likes City because of their approach to the game, bless him.

There is a bigger issue emanating from last night of course…..

IF FIFA's delegates cared about racism, or homophobia, they would have considered the issue before awarding tournaments to the likes of Russia and Qatar. There are more important problems than the summer heat of an Arab state or the transport network behind the now-rusty Iron Curtain. At half-time in the United match, an anti-racism advert was aired by UEFA. All well and good, but it needs a bit more than an advert on UK television to address this problem.

It was a very dignified response from Yaya Toure after the match (and on Twitter – "Hate or racism cannot affect me when so many people are showing me love and support on a daily basis") – I'm not sure I could have been that calm and considered. But sadly, he's probably been in this position time after time.

The clubs themselves are not directly responsible for chants, but they are responsible for the actions of their fans within the ground, and have a duty to deal with incidents rather than ignore them or sweep them under the carpet. This becomes rather more troublesome however if the owners of clubs don't even accept there is a problem, if racism is prevalent in society as a whole, in large swathes of a continent.

We cannot rely on the clubs themselves to fix the problem, which has always been crystal clear. It is up to the authorities to ram home how unacceptable this is, and drag some of these Neanderthals into the 21st century, kicking and screaming. Fines clearly don't work, especially the paltry amounts that are handed out. UEFA seem to think that appearing late for the 2nd half or a player carrying the name of a betting company on his Y-fronts is a bigger offence than a monkey chant. Stop the talk, the banners, the messages passed along the teams as they line up, and

ACTUALLY DO SOMETHING. Start with matches behind closed doors, progress to bans, and force the clubs to deal with unsavoury fans whether they like it or not. Even this isn't perfect, as the ones who need to be punished most are the actual perpetrators of the taunts, so a system must be in place to make sure this happens.

I am being slightly harsh however. It's not that UEFA have done nothing so far - they are finally beginning to react to the problem (see later). So far this season, UEFA has imposed full stadium bans on three clubs - Dinamo Zagreb of Croatia, Legia Warsaw of Poland and Honved of Hungary - for racist behaviour by their supporters while five other clubs have had partial stadium closures. At least UEFA have stated that fines will no longer be the weapon of choice to punish such transgressions, after new regulations were brought in at the start of the season, which sees at first a partial stadium closure, followed by a full closure plus fine. But is that enough? It's just a shame it's taken this long for the penny to drop.

It's deplorable enough to chant racial slurs, but it becomes even more staggering when your own team has two black players on the pitch. What must they be thinking?

CSKA however deny there even being any taunts. So ignore everything I've said- I mean they would hardly make that up would they? Whatever happened last night, it has clearly been a problem in Russia and many other countries previously, and is sadly showing little sign of going away.

Chelsea 2 Manchester City 1: Some Thoughts

Twenty-four hours later, and I'm still angry. I haven't felt like this since Samir Nasri waved the white flag at Robin Van Persie's free-kick.

Oh and I guess there was that FA Cup final too.

As soon as Vincent Kompany's absence was announced by Pellegrini on Friday, the arguments raged over who to pick alongside Nastastic. My pick was Lescott, because he's actually a central defender. So is Demichelis of course, but as he hasn't played for the club yet and was coming back from injury, I doubted his match-fitness and whether this was the best time to throw him into the team. Others even suggested Micah Richards, though when was the last time he played in the centre of defence? It made no sense to me. The general consensus was anyone but Garcia. In the end, Pellegrini went for…..

As usual, it was an interesting team line-up, with Demichelis trusted to make the most difficult of debuts, and Javi Garcia picked in front of him. After unscrunching my face I realised it made sense. With Chelsea playing one up front, City did not want a repeat of the Bayern Munich match where City were overrun in midfield. So picking five in midfield made sense, and it was a line-up that allowed Yaya a more advanced role. The extra man also prevented Chelsea's dangerous counter-attacking capabilities to wreak havoc on the visitors, and it was as usual simple lofted balls that did for City in the end.

The usually excellent Football365's Matthew Stanger didn't agree though, arguing that Mourinho won the battle of tactics. I'm not sure how he came to that conclusion, as he argued that City should have persisted with two up front. But unless one of the front two was prepared to constantly drop back into midfield to help out, I don't see how it would have worked. I'm no tactical expert though, so what do I know?

For all the arguments over who to pick in defence, it was the more obvious picks that in the end that ended up causing the damage. Demichelis may have looked shaky early doors, and there was a lack of understanding that allowed Torres in for an easy chance, but in the end I think he did just fine, as did Garcia. As mentioned, there were bigger issues elsewhere.

It was almost a game of two halves, and I think a draw would have been a fair result. After City had established themselves in the game in the first half, Chelsea took control, and fashioned a number of chances. They could easily have been at least two up at the break. In the 2nd half however, City were the better side, dominant in possession, and they fashioned all the chances, until the game was handed to them on a plate.

It's not just Joe Hart's star that has waned. I have spoke about him previously, and there has definitely been a drop-off in the level of performances from Gael Clichy, to the extent that Aleksander Kolarov is now looking like the better option. How has it come to this? City need a top-class left-back. Clichy was poor for Chelsea's opening goal, and then fell to pieces for a short while afterwards.

So there's no avoiding it any longer. Time to discuss the goalkeeper. Hart has made seven errors that have led to goals since the start of last season, more than any other keeper in the Premier League. I was amazed that people are sharing the blame for Chelsea's winner, when for me it lies squarely at one man's feet. Hart may well claim that he shouted it was his ball, but the fact is it wasn't and he should never have been anywhere near the damn thing as Nastastic headed the ball back in his direction, having been in control of the situation right up to the point that his goalkeeper flew past him. What on earth was he thinking? It just did not require his intervention, unless he thought the windy conditions were going to defeat his team mate. I mentioned in my CSKA match report that he has a tendency to come flying out of his goal every now and then and make "nothing" challenges. He did it for CSKA's goal, and now it has really cost the team. I also commented that he had got over his bad spell and was looking back to his best – and then he goes and does this. The chances of

Malaga's goalkeeper following his old manager north increases once more.

I wouldn't say Nastastic was entirely blameless however. He was concentrating on the ball, but he must have seen out of the corner of his eye a big green man flying his way. A header anywhere else wouldn't have resulted in a goal, but it was laid on a plate for Torres. So, so frustrating.

Now Mourinho might be a grade-A ***** (choose your own swear-word), but Pellegrini should still have shaken his hand. The only surprise is that the media haven't made a bigger deal of this today, because as we have seen in the past, failing to shake the opposition manager's hand has been likened to serial killing, drink-driving or even spitting.

And it's reassuring to know that the Premier League's old guard still influence games as they see fit. A quick word from John Terry in Howard Webb's ear and ten seconds later Pablo Zabaleta was booked for an innocuous challenge.

The fact is that City have played well for the vast majority of games this season, but individual errors are costing the team dear. The players must take responsibility for this. If the mistakes can be cut out, it is not too late to make up lost ground. United fans will point out that City are only two points ahead of an oft-criticised United team, but I would offer in Pellegrini's defence the fact that because we have often played well, we seem more capable of going on a good run and getting back up the table. But only time will tell.

So now it is necessary to put a good run together. City have plenty of winnable games coming up, and can make up ground if they put this bad result behind them and move on. Some of the fringe players will get the chance to stake their claim at Newcastle on Wednesday. Pantilimon will start as was always planned and the media will shriek at it being a sign that Joe Hart's days are numbered.

UEFA's New Policy On Racism More Robust Than It Appears

On the surface, and perhaps below it too, it seems like a limp and impotent punishment, another pitiful response from UEFA and another stick to beat them with in their response to the fight against racism in football. Following racial taunts directed at Yaya Toure, CSKA Moscow have been ordered to play their game against Bayern Munich with a partial stadium closure, with one stand to be closed. That will teach those nasty racists eh? Now they will have to sit elsewhere, and we all know there's nothing racists hate more than having to relocate.

But sarcasm aside, UEFA have not been quite as impotent as has been portrayed (mostly by me on Twitter). Firstly, they have brought in tougher rules this season of which partial stadium closure is just the first step - further indiscretions would lead to fines, full stadium closures and even point deductions and expulsion from tournaments. What's more, the first punishment is not as pitiful as you might think. Anti-discrimination groups have helped push for these new rules as an empty stand has a huge visual effect, embarrassing the club as the world witnesses their shame. They also believe it can help spark debate amongst fans and lead to those fans self-policing racist behaviour thereafter.

This is clearly an improvement on past sanctions, the pitiful fines meted out that helped tarnish UEFA's name especially when coupled with their more aggressive approach to trivial infractions such as arriving on the pitch late or advertising unapproved sponsors.

Some will argue that it is still not enough and that a first offence should lead straight to expulsion, as Stan Collymore has argued.. FIFA too, more specifically Sepp Blatter himself have commented that more stringent punishments are required. I would add that the fine as part of the 2nd phase of punishments is €50,000, a pointless amount for a Champions League competitor.

There is no right answer to what is appropriate, it is merely opinion, but the problem is where you draw the line. Is a couple of fans acting in a racist manner sufficient to expel a club from European competitions? No? How about five? Ten? One hundred? Where do we sit with slurs against a country, or religion? As always nothing is just black and white.

The stringent denials and counter-accusations from CSKA's motley crew of see-no-evil hear-no-evil lackies is a separate issue and you could argue they shouldn't come out of this with a clean slate. It's slander at the very least to suggest Yaya Toure had fabricated the whole affair.

The extra problem though is that further action is required not only from the clubs themselves to face up to the problem, but governments too. Football's ruling bodies can push clubs to action, but getting governments and society as a whole to change its viewpoint is a whole new problem. It also remains to be seen if UEFA's resolve will stretch to expelling a team from Europe – especially a team with great aspirations and good lawyers.

Newcastle United 0 Manchester City 2: Some Thoughts

Phew. The Capital One Cup may not be the most glamorous of competitions, it may be City's 4th priority this season, but every trophy matters to some extent, and any cup tie that goes into extra time is tense. Especially when the dreaded spectre of penalties looms closer and closer on the horizon.

Though if the penalties remain on the horizon I guess a pedant might point out they are at all times the same distance away.

The team line-up was predictable – a selection of players who haven't been getting regular games. It pretty much picked itself. Naturally there was a story led by a vocal minority that Hart had been axed, for a game he was never going to start. Sky ran a loop of footage of him arriving at the ground.

Speaking of which, the Guardian match report stated: "Pantilimon – keeping goal in place of the dropped Hart."

The Daily Mail resorted to a 'Pantilimon Watch' and Ian Ladyman reported this steaming pile of manure: *'City's evening didn't improve much early in the second half, either. If this had been a performance under their previous manager Roberto Mancini, people would have suggested the players were not trying for their coach.'*

The man of the moment Pantilimon was solid, and did everything asked of him, without having to do so much he has immediately usurped Joe Hart in the first team. He made one crucial save in extra time, though Sky, for the first time in their history, did not see fit to replay whether Cisse was offside, as I felt he may have been.

Man of the Match for Pantilimon? Oh dear Sky, you can do better than that. What a pitiful attempt to newly-stir a dying story. Though in their defence, there were no outstanding candidates.

Paranoia!

Like Chelsea, it was a game of two halves, with the added bonus of a third and fourth one afterwards. City started poorly, especially in defence where Boyata was all at sea. I guess when you change a whole team you shouldn't expect them to click into gear and play like the first team. But too often City seem to change players and the change in performance is cavernous - the exit to Aston Villa last season was the prime example. Newcastle should have been ahead at the break as City struggled to gain any rhythm or gain any control over midfield. They were further unsettled by another injury to Jovetic, and you wonder how long we will all have to wait to see him properly.

But City improved in the second half, and came back into the game. Naturally the game gave further opportunities to whinge, and the theme of the night seemed to be how superior Chelsea's second string are, and thus how they are going to win the league and everything else with it.

Now of course I shouted and whinged at the TV screen all match too, but the fact is that City's second string played at Newcastle against what was close to a first-team for them, and won. That's a good thing, even though the performance wasn't that great.

Games like these are always marketed as a chance for players to show the manager they are worthy of more games. Unfortunately it's hard to shine when everyone around you is rusty and possibly not match-fit. It's easier to get a chance in a first choice XI and shine then instead.

But oh god Dzeko was terrible. Couldn't trap the ball, wayward shots, no presence, he is…oh hang on, he's just got an assist. But hey, that doesn't cover his flaws, he just doesn't contribute and too much of the time…oh hang on, he's scored, what a great goal, such a cool finish.
The man continues to puzzle, frustrate, then reward us just when we have given up.

Jesus Navas slightly disappointed once more, but opposition teams often double up on him – at the very least this should have freed some space for his colleagues. Like others though, his influence did increase as the game wore on. It took quite a few players until extra-time to insert their authority on the game.

For awarding a free-kick after Tiote fell over in the second half – for THAT ALONE, the referee should never be allowed to take charge of another football match. Elsewhere, he officiated in the same depressing manner that so many do in the modern game. Free kicks were awarded every time a player fell to the ground, players were penalised for absolutely nothing and he did a great job of disrupting the rhythm of the game. Well done.

And then - the perfect draw. I used to laugh at United fans who prayed for an away draw in cup competitions so that their bank balance wasn't battered once more by their club taking out money as part of their compulsory cup schemes. Now I get it. I can't afford the league games I go to, so whilst I want my team to win everything in sight, the financial side is hard to take and an away draw against the only non-Premier League team left in the competition will do me.

So City come through their run of four away games, one absolute howler away from contentment. Five of the next six games are at home – make it count City, make it count.

Manchester City 7 (SEVEN) Norwich City: Some Thoughts

City's 1st home Saturday 3pm match in 7 months, and it seemed like an age since I had been at the stadium, after 4 away games on the bounce.

As always with results like this, the question will be asked whether City were great or Norwich were terrible and as is usually the case it's a mixture of the two. Norwich were the worst side to tip up to the Etihad since United came to town (a few even argued that they were worse!). It's always nice to see your team's score spelled out in brackets.

It's not a good pointer for the future of the Norwich manager's future though. His players did not seem up for the battle, and after heavy investment in the summer, their season has been a huge disappointment.

So the story about Hart being dropped turned out to be true. City seem to have more leaks than a Welsh farm (I haven't thought that through if I'm honest), as all newspapers led with the story immediately after City's press conference on Sunday.

The debate over whether Hart should have been dropped has been done to death now. There is no right or wrong answer of course, and the most tedious element of the week was the expert opinions from ex-players, which naturally contradicted each other. By the weekend, it was clear that dropping Hart would be the making of him, whilst at the same time it would destroy his confidence. I didn't want to tempt fate by saying it, but this was always probably the best time to do it anyway, and the decision was never going to make much difference to the game itself, with City's Romanian stopper having little to do bar the odd bowl-out, kick, one save and the odd plucked cross. One last thing I will say though is that I have seen many argue that for all his mistakes, Hart has saved City on many occasions too – but that is his job, and no team can afford a keeper who regularly makes mistakes. Perhaps Hart has been unlucky – all goalkeepers make mistakes, but his inevitably lead to goals.

Even Sky couldn't give Pantilimon man of the match for this game.

Dwight Yorke may be the most inept commentator in the history of the game (some going that), but his rather bizarre comment that the score line somewhat flattered City had an small element of truth in it. It was one of those days where everything went City's way, including for once a couple of flukey goals early on to destroy

Norwich's confidence, but it was also one of those days where it was clear from the start that City were going to win.

Match of the Day – as usual, a pitiful level of analysis followed the highlights, as expected. City's biggest ever Premier League victory received scant praise, and Alan Shearer took the human race back 200 years with his insight. I only watch the programme for the football so it's not that big a deal, but it's worth noting that Gary Lineker was vociferous on Twitter last month defending the programme after a scathing review from the Guardian's Barney Ronay. He pointed out the ever-healthy viewing figures, but he missed the point completely – the only terrestrial TV football highlights programme for the Premier League will always have good viewing figures, irrespective of the banal punditry that accompanies it.

For all the talent in the squad, for Yaya's wonderful free-kicks, for the dazzling play and sublime goals, why can we still not field a player who can take a good corner? It seems to have been this way for a generation.

*OMG! OMG! Wifi in the ground! Amazeballs. Well not quite – the Wifi was trialled for the first time, and worked some of the time for me, and some of the time it did not – which is still a huge improvement on what went before.

The problem with knee-jerk reactions is that they can quickly look stupid. From last week's widespread disappointment at the Pellegrini regime and the oft-quoted fact that we were only 2 points ahead of the widely-slated Moyes-led United team, this week City find themselves a single point behind Chelsea. And without the Hart blooper last week, we'd be two points ahead of them. City are still two points ahead of United, but they were always being written off far too early, and are sadly still going to be contenders.

Jamie Carragher honoured us with his opinions on Pellegrini this weekend. Thankfully Carragher's thoughts were in print, so I can report everything he said, even if it did require visiting the Daily

Mail website. Carragher argued that City have gone backwards under our new manager. It's this sort of knee-jerk reaction that will slowly drive me to insanity. Ten games in and with two so-far successful cup competitions in progress, it's hard to see how we have gone backwards, apart from some recent issues in defence. By this time last season, City had already put in 5 poor performances, and under Mancini we conceded at least three goals on 8 occasions last season (ok seven, I can't put the last day defeat to Norwich down to him), and 2 goals on 6 other occasions. Some people will pine for Mancini until the day they die. It continues to stagger me that our new manager is supposed to implement a successful blueprint on the club immediately, and that the inevitable comparisons with his predecessor are done using results alone when it was widely reported that Mancini was not sacked for poor results, and that his successor was brought in to prevent a rerun of such problems within the club. But hey, we lost to Cardiff, so that means it was a huge mistake sacking Mancini. <sigh>

Manchester City 5 CSKA Moscow 2: Some Thoughts

Sometimes, there are more important things than a football match. Sometimes there are wider issues that need dealing with, that cannot be swept under the carpet, that cannot be forgotten by covering our eyes and ears and pretending that everything is ok. There is a cause at stake here, there is a persecution against a group of people that shames the government of Russia and shames also its people.
Free Pussy Riot.

So City are though to the knockout stage of the Champions League, and with two games to spare. Naturally, the pro-Mancini camp will argue that he would have qualified from this group, but let's forget the past and just acknowledge a job professionally done. Mancini struggled against Ajax and even at home to Villareal, but what's done is done.

And let's not forget that City can still win the group. This may seem unlikely, but the game against Bayern Munich will be a dead-rubber of sorts, and there may be some reserve players on show. It may well resemble a glorified friendly, but City will be keen to avenge the defeat in the Audi Cup final (and that other game).

But looming on the horizon is the distinct possibility, perhaps a probability, that City will face a top, top team in the last 16. Should they lose, will the team be considered failures once more? Probably by some.

Qualification with games to spare though is a huge plus considering the log-jam of games in December.

With that in mind, it seems to have got to the point that we are so spoiled as City fans that an opposition team actually having some chances, or scoring a goal is now unacceptable and a sign of our frailty. Of course the defence has made some poor decisions this year, but sometimes other teams construct a good move, a player does something brilliant, and balls fall their way. Quality players will sometimes get past our full back or win a header in the six-yard box. It happens. And to state the obvious, a more adventurous style leaves gaps at the back and works the defence that little bit harder.

How humorous to observe the debate in the media over the past fortnight or so as to which was the superior front two - Van Persie and Rooney or Suarez and Sturridge - well who cares, because there is no one better than beauty and the beast (a cringeworthy description even if it is actually quite accurate). Add a revitalised Nasri and Silva and that is a front four of supreme talent, that can score 12 goals in 2 matches without even appearing to break sweat (more than an entire season under Stuart Pearce). And into that mix will come Jovetic. If Aguero can stay fit (if), he should break records galore.

And well done to Kun, City's leading ever European goal scorer. He does alright.

We still can't take corners. There must be someone better at them than David Silva.

Another underwhelming atmosphere. I have commented before that the Champions League has not captured the imagination of City fans, but this is not helped by Group games. It can be guaranteed that the atmosphere for the knockout stage(s) will be somewhat different. And to go over old ground, the lack of a full stadium is not an opportunity for playground taunts, but a damning indictment of the cost of modern football, the tipping point already reached for many.

Jamie Jackson managed to get SHEIKH MANSOUR'S BILLIONAIRES into his match report. Again. Impressive work.

The racism issue hung in the air all night. I might have a Russian GCSE but I can't understand a word of it anymore to be honest (I couldn't then either), but there seems to have been little incident on the night, bar some vile cards left on public transport and the dreaded lighting of a flare, a crime worse than GBH. The CSKA fans before the match seemed more interested in taking photos of their pints of bitter - I guess they don't have Robinsons' Dizzy Blonde in Moscow.

I didn't quite understand the booing when the Russian announcement came over the tannoy. Do City fans now hate the Russian language too?
Down with the Cyrillic alphabet!! Death to the funny letters, especially the B that is pronounced like a V!

For the first time I got the tram back to town, and it wasn't bad at all. Apart that is for the fact that there were no trams waiting at the stop after the match, or for some time afterwards, but let's not be harsh on Metrolink. After all, how could they possibly have anticipated a thousand people suddenly needing a tram at 09:40pm on a Tuesday night?
But once trams appeared, it took 12 minutes from queue to Piccadilly station. Not bad at all.

The Fictional Mutiny Against Roberto Mancini: by Edin Dzeko and Rudyard Kipling.

To take the euphoria away form a 7-0 thrashing, the press needed something to hit Manchester City with, so cue a conveniently-timed article in the Sunday Mirror about Edin Dzeko slating his ex-manager. Paranoid, me?

Edin Dzeko admits Manchester City dressing room DID turn on Roberto Mancini
*Edin Dzeko has **confessed** that he was part of the dressing-room revolt that saw Roberto Mancini sacked as manager of Manchester City.*
The Bosnian striker admitted that he spoke to chairman Khaldoon Al Mubarak on several occasions to voice his displeasure about how Mancini was running the club.
"When the new coach arrived, the chairman asked me, informally, whether I was now happy… I had complained to him a few times about the former coach and my situation... He was aware that I didn't feel happy about what had happened to me over the last two years."

The problem is that Dzeko said nothing mentioned in the headline or opening gambit. Read that extract above again – it's no wonder he penned a furious missive on Twitter. He commented that he had expressed to the chairman his dissatisfaction at a lack of playing time, he mentioned having a difference of opinion with Mancini over this and his frustration at being benched so often.

No mention was made of mutinies, by him or team-mates, or wanting Mancini out, or of a dressing-room coup. Elsewhere in the interview he says he couldn't complain as he was thankful to Mancini for giving him a chance in English football. The mutiny was all fabricated in the head of the journalist, a staunch City supporter, which makes it all the more depressing. And all this from an interview two months ago – strange how it took this long to come out.

You could argue that Dzeko shouldn't have been so honest in the interview. Players should know that anything they say may have the truth they've spoken twisted by knaves to make a trap for fools. Or you could accept that footballers are allowed to express opinions, especially ones that aren't particularly controversial, and not succumb to a hysterical overreaction as a result.

The problem with newspaper headlines is that due to their brevity they are not subject to the same libel laws as the main article. Thus they have a near-free reign to twist the facts, something sub-editors (who write the headlines) are all too good at manipulating. What these sub-editors and journalists know, a fact backed up by various studies, is that people tend to have a short attention span and as a result often don't get past the headline and first paragraph in an article.

And thus it was with Edin Dzeko. He mentions speaking to the chairman about being unhappy, and this is translated into being part of a squad mutiny. In my opinion, it's utterly pathetic.

Sunderland 1 Manchester City 0: Some Thoughts

So for the fourth season in a row we witnessed abject failure at the Stadium of Light. Every year we manage to lose a different way, and the referee is often their man of the match, but as usual we only have ourselves to blame.

And whilst Sunderland should have been down to ten men for most of the match, and whilst there was a foul leading up to the goal, thus giving credence to the argument that a draw was deserved, the inability to score against a depleted and out-of-form Sunderland is quite simply unacceptable.

And to state the obvious - what a frustrating, annoying, gut-wrenching, insipid performance.

And to state another obvious point - HOW DOES THIS KEEP HAPPENING??!

One problem is that we are too reliant on key players, with insufficient cover should they be absent. In previous weeks the loss of Vincent Kompany has been felt heavily and this weekend it was clear to see the drop in the level of the performance without David Silva. Add Sergio Aguero to the mix and you probably have a spine there that City need to keep fit to perform at their best. This has to change.

And all this against a side with two players suspended, barely a fit left-back at the club, and two dinosaurs patrolling the centre of defence, one of whom has been injured for 22 months. And despite all that, and all the domination of the ball, and the numerous shots, the keeper was only really tested once.

And thus we gift Sunderland's first clean sheet of the league campaign. Only Peterborough have failed to score against Sunderland before yesterday. Though whilst they had only one victory from the previous ten games, most of those winless games were watched over by an angry fascist.

When you lose various players to injury all at once, is it really sensible to swap round other players also? Why did Pellegrini feel the need to swap round the full backs? Zabaleta has not had his greatest season, but he is still a better option than Richards at the moment. The Daily Star (yes, I know) reported yesterday that Arsenal are to revive their interest in Richards. I'm not sure how to feel about that.

Javi Garcia – the ultimate stick to beat Pellegrini with. The Chilean does not help himself when he continues to pick this player. The stats show him as one of the most accurate passers in all of Europe, but that somewhat masks his many other deficiencies. We can surely do better. Yes the manager's hand was forced somewhat by the raft of injuries, but there were still numerous options available to him. Milner in the middle, Navas stretching them out wide, even Kolarov in a more advanced left-sided role. Anything.

Still, Javi Garcia isn't to blame for City failing to score. Or for the goal that they did either.

And what great timing for Yaya Toure to have one of his "can't-be-arsed" days. For all his immense class, he has days where you want to throttle him. It's a shame no manager seems prepared to substitute him.

I'm a staunch supporter of Pellegrini (hey, I staunchly supported Alan Ball for almost a fortnight), but for the first time I doubt some of his actions. The tinkering is too common for me, and he had not yet got the whole squad to apply his ethos – but these things can take time.

The away form must improve - will we still be chanting this mantra in March? The problem slowly dawns that the unthinkable could happen - finishing outside the top four. It's a bit early to be panicking on that front, but if the away form doesn't pick up soon...

And has there ever been a great dichotomy between our home and away form?

With every poor away performance comes extra pressure in the following match. And that match is Spurs, who whilst also having their own rough patch, are above City in the table and have an excellent squad. In the meantime the players and fans alike have a fortnight to stew over the defeat. The defeat also puts extra pressure on maintaining the excellent home form. If that tails off at any point, then City really are in trouble.

And yet the league remains wide open. It was a weekend of big teams falling over in spectacular fashion. It was also a weekend of sterile domination. City, Spurs and Arsenal all dominated in the stats, with greater possession, shots and passes and all lost. And whilst no City fan should ever support United at any point, their victory has helped keep the pack close. The clubs with new managers have had troublesome starts as three new men attempt to impose their new ideals on the team, whilst the longest-serving manager sees his team at the top. This may not be a coincidence.

(Of course many City fans wouldn't allow Pellegrini six months of failure, let alone eight years.)

And perhaps linked to the above, City remain favourites for the title. So whatever the bookies know that we don't, let's keep calm for now. At least the international break has come at a good time considering the injury list. God bless the World Cup play-offs.

I didn't watch the match live due to a christening, for a beautiful little girl with her own battles ahead in life. It was all the perspective I needed – it is, after all just a football match, and sometimes we'd all do well to remember that.

I'm still p***ed off though.

City's Squad Cost & Value

For no reason whatsoever, I have taken a speculative look at the Manchester City squad value as it stands now, compared to what it originally cost. Not surprisingly, the squad didn't cost a billion pounds after all. Market values are also predicted on the assumption that the player is under contract and thus not available on the cheap.

I have added afterwards the market value as predicted by the usually excellent transfermrket.co.uk in italics. Many of the transfer costs are taken from their statistics too and raised my eyebrows a few times – you may disagree at some of these fees quoted.

Joe Hart - £792,000 from Shrewsbury. The subject of a million debates, the player seen as both world-class and a liability is clearly worth a lot, lot more than what City purchased him for. Still clearly England's number 1, he put a shaky period behind him, and conceded just the 4 goals in England's 10 qualifying games, before the boob against Chelsea ruined everything. He should however have over a decade left in the professional game. On the presumption that he would be sold domestically and taking the English player premium into account, but then realising that goalkeepers do not fetch as much as outfield players, I would value him at around **£20m**.
(I'm guessing many will disagree)
Transfermrket.co.uk value - £21m

Costel Pantilimon & Richard Wright –cost little (£0 and £2m), worth little. As you were.
Transfermrket.co.uk value - £2.2m & £225,000

Micah Richards - £0. An academy player, so cost City nothing in transfer fees. Once linked with a £25m move across the City, then his star waned, now it is flickering once more. The unfortunate factor is that he could injure himself cleaning his teeth, and this must affect his value, and it seems to affect his form, as he is hardly setting the world alight again. But he is English. So I reckon - **£11m**.

Transfermrket.co.uk value - £14m

Pablo Zabaleta - £7.6m. The person every man wants to be, which must be good for his transfer value. Consummate professional, workhorse, passionate, committed. Not lacking in skill though not top of the tree in that respect. Not firing on all cylinders so far this season, but I doubt that would affect his value much. I would guess at - **£20m.**
Transfermrket.co.uk value - £16m

Vincent Kompany – £7.48m. a value that can be measured on and off the field, but he can now also be considered to be officially injury prone and also attracts ridiculous red cards like the Manchester United Megastore attracts glory-hunters. Defenders rarely fetch top-whack prices, and Barcelona were laughably linked with a £20m bid in the summer, but his absence is felt stronger than any other City player, so I will plump for - **£28m.**
Transfermrket.co.uk value - £31m

Martin Demichelis - £4m. As he was been injured since his arrival until recently then presumably his value remains the same. It seemed a fair price – an experienced performer approaching the twilight of his career. A few games later and he has performed ok, so nothing has really changed. **£4m.**
Transfermrket.co.uk value - £2.6m

Matija Nastastic –£13.37m. A transfer that was somewhat of a rarity, as it involved a partial-swop deal with Savic. A revelation last season, a bit more suspect in the early weeks of this, his value has probably not fluctuated too much. He is still an excellent prospect who has shown great maturity but who has understandably still got plenty to learn and misses his captain next to him. I would speculate that his value at the moment is about the same as when he arrived. You'd hate to see him go though, as there's a whole lot of potential there. And let's not forget – he is a mere 20 years old. Value? About **£20m**
Transfermrket.co.uk value - £18.5m

Joleon Lescott - £24m. No doubt that his current market value is much lower now. Age has taken its toll, and City always overpaid THE CHOSEN ONE anyway, but he certainly paid his way in the end and has been a consummate professional. Would probably fetch about **£5m** right now, if anyone would pay his wages.
Transfermrket.co.uk value - £7.9m

Gael Clichy - £7m. A solid performer throughout his stay at City, if slightly frustrating. £7m seemed a steal at the time for an experienced premier league performer, and he is probably worth more than that to this day. My nagging suspicion is that City may strengthen the left-back position in the future as he doesn't really excel enough, and is showing a few signs of regressing slightly, which is shown in my valuation - **£12m**.
Transfermrket.co.uk value - £14m

Aleksander Kolarov – £16m. Where to start with Kolarov? One moment he's scoring a wonderful free-kick and putting in 5 magnificent whipped crosses, the following week (or minute) he's a liability who we'd do well to give away. He seemed destined to leave after the acrimonious end to last season, but now he is threatening to usurp Clichy in the first team. God knows what his value is – so I can only speculate, after much thought, at - **£12m**
Transfermrket.co.uk value - £21m(!! x 10)

Dedryck Boyata - £0. Cost nothing but has never really looked like breaking into the first team for more than the odd match or two, often in the cup competitions. Not sure what we could get for him – would suggest around **£5m**
Transfermrket.co.uk value – not listed in squad.

David Silva - £25.3m. Or Merlin as he is also known (hmmm). There's nothing more I can say about City's magnificent Spaniard, except to point out that he seems to be back to his best. A first team pick for the world champions, it's fair to say he has a high market value. Hugely missed as soon as he got injured. I'll go for - **£35m**
Transfermrket.co.uk value - £35m

Fernandinho - £30m? Like Carlos Tevez before him, people are still arguing over what he actually cost. Various journalists are insistent it is the substantial figure quoted above, so who am I to argue, considering their impeccable track-record? The fact is that his role in the team is an unglamorous one, and five years of world-class performances would probably not raise his value a cent. His current market value is probably what he should have been purchased for, perhaps slightly more as he continues to improve with every match, so I will take a vague guess at - **£23m**. *Transfermrket.co.uk value - £28m*

Samir Nasri. £24m. Hmm, tough one this. He seems to have got his mojo back this season under Pellegrini, and is getting more match-time as a result. There's no doubt he is a supremely talented footballer, the only question is over application and mentality. He also gets plenty of playing time in the French national squad – I would argue his value is around **£25m**, a fair rise on his value at the start of the season. *Transfermrket.co.uk value - £16.5m*

Jack Rodwell - £12m. Tough one to call this. There is clearly a £20m footballer in Jack Rodwell. But as we all know, he is more injury-prone than Wile E. Coyote. For that reason alone I reckon he would only fetch at the moment, at the most - **£10m** *Transfermrket.co.uk value - £13m*

Yaya Toure - £26.4m. The "Barcelona reserve", as Brian Reade memorably described him, is now one of the most revered midfielders in the world. As for his worth should we bizarrely decide to sell him – I would want **£25m**, and not more because he is getting on a bit. *Transfermrket.co.uk value - £26.5m*

James Milner - £24m. The much maligned Milner is an important part of City's stellar squad, but there can be no doubting that his value is much lower than what he was purchased for. Part of a £16m + Stephen Ireland deal (so £16m then – ha! I'm so funny!), he was another player bought for over his market value as the

selling club wrung every last penny out of cash-rich City. I would rate his current market value at - **£14m**.
Transfermrket.co.uk value - £16m

Javi Garcia. £17.7m. Oh dear. Garcia sometimes gets called up to the Spain squad. Garcia played for a successful Benfica side for many years. Yet Garcia seems to have few redeeming features in a City shirt. Perhaps he is just not suited to the English game, as he didn't get this far in the game without many redeeming features. What would he fetch now? A continental side may well spend **£12m?**
Transfermrket.co.uk value - £16.5m

Jesus Navas - £17.6m. I'll be honest, he had slightly disappointed me since his arrival. Started on fire, but has cooled off somewhat in recent weeks. His value has probably not changed then, but his form over the past couple of weeks bodes well, and I hope this figure will rise over the next year. **£17m**
Transfermrket.co.uk value - £17.5m

Stevan Jovetic - £22.8m. Struggled to gain full fitness since his arrival, so apart from a starring role in the Capital One Cup game against Wigan, we've seen little of him, and thus his value remains where it was - **£23m**
Transfermrket.co.uk value - £23m

Alvaro Negredo - £16.4m. The beast. Eased into the first team, he has quickly established himself as one of the first names on the team-sheet, and forged a great partnership with Aguero. It's probably too early to say he is worth more, but his value has surely risen at least slightly since signing, and he is getting some playing time in the Spain team too. **£25m**.
Transfermrket.co.uk value - £22m

Edin Dzeko - £27m. The man who splits City fans right down the middle as much as any other player. Either way, I can't us seeing us recouping our money should the time inevitably come when he moves on to pastures new, probably to Borussia Dortmund (or even Arsenal).

But, but, but. He may frustrate, but he still keeps up a healthy scoring record, scores important goals, responds when he seems at his lowest, and also is a successful international on his way to the World Cup Finals. We'd probably get around **£18m**. Dortmund are rumoured to be offering £15m, but City want more.
Transfermrket.co.uk value - £24m

John Guidetti - £0. Another academy prospect, so no initial cost, and very hard to value due to long-standing injury concerns. Currently on the verge of another comeback, and prolific when he stayed fit for a year in Holland, many City fans want to see him get first team action despite having never seen him play. Would guess wildly that he could fetch around **£10m**.
Transfermrket.co.uk value - £5.3m

Sergio Aguero - £38m. It is saying something about Aguero's time at City that he could have cost so much yet has almost certainly risen in value since. He hasn't been perfect (who is?), and was badly hampered by injuries last season and thus less effective, but recent weeks have reminded us all what he is capable of. At the time of writing, he is the top goal-scorer AND the top assister in the Premier League.
With another spurious transfer rumour last week about Barcelona (and Bayern Munich) preparing a £40m bid, I reckon that if City ever had to sell him they should not accept a penny under **£50m**. And for the record, I wouldn't sell Bayern Munich a virus. Our Spanish executives probably wouldn't sell Barcelona one either.
Transfermrket.co.uk value - £35m(hmmm)

There are many other players swishing around of course. Youngsters on the brink, on loan and those in limbo that all have some value or other. But at least those in the first squad have not been the drain on resources that their predecessors were. The current purchasing policies seem to have produced players that have a sell-on value, whilst lowering the wage bill on those that went before.

Cost of squad to purchase - **£363.50m**
My current squad value - **£426.00m**
Transfermrket.co.uk value - ***£420m (approx)***

The Football Blogging Awards – Urbis

Towards the end of November I attended the Football Blogging Awards at the National Football Museum, Urbis, as part of the nominated Bluemoon Podcast team. Situated on the back table, we worked out we hadn't won, and were proved right, but a good night was had by all, we got interviewed by the Mancunian Matters website, chatted to the Manchester Evening News contingent, met Natalie Pike, ate the worst buffet of all-time, and went home with a goody bag the Oscars would be proud of, containing some Haribo, a Milky Way and a can of Coke (full fat). Read it and weep Tom Hanks.

Manchester City 6 (SIX) Tottenham Hotspur 0: Some Thoughts

Wow, and once more – wow.

What I thought would be a tight game, settled by one moment, either of genius or perhaps one ghastly mistake, proved to be just that for a good 14 seconds.

As usual the team line-up provided plenty of ammunition for the Pellegrini doubters, due to the big issue of the month – the goalkeeping spot. I, like many others, presumed Hart would be back in the team after the international break, especially after his strong performance against Germany. However I have since seen some logic in Pellegrini's actions. Whoever was picked did not significantly alter City's chances of victory, and it can be seen as quite clever from the manager to draft Hart back in for a game of less significance on Wednesday. Thus, Hart can find his feet without the media spotlight that would have accompanied him at the weekend, and what's more, by sticking with the same keeper for the Spurs match, the game was about the football, and was not clouded by other issues. Hart will start on Wednesday, and after that, who knows?

So City scored after 14 seconds with their second shot after Spurs had kicked off. And it wasn't a bad goal celebration from Navas either, after what was probably the earliest goal I have ever seen at a football match. That's one way to settle the nerves.

Spurs threatened only briefly, between the first and second goal, but they looked dangerous and it was important that City came through that period without conceding. Once the second goal had gone in however, there was little to worry about thereafter.

But for City's dynamic duo upfront, new heights were hit yesterday. Aguero was undoubtedly the best player on the pitch, often unplayable, always a nightmare for Tottenham's defence. Negredo was not far behind, and the understanding between the two is as good as anything I have seen. By the time Negredo smashed in the fifth goal, I had run out of words to describe the attacking display. And it could, and perhaps <u>should</u> have been more than six.

In fact, the attacking players were so good, I forgot David Silva existed. Sorry David.

Navas was superb from beginning to end, showing us exactly what he can offer. Some of his crosses were sublime, precise and deserving of more goals. For a player who supposedly cannot shoot, a brace of goals is very welcome indeed. He should start again next week.

A shout out too for Fernandinho, who continues to be magnificent, and Joleon Lescott, who did well when he came on. Demichelis too was fine, a player already getting plenty of criticism for reasons that escape me as he is a squad player filling in and doing his job.

This side lost at Sunderland. Repeat that to yourself, as it really does beggar belief. This is surely a psychological or tactical problem. City need to approach their away games in an identical matter to those at home. Perhaps some form of hypnosis would help?

Some stats: Sergio Aguero has scored more goals than the entire Spurs side. Manchester City have scored more goals at home than any other side has home AND away, a record total at this stage of the season for the top division in England. That cherished "scored most goals after 6 home games" trophy is the one piece of silverware that has continually eluded City, so that's another monkey off our backs. It should also be noted that City have scored an average of 2.7 goals per game over the past fifty home league games and have now scored in 56 consecutive home league games. City also have the best home defence.

But proof that stats are sometimes irrelevant can be seen by the fact that Spurs had 53% possession yesterday. What's more, away from home, City have made more passes than at home, have a better passing accuracy, on average 6% more possession, and only 2 fewer shots than at home. Go figure.

The Nasri penalty appeal. There's no doubt in my mind it was a penalty and a red card. Of course Sandro did get the ball cleanly at first, and it can be construed as a good tackle – and every referee will see it that way to avoid making a tough decision. But touching the ball is irrelevant if he takes the player as well, and as far as I can see that is precisely what he did. If that had happened outside the area a free-kick could be guaranteed, but I will say that if it had happened the other way round I'd probably be applauding a fine tackle, so perhaps I should move on.

How Kyle Walker gets into the England squad remains a mystery, even in a squad as underwhelming as the current one. It's just increases the shame that Micah Richards is made of glass, and to think that Walker beat Aguero to Young Player of the Year remains one of the most ridiculous decisions ever.

Cardiff City ensured a perfect day with their late equaliser against Manchester United, and City suddenly find themselves in the top four.

Oh, and for balance, Alan Shearer did something approaching analysis on Soldado. See Alan, it CAN be done. And do try and check out Soldado's "heat map" for the game. As he takes kick-offs, there is a huge glow in the centre circle.

Just the one player in Garth Crooks' team of the week. I wonder what we'd have to do to get two players in there?

So nothing to moan about after thrashing key rivals 6-0, right? Ha, don't be ridiculous! Whinging at the line-up, whinging afterwards on radio phone-ins and message boards at our defence (half of which is now injured/ill), Jason Manford's singing, and the substitutions, the WIFI or even the tram queue. It's what we do.

I'm not sure how Messi's going to get in this team.

Manchester City 4 Viktoria Plzen 2.

City came through a nervy match with the three points and another four goals to add to their rather impressive home tally, but it was a hard-fought victory against the group's whipping boys who gave as good as they got, and more, for most of the match.

With seven changes, it was hardly surprising that the team rarely lived up to Sunday's star billing, especially with the stakes so much lower. As is seemingly always the case with City, when significant changes are made, the performance dips alarmingly, but here was a team that contained many players whose time could soon be up at the club, and it was a performance that reiterated why City often start matches with little or no English representation in the team. Throughout the match there were gaping holes in the midfield and defence, and City were often carved open at will. Thankfully the returning Joe Hart put in a commanding performance, and along with sloppy finishing, City escaped enough times to gain a victory due to their constant goal threat at the Etihad.

The other problem though is that City's second-string drag the first-teamers down with them. Fernandinho was ill-at ease (though not poor) having to partner the cumbersome Javi Garcia, who helped contribute to the ample room given to Plzen's attacking players. Only Nasri rose above it, once more covering Silva's absence admirably in his 100th match for the club and he was a deserving winner of Man of the Match.

The paranoia merchants (all of us) had plenty of ammunition as the Tyler/Quinn double-act continued to scrape barrels on commentary duty with fevered passion, Tyler's high-pitched voice attracting cats within a 10-mile area every time Plzen got near the City area. Once he had spat out the words "Slamir Nasri" after the Frenchman had hit the woodwork, I knew we were in for a long night.

But what was clear is that Edin Dzeko is a player shot of confidence, a man clearly unhappy, who may need to leave for everyone's sake (see the next section for further details). His understanding with Aguero was a million miles behind what Negredo has with the Argentinean, and as soon as Negredo came on, we saw the difference in performance levels. Still, this was typical Dzeko – balls bouncing 10 yards off his leg, disinterested, nothing coming off and then of course he scores, and maintains a very healthy goal ratio. Nobody is better at headed goals whilst facing the wrong way. Try smiling Edin, you might enjoy it.

There was just time for Yaya Toure to pick up the yellow card that will see him miss the final group game, a suspension that Martin Tyler had alerted the world to, so expect stiff action against the club now as no player has ever executed such a blatant act before.

But job done. Another four goals in the onion bag even if it was a score that was harsh on the plucky full-timers from the Czech Republic, and the crowd saw Edin Dzeko score the 41st goal at the ground this season. It's like Brian Horton never left.
So City can still top the group, needing the small matter of a three-goal victory away to Bayern Munich, which should be easily attainable, I think we can all agree. It's unlikely that Pep Guardiola will play a scratch side as the league is already going their way, and they will want to cement the top place, so ahead lies a hugely

difficult knockout match. That's in the future, for now let's just hope that Sergio Aguero is ok, and we get a near-fit squad back as soon as possible.

Edin Dzeko – This Is The End

(I can't get them all right, ahem)

As the ball hits the back of the net, we all expect a smile. Maybe a finger pointing to the heavens, an elaborate, vomit-inducing dance routine, a slide along the hallowed turf or a shirt-based personal message thanking a deity.
But for the Edin Dzeko of 2013, there is nothing. No joy, no smile, nothing.

Edin Dzeko clearly isn't a happy man. Quotes keep popping up in the press to suggest this, his demeanour merely confirms the suspicions. He wants to play and he thinks he deserves to. Then he does occasionally play, we wonder why he thinks he deserves to play, then he scores and we all feel a little confused.

It has always been this way for Dzeko and City though. In the interview he gave on Bosnian TV in September he mentioned his difference of opinions with Roberto Mancini at his lack of playing time, his ire directed especially at the time he was dropped having just scored four goals at White Hart Lane. He has often been considered City's "super-sub", a player who regularly scored goals but often from the bench and often when they were most needed, be it an equalizer at Notts County in the season City won the FA Cup or the equaliser on THAT day against QPR.

The problem is of course that when he starts, he seems so less effective much of the time. A confidence player, he can be on fire, or he can be a near-liability. When down, which is a lot of the time, his touch deserts him, his head drops and he comes across as lazy and disinterested. His goal ratio remains healthy throughout, but a team with City's aspirations needs more from a striker than goals alone, and now that his competition has gone from the oft-uninterested and lazy Balotelli to the industrious, powerful goal-scoring beast that is Alvaro Negredo, the penny should have dropped with Dzeko that things aren't going to improve. A new manager has changed little.

Dzeko had his chance to shine and to impress earlier in the season, when he was favoured over Negredo for a few weeks and he failed to grasp the opportunity. When Negredo started, the difference in performance was obvious to all. Negredo has not looked back and forged the best striking relationship with Ageuro that the club has seen in decades.

In a season leading up to a World Cup, players are desperate for playing time to keep their place in national sides. For Dzeko this probably won't matter as he should start for Bosnia in Brazil come-what-may. But he is at the stage of his career when he should be at his peak and it serves little purpose for either side to see him marooned on a bench. He will probably be a success wherever he goes next, be it Borussia Dortmund or Arsenal, but it's time to finally admit that the Edin Dzeko/Manchester City journey has almost reached its end.

Manchester City 3 Swansea City 0: Some Thoughts

So another comfortable home win – eventually. For once, City were made to work fully for their victory, but their superior class told in the end.

Swansea offered far more in that first-half than most visitors to the Etihad, after another storming start from City. Yet again we could have scored in the first minute, and once Negredo had scored many naturally felt another procession was on the cards. We have become spoilt of course and expect this as standard, but Swansea had other ideas. They pass the ball about superbly, and caused City plenty of problems and could have gone into the break level if not for some very wayward finishing.

There is a point to make here though that this is what separates the top teams from those that occupy mid-table and below. All teams can fashion chances, but the top teams tend to be more clinical – and so it proved on Sunday. Some of the play continues to be breathtaking – the best I have ever seen.

But in that first half it seemed too open, with too much space for the Swansea players to break into. Pellegrini tightened things up in the second half, though City probably also wore down their opponents as is often the case nowadays. By the end, the Swans were all at sea (Ha, hilarious! I should be a headline writer!).

You wonder what damage Swansea could have done with their first choice strike-force available, but then City were missing their first-choice central defensive pairing, so it evened itself out.

The stats: that's 8 goals in the last 7 games for Alvaro Negredo. His free-kick was the fourth one scored by City in the league this season (there have been 19 scored in the league in total so far). Samir Nasri has scored more premier league goals this season already than last season (3) and has scored more than once in a game for the first time since December 4th 2010. In total, that's now 29 home goals in the league this season, two more than any other side has scored home and away (thanks to @OptaJoe for all that).

Joleon Lescott and Micah Richards have been in the papers over the weekend, talking of leaving if they cannot get playing time. Of course Lescott is doing just that due to injury and was great against Spurs for 45 minutes, shaky against Plzen and good again against Swansea, but he knows he is back up and that will not change. Like Gareth Barry, he is approaching the twilight of his career, a career that will end elsewhere.

Richards is a different kettle of fish however. It's hard to truly judge the player when he injures himself on such a regular basis, but the Richards of now bears a striking resemblance to the erratic Richards under Mark Hughes that seemed to spend too much time in the gym and not enough on the field. He is a link to the old days, the Jim Cassell academy, he is a popular figure and a club cheerleader and we all hope he stays, but I cannot justify a first team place for him at the moment and if he demands time on the pitch, this could prove the tipping point.

If Lescott and Richards were to leave it would naturally lead to media criticism over the de-Anglicisation of the team, but the fact is that the English players would get more time on the pitch if they were as good as their team-mates, and I'm not sure they are anymore (for everyone's sanity we'll leave Joe Hart out of the argument). The new academy and the batch of youngsters ripping up trees bode well for the future, but there may be a gap of a few years before we see a new English element in the first team.

As Paulinho put in another underwhelming and error-strewn performance earlier in the day against United, it becomes more baffling with every match that Fernandinho is overlooked by the Brazil manager. The selection for the team is often erratic, but let's hope for the player's sake that a move to a higher-profile league gets him the recognition he deservers. If Jo is regularly getting on the pitch for Brazil, what possible justification is there not to give Fernandinho a run-out? Maybe his style just doesn't suit in a position that Brazil are quite strong in at the moment.

Another poor turnout from the away team's support. This is not criticism, simply pointing out that if you insist on charging fans £50 a pop then ask them to make a huge cross-country (sorry, countries) trek on Sunday, we shouldn't be surprised when the majority say "sod that". Half-price tickets for City's match at Fulham are a start, a move replicated by other Premier League teams, but it needs to go much further than the odd reduction. £20 needs to be the norm, £30 at the most.

The true tests are almost here. Two tricky away games where anything could happen, that could shape City's title campaign at such an early stage. Here's hoping that Manuel Pellegrini has worked out how to solve this particular problem. For the record, City are not alone in this respect. United have conceded 20 goals in their last 10 away games and have failed to keep a clean sheet in their last nine. But then they have Tom Cleverley in midfield.

Calling Negredo the beast gets creepier with every passing week. As for "feed the beast…" – just NO.

West Brom 2 Manchester City 3

We won away! Never felt more like singing the blues…..

Well on the whole that was better – the home form replicated, at least for a while.

The MCFC twitter feed promised surprises ahead of the line-up announcement, an announcement guaranteed to strike fear into the hearts of City fans.

And whilst the team was hardly surprising, it did kick off a new wave of online angst. Dzeko came in for Negredo, and the left-back spot was rotated once more with Kolarov back in, Demichelis was favoured over Lescott and Pantilimon keeping his place as expected. The better news was the return of Kompany, which triggered off an aftershock of panic that he had been brought back too early and would end up limping off the pitch at some point.

The return of Dzeko may have frustrated many, but he did score all the goals against West Brom last season, and Negredo's goals have come largely at home. This is something of a false argument however, as all the team have tailed off away from home so you can't place the emphasis on Negredo – City have quite simply scored a lot more at home. Secondly, what Dzeko did last season is irrelevant.

However, with three games in six days, there was always going to be changes, and this was the game Pellegrini had probably identified as the more winnable of the two away games this week.

But whilst rotation is to be expected, it is still acceptable to question if it has been done the wrong way round. City are struggling away form home and utterly imperious at home. Would it not make more sense to play the strongest eleven away and make the odd change at home?

So a non-English starting XI for City. I look forward to Neil Ashton's "the day football died" article in the Daily Mail. City's English contingent were reduced to throwing chewing gum at the coaching staff on the bench. I guess it passes the time.

Heavy traffic meant yet another new kick-off time – 8:15pm. The Bleacher Report's American correspondent wonders how this could happen when the kick-off time was announced weeks ago. They obviously don't have traffic jams in America.

Onto the match, and for half an hour, City were irresistible, that home form finally transferred away from Manchester. Aguero missed a sitter before he scored, Dzeko battled and ran and was involved in everything, and City should have been five up, but for wasteful finishing, the wrong run or the odd mis-control.

Having not put the game to bed though, the worry surfaced that City would pay for their profligacy, and West Brom came into the game as the first half drew to an end. Thankfully there was no real incisiveness in the play. The second half continued the theme, with City content to protect a lead and chances were at a premium. With the third goal came a chance to relax, but history shows that to be a foolish notion. City eased off, and there was still time for the token calamity goal before a minute of panic at the end. But three points is three points, our goal difference is a mile ahead of everyone else, so there was no need for a sleepless night (unless you like cricket).

The truth is that City's failure to assert themselves for longer was slightly disconcerting, but we can't expect them to batter any team for ninety minutes. My main worry with Pellegrini teams remains the same – the team is quite "open" and doesn't look set up to close out games. Maybe that will come with time.

Demichelis impressed too for a while, as for all his wild swings at the ball, he has the experience to anticipate well, and cover for colleagues. He was undoubtedly poor for West Brom's second goal though, and Pantilimon's huge frame prevented him getting down quick enough.

Man of the Match? Fernandinho. He almost spared us more talk about Gareth Barry, but then Everton went and won at Old Trafford. The Brazilian was everywhere, mopping up, setting up attacks and he continues to impress.

And not far behind was our captain. Kompany did everything we expect of him – intercepting, tackling, blocking (with one notable goal-bound block from Berahino standing out), bursting forward and marshalling the defence. He has been sorely missed away from fortress Etihad.
Jamie Jackson mentions today that he was dubbed the "Glassman" whilst at Hamburg due to his fragile physique, and we can only pray that he improves his injury record in the future.

And now for two more stern tests, in what now looks like a three-horse race for the title. Agent Moyes is doing a sterling job over at Old Trafford, but Arsenal continue to win as do Chelsea despite their faults. Southampton away and Arsenal at home will help shape the season further, and a defeat in either would be costly. Play City's strongest eleven please Mr. Pellegrini.

Elsewhere? I hate him with a passion, but those goals by Suarez last night….my word. (*Norwich at home I am guessing…*)

Final thought – we may all mock United at the moment (and rightly so), but be careful – it wasn't all bad news for the club last night. Massive floodlights? Pah.

Wednesday night's Barclays Premier League tie between Manchester United and Everton, broadcast across the globe, will be a world first as the club debuts the largest, brightest and clearest pitch-side electronic boards in football.

The pitch-side digital platform will be used to connect the fans to the club digitally, not only linking to social media activities, but also communicating key information.

This new system has been specially positioned at pitch-side so that the view of fans inside the stadium will be unaffected, despite the panels being the largest in Europe.

The crystal-clear quality will further develop the club's strategy of single sponsor visibility, giving a premium and clean look whilst avoiding the need for jumbotrons or multiple displays within Old Trafford.

Sir Bobby Charlton said: "This development is consistent with United's history of a pride in being the first in the world, and the best at what we do. While I am continually amazed at just how far around the world the coverage of our games goes, the work that is done by the club to communicate with fans both at home and abroad using the latest technology has to be good for everyone involved."

Be scared. Be very scared.

The Bumper Bundle of City Slurs: The Journalist Files (Part 1)

A long time ago, in a place not very far away, some wise men came from the east to transform an ailing football club. City fans couldn't believe their luck, and thanked every fictional god for their change of fortune. Not everyone took it so well though. Rival fans were predictably none too pleased as the death-knell was rung on football as we knew it, but plenty in the media took an instant dislike to the blues too. Here's the first part of a selection of buffoonery from Her Majesty's press over the past 6 years. Sit back and enjoy.

All excerpts in bold are my favourite bits.....

It starts with a match report. I wouldn't wipe my backside with the Sun newspaper (it would be impractical anyway), but this was the sort of coverage you could expect in the early days of the new regime. Neil Custis took a particular dislike to all Brazilians (the players at least)…

Neil Custis Match Report

*Robinho was left on the bench and as for **that waster Elano**, the sooner Hughes gets him out the better. A sub once again, Elano **pranced around like a pop diva** as he warmed up. He even kissed a young fan on the head, causing more little ones to queue up in the hope of the same. **Who on earth does he think he is?** When he and fellow Brazilian Robinho saw Ireland put City ahead on 28 minutes, they just stood still and clapped. Would you really want this pair in the trenches fighting alongside you? When Robinho finally came on just past the hour mark, he responded with one weak effort on goal. **Pathetic.***
*It is a shame he and Elano have **not got the passion that Ireland displays***.

Others though have spent six years praying for City to fail. Bless 'em.

Ian Winwood, Daily Mirror

Dear Santa Claus,
Santa, my request this year is quite simple: I was wondering if it might be possible for you to ensure that Manchester City are relegated from the Premier League?
*....Basically, I would like Manchester City to be relegated **for the good of football itself**. I have nothing against the second team in England's third city, apart from the fact that they are the latest club to believe that the recipe for football greatness contains just one ingredient: **money**.*
*Down at the City of Manchester Stadium – the Middle Eastlands, if you prefer – there is crazy money – and with it, **crazy talk**. **There's mindless chatter of triumph and glory, of capturing every great football currently playing the game**, just like those cartoon aliens did with basketball players in the film Space Jam.*
*There's talk of £200,000 a week contracts, maybe more. It might not come to this, but you can bet your offshore holding account that **Frank Lampard's £130,000 a week at Chelsea will soon be eclipsed**.*
10 years ago, would you have believed that some players would be making a million pounds every eight weeks?
No? Well, what's to say that these things won't continue to defy belief?
I want Manchester City to be relegated simply because no one really believes that it can happen. Relegation doesn't happen to the rich clubs, so it seems; it's for the Stoke City's and West Brom's of this country.
*But most of all I want City to go down because they are the just the latest **bad example football is setting for a whole new generation of fans**. They spread the idea that being a football fan is only about one thing, and that thing is success.*
Worse still, it seems that the only thing that can buy this success is money.

United fans took a similar different viewpoint, their argument somewhat at odds with the fact that the football club they tried to deride was founded in the 19th century. They weren't very big on irony either, as the following shows:

Rick Boardman of the band Delphic said in a interview, talking about City fans:

"They care more about us losing than winning games themselves – I just don't get that. It could all change but I've got confidence in our club. And whatever happens, we'll always have the history."

But it's not just about history where United dominate City of course. It's also about the most important factor in any club's standing in the game – global popularity. This gem appeared on manutdtalk.com in July 2009:

Man Utd are bigger than Man City ever will be.
(carefully selected excerpts)

My recent trip to Malaysia to watch Manchester United's pre-season friendly against a Malaysian XI highlighted why this club is so great and why **Man City are decades away from usurping Manchester United – and there is only a small, tiny, improbable chance of that happening.**
Arriving at Kuala Lumpur International Airport on Friday morning, my mates and I bumped into fellow reds, who promptly redirected us to the Bunga Raya VIP complex. There we met **Man Utd fans from all over Asia: Singapore, Malaysia, Thailand, Indonesia, India and Vietnam.**
Fans of all ages and backgrounds were there to greet our heroes. Some waited for hours just to get a glimpse of their heroes. Luckily for me, we were late and so only had to wait a short while before seeing Giggsy and co. **How many fans would turn up to greet Man City at an airport in Asia?**
Does Man City even have an Asian fan cub outside of Thailand?
The next stop was to book in at our hotel and rest before heading for the training session that afternoon. An estimated 40,000 people showed up just to watch the reds train!
How many people would turn up to watch a Man City training session?!
The next day, a whopping 100,000 people showed up to see their heroes in action!
As former British colonies, **there are really only two teams that**

matter in Malaysia and Singapore – Manchester United and Liverpool. The same pretty much applies for most of Asia.

Bitter rival fans simply cannot comprehend **how deeply the love for these two clubs runs in the veins of Asian fans.**

This kind of passion is built up over decades.

Fans from all over the world have been taking Manchester United to their hearts for decades. They have done so because of the swashbuckling football, because of the heroic players, because of Sir Matt Busby's ability to turn the nightmare of Munich into the fairytale of Wembley and because of all the amazing moments in the Theatre of Dreams.

Modern day rivals like Chelsea and now Man City still have to earn that right. That honour of being truly established in the hearts of fans around the world. United has a rich history of iconic players like Best, Law, Charlton, Whiteside, Robson, Bruce, Keane, Cantona, Giggs, Scholes, Cleverley, Beckham and more recently Rooney as well as Ronaldo.

Who do Chelsea or City have?

Even if Man City have the financial clout to buy a star-studded squad like The Galacticos, it doesn't guarantee success and it doesn't guarantee **a loyal GLOBAL fan base like United has**, because United earned that fan base with its history, legendary players, attacking football and yes, **clever marketing**. But unlike Chelsea and now Man City, United were not bank-rolled. No, United enjoyed the fruits of their own labour and foresight.

I do not begrudge Man City fans the right to be positive about the future and I do think it's reasonable to say that **they will be challenging for honours soon**, but what I take exception to is the exaggerated statements about Man City nearly being a bigger club than Manchester United.

Boys…. You are decades away from even getting close to Manchester United!

Man City supporters are simply kidding themselves if they think they are going to magically become bigger than United or even a top four club overnight.

Man City will do well to get into the top 6 this coming season and they might well challenge for honours in the near future, but please, please spare me the nonsense that you are a bigger club than Man United.

You are decades away from usurping us – and there is a very slim chance of that happening.

You do not have the players, nor do you play the kind of football that captures people's imaginations and most of all, you cannot buy class or an identity.

The little shred of identity that Manchester City had went out the window when you decided to bend over and remain silent when Thaksin bought your club and then sold it to the Arabs.

Who are the real glory hunters?

Contrary to popular belief Manchester United built their success on good policies and good management. Man City spent £180million more than United and still were a mid-table club last season. You can buy mercenaries, but you cannot buy class.

Decades, boys. Decades….

Author: RedForceRising

(oh ok, I admit I added the Cleverley bit…)

But with things progressing nicely, there was still plenty to criticise City over, and not just off the pitch. Emmanuel Adebayor's ASSAULT on Robin Van Persie (he could have been killed) for example made the headlines for over a week. The fall-out from his goal celebration against the same time rumbled on for even longer:

Former Met Police commander John O'Connor said: *"I am sure the police will want Adebayor to be made an example of. From a police perspective, Adebayor could have been arrested and then charged with actual body harm for the incident with Van Persie. He would then have faced the prospect of standing trial in court."*

Simon Hattenstone said *"If even now all he wants to do is take out his revenge with his studs and provoke crowds into riots what's he going to be like when things go bad?"*

Alex Stepney said, *"I seem to remember George Best got a six-week ban in 1970 for knocking the ball out of a referee's hands so I think Adebayor did get off lightly. These incidents are more noticeable nowadays."*

Henry Winter: *"So whose emotion do you want most in football? A multi-millionaire itinerant footballer crowing in the face of erstwhile employers who nurtured him, paid him handsomely and cherished him until he was tempted away by riches elsewhere, or fans momentarily allowing their passions to run away with them in defending their club? Thursday's decision by the Football Association not to punish Emmanuel Adebayor for inciting Arsenal supporters at Eastlands on Sept 12 is devoid of logic, defies police evidence and makes a mockery of its chief executive's stance. In every sense, Adebayor went too far. A one-game ban would have reminded him and his immature peers of that. It's not difficult."*

Oliver Holt compared it to Cantona's kung-fu moment. Archbishop Desmond Tutu's spokesman said Des had called for "an end to thuggery on football pitches" (ok, I made that one up). Alan Green said the book should be thrown at Adebayor – having admitted he hadn't seen the incident. Stan Collymore said he should have got a 2 match ban for the goal celebration alone. Bobby Gould said that the whole affair would cost England in their bid for the World Cup.

If he'd done that in the street, etc etc……

Over at the Guardian, there was one journalist that kept providing little nuggets of gold. Step forward Paul Wilson:

"They (City) keep trying to throw squillions of pounds at marquee signings who plainly prefer staying where they are…"

"Younger players who could give City some of their best years and still have a trade-on value….that is the very blueprint United are now following, while City seem to have abandoned the notion…"

"Throwing suitcases full of bank notes at a new trickster…"

"They (United, in the transfer market) accept defeat with dignity and look elsewhere."

"It is not United's style to lay siege to rival clubs or try to wear down their star players with repeated offers.."

"City could learn a lesson or two in humility from their illustrious neighbours."

"None of the top-four managers seem unduly concerned by project Eastlands…"

"City have just paid top whack for a United reject…" (Tevez)

"With Ferguson you can be pretty sure you will get one an answer. He answers questions directly – at least when in a good mood and away from the immediate stresses of the season proper. Get Fergie to chat and you are bound to end up with something interesting…"

"The first is that he (Ferguson) enjoys talking about football, and will happily deal with sensible questions instead of regarding press conferences as an unpleasant chore…"

"Fergie even has City fans hanging on his every word…."

"….the Everton chairman must realise that sooner or later City will come calling for Moyes. Being City, they will probably aim for José Mourinho first, yet top Champions League managers tend to go to top Champions League clubs and City have never kicked a ball in the Champions League."

And then the big news began to filter through. A little nondescript club called Manchester City had bid over £100m to buy a footballer. They were going to offer him half a million pounds a week, and lots of other stuff too. The transfer amount changed during the day. It went up to £150m, back down to £120m, back up again, and so did the wages. At one point he was rumoured to be earning almost as much as a mediocre film star or a racing driver. Football was being read its final rites. This club weren't in the Big Four. They weren't in the epic Champions League every season, weren't part of the G14 (R.I.P.). They didn't even have members on the FA Board. They certainly didn't usually feature in Sky Sports' Special Super Grand Slam Spectacular Sunday.

So back to the Sun we go and another piece of award-winning journalism.

WHERE ARE THE A-LISTERS AT CITY?

STEVEN HOWARD

(Steven is the Sun's CHIEF SPORTS WRITER. The crème de la crème. This guy has muscled his way to the top past quality writers like Neil Custis, or that other Custis (the one who wanted David Beckham as England manager)).

*THEY were the club who **announced they intended to sign Lionel Messi, Kaka, Cesc Fabregas and Juventus keeper Gigi Buffon. Oh, yes, and Cristiano Ronaldo was also on his way to Manchester City – in the January 2009 transfer window for £135million.***
As the Manchester United fans waiting for the tram that would take them back into the city centre after the 3-0 win over Newcastle last Monday chanted: "They wanted Kaka and got Bellamy – City are a massive club."
To date Sheikh Mansour has splashed £355m on transfer fees, including £130m in the close season alone.
Throw in £488m in wages, the £210m cost of the takeover and a further £20m capital expenditure and we're already up to an incredible £1billion.
Kamikaze spending.
Yet City still can't get the mega-stars. *Instead, they have been forced to settle for second best.* ***It's David Silva not David Villa. It's Mario Balotelli not Fernando Torres.***
The same David Silva who will remember Spain's World Cup-winning triumph in South Africa as the time he lost his place in the starting line-up.
*There are also massive question marks over **holding midfielder Yaya Toure (£24m)** plus defenders Jerome Boateng (£10.5m) and Alexsandar Kolarov (£16m).*

Yet the key to buying the title is an out-and-out goalscorer.
As Blackburn proved when they broke the British transfer record
by signing Alan Shearer for £3.3m in 1992-93.
As Chelsea confirmed in 2004 when they paid a club record £24m
for Didier Drogba, the hottest young striker in Europe.
City are paying through the nose for supporting cast players.
Top of the bill headliners like Messi, Kaka and Ronaldo remain
as elusive as ever.

Mark Lawrenson questioned how City could be throwing obscene
amounts of money in trying to sign Kaka:
"At a time when people have been left devastated by the credit
crunch, football is in danger of shooting itself in the foot. It would
be bad enough during a boom time, but during these tough
economic times it is sick. If City do this then they will lose the
sympathy and support of fans who will begin to question the
morality of how someone can spend that sort of money on a player
rather than build a new hospital or pay for some lifesaving
medical care. People will turn round and say: 'The world has gone
mad. I'm not sure about football any more'. How would you feel if
you can't pay the bills while a player at your club is on mind-
boggling money?"

Lawrenson was right. I lost count of the number of fans that came
up to me in the street in 2009 and said to me, "the world has gone
mad. I'm not sure about football any more."

PFA chief executive Gordon Taylor then told the world of his
disapproval of City's bid for Kaka.
"It is a bit bizarre that, in these times of credit crunch, we are
talking about a club paying £100m for one player," he said.
"One of the things we have to ask is…is football sending out the
right signals given the current financial climate? Football needs to
set a good example to the rest of the world, as we do with our anti-
racism programmes and community projects. Football cannot be
immune from the credit crunch and whilst City are an exception to
the rule, the game has a duty to show financial propriety at this
moment in time."

(Apropos of nothing, Gordon Taylor is the highest paid union official in the world. Taylor earns a £1million yearly salary – five times the remuneration of the second highest-paid union official and around ten times that of the average League Two player.)

Andy Gray had an opinion, naturally.
"If Manchester City's pursuit of Kaka suggests one thing it is that football is losing touch with the real world and the genuine supporter. Don't get me wrong. I am excited as anyone about the prospect of seeing the Brazilian in the Premier League BUT it has to be for the right reasons and at a sensible price of £50m-£60m."
What Andy was saying was that if City signed him for £60m, it was a sensible deal. But if City signed him for £100m, football was dead.

The time had come for Simon Hattenstone to enlighten all City fans.
"Arsène Wenger says Manchester City are not in touch with the world, that we're destroying football and the global economy by creating inflationary pressures in deflationary times, that we lack values and have no sense of reality. How dare he?
Very easily, in fact. **And any true Manchester City fan, however hungry for success, would agree with the Arsenal manager.**
For years I despised Chelsea for bringing the crass loadsamoney culture to football. Now City, my life-long club, are making Chelsea look positively Shylockian. City have been a comedy club for years, but people used to laugh with us rather than at us. Not now. **A billion quid a week for Kaka and it looks as if he might be coming. And he calls himself a Christian. Jesus.**
Ah, but these are exciting times at City, enjoy, friends tell me, roll with it, as those Oasis boys would say. **Pardon me? Being knocked out of the League Cup by Brighton, hammered in the FA Cup by Nottingham Forest and perilously close to the drop zone is exciting?**
No, exciting times were doing the double over Manchester United last year, and challenging for a top-four slot for half the season with a hybrid team of homegrown kids and foreign imports. *But let's not be rose-tinted.*
So to yesterday, and our Abu Dhabi saviours who **announced they**

*were going to sign up a 20-strong squad of £30m plus players as if that were a guarantee of success, and that **they were going to break all records in terms of transfer fees and wages**, as if that in itself was a measure of success.*
*I still can't believe Kaka will sign. I don't want to believe that one of the world's leading footballers would **stoop so low as to join us**. But say he does, and just say we go on to **buy up the entire Brazil squad for a few trillion quid**, and they did gel, and we did win the league with the most expensive team ever assembled, would it really feel like a triumph? **I hope not**.*"

Matt Hughes went further. By even entertaining the notion of moving to Manchester City he said the Brazilian was jeopardising his reputation as a high-class footballer consumed by chasing the biggest prizes and risks cheapening his status to that of a mere mercenary. It would be a tacit acceptance that his earning potential was more important than his achievements. It would be sad to see him effectively abandon his professional aspirations in his mid-twenties.

Strangely, such worries were absent when Real Madrid were rumoured to be paying £100m for Ronaldo, or when Chelsea themselves bid 100m euros for Kaka in 2006.
Another concern that had the nation frothing at the mouth was the sad demise of the club's youth academy, which was definitely going to decline now, as City would never play a youth player again and the England team, which contained no City players and had had no success for over 40 years, was now going to suffer as a result.

Bobby Robson had his say (disgusted), as did Alan Shearer (dismayed), Dave Whelan (shocked), Ian Wright (outraged), Joe Royle (upset), Martin O' Neill (quizzical), Paul Merson (confused) and of course Alex Ferguson (dismissive). In fact, Sky Sports News asked every Premiership manager for his opinion.

Gordon Waddell was furious, as shown in his article entitled **"Football will die if Manchester City sign Kaka".**
"When Manchester City sign Kaka, stick it in your diary as the day

the people's game died forever. When a footballer is paid enough to keep a factory of 1000 people in wages for a week? In this economic climate?
Kaka's good – great, even – but the Brazilian is human.
That's why his signing has nothing to do with football.
And why it will spell the beginning of the end for a lot of punters.
I rarely wish failure on anyone but in this case I'll make an exception. For the sake of the beautiful game."

Kenny Burns was ill with revulsion.
"I CANNOT get my breath with all the talk of Manchester City paying more than £100m for AC Milan's Kaka.
And paying him £500,000 a week.
The world and this country has gone completely mad. It is disgraceful, embarrassing, stomach-turning really.
This kind of money should be saved for throwing around to make star-studded teams on those computer games, not for the real world.
The owners should wake up and smell the coffee. There is a credit crunch on and the country is in meltdown."

Martin Lipton in the Mirror was next in the queue.
"The snub could not have been more public, a bruising of Dubai pride that will take many months to ease.
*But as Kaka last night effectively told Manchester City they may **know the price of anything but understand the value of nothing**, it may have been the **best embarrassment the club will ever undergo**.*
*And it could be **the best thing that has happened to English football in years**.*
City were close to becoming the wealthiest laughing stock the game has ever known.
*Trying to run before you've really learned to walk is an elementary error, the sort of mistake **immature clubs with immature owners** make.*
City have tried to build a glittering palace before they even started to lay down the foundations.
*Last night City looked what they are, **jumped-up, arrogant and***

out of touch. *But it could be the most important night of the new era – if they learn their lessons."*

And then along came "freelance journalist" Michael Henderson, to make an abject fool of himself.

"They might not be chortling in Miles Platting right now but everywhere else people are roaring. At a time of global uncertainty you can always rely on 'Cit-eh' to don red noses in the noble cause of cheering us all up, and they have not disappointed.
Being a laughing-stock in England was never enough for a club of such overwhelming ambition. Now, after a week of buffoonery unparalleled in the history of football, they have finally achieved the international recognition they craved for so long. Manchester's little-regarded other team is now a laughing-stock throughout the world!
Comedians to the world! Even the great Morecambe and Wise couldn't pull off that trick. Yet, by reducing Mark Hughes, a manager of some promise, to the rank of errand boy, endorsing a transfer policy that values Craig Bellamy at a cool 14 million smackers, and now, after the humiliation of Milan, hurling insults at one of the world's grandest clubs, the former sportswear salesman (Cook) has won the gratitude of millions.
When the mouthpiece of a club synonymous with high-spending failure accuses Milan of lacking 'sophistication', it is surely time to start counting the spoons. To demean the club you represent so shamelessly in public does not merely insult Milan; it insults the game itself.
The mood may be changing because it is clear that a growing number of City fans are deeply ashamed of their club's conduct."

That was City told…….

To be continued…….

Away from City, and I think it's fair to say we are all taking United's struggles with good grace – far be it for us to make things worse for the poor mites by winding up any united fans we might know. Alex Ferguson really did leave a mountain-sized poo on the manager's desk before departing for pastures and vineyards new. A star strker who wants to leave, a weak midfield, and an ageing defence. Recommend a manager who has never won anything and has no pulling power, a man who still can't seem to believe his luck in getting the job, and bob's your uncle, mission accomplished, and a fine mess United have got themselves into.

It would be fitting if United didn't finish in the top four. They helped set up the cosy cartel that ensured, that along with the likes of Arsenal, their revenue would always outstrip everyone else's, their participation in the Champions League kept the status quo, and they set up a system, aided by their letters to Michel Platini to force through Financial Fair Play rules , rules that they have now managed to persuade other Premier League clubs to agree to, even though these rules prevent the other clubs from ever competing at the top table. So how fitting if having done all this they don't qualify for the CL cash, and the Glazer model whose survival depends on massive revenue from such competitions is sent crashing to the ground. I guess you do occasionally reap what you sow.

Remember the barrage of criticism City got for their so-called pitiful defence of the title last season? Well I don't recall us slipping to 10th in the table at any point, 12 points off the lead. Let's see how many bile-filled pieces are submitted from fleet street this week. Suffice to say you'd be able to count the final number on Abu Hamza's right hand.

Still, there's still plenty of room for United sycophants to remain in the media and beyond, so it was only fitting that United's latest great young hope, whose sole achievement so far is being likened to Duncan Edwards, Franz Beckanbauer and Maradona all rolled into one, whilst playing about 4 games, has thus been nominated for YSPOTY. No doubt the jury that came to this ridiculous decision was made up of Paddy Crerand, Lou Macari, Gary Neville and Greg Dyke.

Southampton 1 Manchester City 1: Some Thoughts

For the second season running, a 90 minutes at the St. Marys Stadium that felt like three hours. A point is no disaster, but the performance brought back worrying issues over City's performances away from home.

So City move 7 points clear of the reigning champions, surely putting them in pole position for a 2nd Premier League title....oh, hang on.

The line-up for once contained little to surprise, the only bone of contention being James Milner coming in for Jesus Navas, whilst Kolarov retained his place. You could see the logic behind it though, Pellegrini seeking Milner's graft to shore things up. It didn't work though.

For all Southampton's merits, they were missing key players and were coming off three defeats. It should have been a good time to play them.

But yet again the formation seemed all wrong. City's poor performances away often result either from individual mistakes or from losing the midfield battle and with only four in midfield City once more lost the midfield battle (not overwhelmingly, but still...), often seemingly outnumbered in the middle third. Having said that, as mentioned later, a change in formation in the second half changed little.

Worryingly, the team also seemed tired, which considering the run of games coming, is disconcerting (if true).

For all the criticism every time Edin Dzeko starts, Alvaro Negredo has offered little more away from home, and this game was little different, as he offered less than Dzeko did midweek. As I have also mentioned though, this is not just about him, as he is part of the wider picture, a whole team that fails to perform much of the time when away from Manchester.

City started brightly, were creative and took the lead through Aguero. All seemed well, and then yet again they lost their grip on the game. The team continues to struggle against teams that harry and press high up the pitch, especially when that team is adept at passing.

City's front two looked sluggish, though things may have panned out very differently if Negredo had controlled better when through early on or if Aguero had not thrashed the ball over in the first-half, as did Nasri late-on and early in the second half. Having said that, you could not argue that Southampton did not deserve at least a draw, and City created virtually nothing of note in the second half. Again.

Apart from one cross that he should have intercepted that resulted in a header wide for Southampton, Pantilimon did well, and was the best of a bad bunch, with one stand-out save in the second half. There is no sign of Joe Hart returning to the league side in the foreseeable future.

What the game reiterated is the need for reinforcements in central-defence. Demichelis has done ok, but he is certainly a tad rash, dives in too much for my liking and has been well-documented, is not the quickest. He is fine as a back-up defender, perhaps our 4th choice, but if he is to have a long run in the team it puts the team at risk. Lescott is on longer good enough either for a long-run in the team (nor Boyata) and with an injury-prone first-choice pairing, another body is needed in the squad.

As for Vincent Kompany, his performance was less assertive than his comeback match, and he struggled along with everyone else, turned repeatedly for the goal and almost giving Osvaldo an assist in the second half.

It's rare you see City come away from a game with only 45% possession, fewer shots than their opposition and a mere 74% pass completion rate. On this occasion the stats portray a fairly accurate picture.

At least we have a manager who is prepared to make difficult decisions. For all his skill, it is about time Yaya Youre got substituted, after another half-arsed performance. That might be a bit harsh, it might not, but he more than anyone struggles against a team that presses hard. And for all his and Fernandinho's talents, neither is a natural ball-winner in the way De Jong was and both do leave space in midfield.

I'd suggest Jack Rodwell as another option, but he is quickly becoming the forgotten man of Manchester City.

Eventually Pellegrini did change things around, with an extra man in midfield and with Yaya Toure pushed forward when Negredo came off. It made little difference to the pattern of play and nor did resorting back to two upfront when Dzeko came on. No subs made much of an impression.

In isolation it was not a bad point, especially in conjunction with the United and Chelsea results, but the problem is that City are playing catch-up for previous errors and there is little room for manoeuvre unless Arsenal implode, which I do not believe they will.

But let's look at the positives – it was a better performance than we put in there last season. And somehow, City are still favourites for the league – though may not be by the end of the weekend.

It's just as well that Tuesday's match is not a must-win, as Bayern Munich won 7-0 away this weekend, without an injured Arjen Robben. Who knows though what teams will line-up for the final group game.

Bayern Munich v Manchester City: Match Preview

December 10, 2013

Manchester City are through to the knockout-stages of the Champions League and play Arsenal on Saturday, so will rest some players. Even Jack Rodwell might play. Maybe.

Bayern Munich are through too, so will probably do the same (apart from the Jack Rodwell bit).

But then again they may not, because they don't like City and might want to rub it in, with the league going their way as usual. At least Robben's out.

But then City could win the group if they could register a 3-goal victory. In a similar fashion, I could win the lottery this weekend. Well I could if I ever bought a ticket.

City have come a long way. They once played Macclesfield. No, seriously. In the league!

Joe Hart's back.

Predictions:

City may pack the midfield and stick 1 up front. They may not though, and stick to 4-4-2, which could be a dangerous tactic.

Yaya Toure won't play as he's suspended, but I bet Edin Dzeko does and Garcia and James Milner and I bet Clichy does too.

That's unless they are injured, I haven't checked. Did Rodwell travel with the squad? I don't know.

A lot of the away end will be intoxicated.

Derogatory comments about Javi Garcia will appear online at precisely 6:45pm, and at regular intervals thereafter.

City will get someone really good in Friday's draw. Eek.

(is it on Friday? I've no idea.)

Cue the music. Evocative, isn't it?

Bayern Munich 2 Manchester City 3: Some Thoughts

Well I will be honest – I didn't see that coming.

A dead rubber, a match that didn't matter – that was the public line and the line I had taken to give myself a relaxing night in front of the television. Nothing to lose after all, as we would be finishing second in the group and there was merely pride at stake.

But with Arsenal on the horizon, there was a general consensus not to play our strongest side and Pellegrini certainly agreed. The team was similar to how I had envisaged, and I had no problem with it.

But then I changed my mind, because I saw their team and everything went horribly wrong. So the following match thoughts have been split into two sections:

1. <u>After 15 minutes:</u>

There is logic in playing a weakened side, for obvious reasons, but was it really sensible to pair Demichelis and Lescott in central defence against the best team in Europe? This may be portrayed as a meaningless game, but an absolute caning would not only be embarrassing but possibly damaging to the players and manager.

Here is a back five of whom none of the players may be at the club in a couple of years. And I can see why.

Joleon Lescott especially had a horrendous first fifteen minutes. He resembled a rabbit in the headlights, as did many of his colleagues. The second goal was appalling defending. More slapstick defending almost resulted in a third goal.

And thus we see what happens when you put English players in the team. James Milner continues to frustrate me – I really just don't believe that, for all his qualities, he is of a standard to take this team forward.

But for Joe Hart, some sympathy. You get the feeling he has been thrown to the wolves tonight.

2. At Full-time: A Road To Damascus Conversion

What a turnaround. What bottle from the City team.
Let's be honest. After a quarter of an hour, every City fan on the planet expected a huge defeat, a morale-sapping spanking, a result to reinforce Bayern's superiority over City, a score that would put us firmly in our place.

But the response from the team was everything you'd hope for and probably least expected. Slowly they found their way back into the game, slowly they saw more of the ball and kept hold of it, pushed Bayern back, and got their rewards. Bayern Munich had a strong five minutes before the break, but offered little in the second half. The vagaries of the qualification rules left us with the bizarre situation of Bayern Munich holding the ball in the corner despite the fact they were about to lose their long unbeaten home record, but you can understand their logic. Topping the group was always their priority.

James Milner eh? Two assists and a goal, he was superb for the final hour and proof that knee-jerk reactions about players are to be tossed away into the ether where they belong. His distribution will always frustrate me sporadically, but he clearly brings other things to the table. And he's English!

(And yes, five English players appeared on the pitch at some point. The media will no doubt go to town over this.)

David Silva – welcome back. For all of Samir Nasri's superb play over the past few weeks, what a joy it was see the diminutive Spaniard back on the pitch. He is simply a class above.

But then there is also Micah Richards. His tweet apologising for getting injured was almost heart-breaking and he will be hurting in more ways than one today. We all want him to stay fit and be a success, to be a part of all of this, but he is injured so easily it is becoming untenable to pick him. It pains me to say it, but the team performance rose significantly once he was replaced by Zabaleta (though it's harsh to put it down to this one factor). His future at City is only assured because his injury record prevents anyone buying him. I desperately hope he can turn things round.

PARANOIA KLAXON!!
Manuel Pellegrini unwittingly diverted attention away from the match (much more on that later), but that aside there was yet again a pathetic level of coverage of City's amazing comeback. At half-time Graeme Souness (one of my favourite pundits) said the 2-1 score line flattered City (it did not), but it was Glenn Hoddle that truly took the biscuit at full-time, the usual tactic used of calling the opposition poor rather than daring praise City instead. To turn the paranoia-meter up to 11, I wonder how coverage would had differed if United had pulled off a similar performance, or Arsenal for that matter. Whilst Dan Walker of the BBC dared buck the trend by calling to one of the top five away performances by a British side in the Champions League (kudos for Henry Winter also for his compliments), Raphael Honigstein could see no positives in City's performance in what was a dead rubber, despite the Times' Tony Barrett's attempts to point out how much belief this could give a side that may previously have been carrying around an inferiority complex in Europe.
Naturally the majority of newspapers made United's 1-0 victory over Shaktar Donetsk as their main story on the back pages, because…well, I've no idea to be honest (sells more papers I guess).

I've given up talking about Niall Quinn.

Typical City lives on and the club manage to travel to Munich and contrive to get the press talking about something other than the result. Again. Pellegrini's post-match comments, coupled with James Milner's later on have certainly caused a stir in the press and amongst City fans. Whilst you cannot fathom how none of the coaching staff were aware that City only needed one more goal to top the group, the comments of Pellegrini, even if they were in pigeon English, left me in little doubt he thought City needed to score five. There is always the possibility of course that he has been misinterpreted, but his English is not that bad, so I doubt it. You can understand City not expecting a match scenario where a fourth goal could take us through for the simple reason that the scenario was so, so unlikely, but it is gross amateurism if (IF) the club were not aware of the options as the match drew to an end. We can argue until we're blue in the face about what the coaching staff may or may not have known, but the introduction of Jack Rodwell with three minutes to go surely reinforces the notion that Pellegrini was not looking for another goal. Of course, football is not so simple that simply introducing another striker means more goals will come and changing the shape of a team can be more productive sometimes, but once City found themselves a single goal away form topping the group, to not bring Aguero on at any point seems ludicrous.

Maybe Pellegrini doesn't care who we meet. Maybe victory meant more to him than topping the group, his first ever victory over a Pep Guardiola team at the 11th attempt. Either way, you'd expect an engineer to grasp simple mathematics. The spirit of Alan Ball lives on.

(As for the argument that it doesn't matter anyway, because no-one will want to play us (Carlo Ancelotti – "City are the most dangerous rival in the upcoming draw") and you have to beat the best teams to win the competition, that is nonsense. You stand a much better chance of winning the Champions League if you only come up across two top teams than if you have to beat four.)

Still, it seems many are wise after the event.

Barney Ronay 9th December: *City need to beat Bayern by three clear goals in their own indomitable illuminated doughnut of a stronghold to overhaul them at the top of Group D rather than simply qualify in second place.*

Barney Ronay – 11th December: *At the end of a dramatic night it seemed a shame a misunderstanding of the rules should overshadow a fine result, however briefly.*

Typical City lives on elsewhere too. Having achieved the feat of elimination from the group stages with ten points, City have now broken all records by finishing second in a group with fifteen points (two points more than our previous two campaigns combined). Bravo!

With the Ballon D'or on the horizon, how fitting it would be if Franck Ribery gets nowhere near the award (as will surely be the case). A bigger cheat you could not hope to see (ok, one person springs to mind), making Ronaldo seem almost angelic in comparison. The clutched knee/pained face/I think I've been shot impression is wheeled out at least five times a game in an attempt to get an opposition player cautioned/dismissed.

Some stats? OK then. This was the first time in 38 years that Bayern had lost after building a two-goal lead at home. It ended a run of 10 consecutive Champions League victories and 18 consecutive home victories for Bayern. Travel-sick Manchester City finish the group stage with three away victories, despite only having 40% of possession against Bayern.

And then there's the money. 5m euros in bonuses and a boost to City's coefficient means there is more to results like this than a bit of pride.

But surely the greatest joy in all of this is the bitter blue in me cocking two-fingers at every person Bayern-related. From their tax-dodging president to their arrogant executive chairman, they can stick their David Conn eulogies where the sun don't shine, the fan-owned club took one hell of a beating (ok, a small one). They are the Manchester United of Germany, and their hoovering up of the best talent is anything but fair. The TV pictures of their glum faces in the closing stages because for once everything wasn't going their way was a truly beautiful sight. This wasn't in the script.

Sunderland > Bayern Munich.

Manchester City 6 Arsenal 3: Some Thoughts

Blimey.

So it was six in the city as Arsenal were gunned down at fortress Etihad as City slickers fired a ferocious….ah sod it, my heart's not in this.

This was the biggest game of the Premiership season so far, and the stakes at this stage of the season couldn't have been much higher. Victory and City were right back in the title race and Arsenal would have been hauled back into the chasing pack. Lose and City would be nine points behind the leaders.
The team line-up was as expected. Move on, nothing to see here.

But what a game. At no point did it let up, an amazing spectacle that had my heart pounding until the final whistle and beyond. It would be easy to go to town on the defence, but I don't feel it is necessary after this game. Both teams have a world-class array of attacking talent and they went at it hammer and tongs for the whole match. Goals were bound to follow, and each defender on both sides did plenty of good things but they were worked to the bone and for once it may be best to focus on the positives and not pick holes in player performances.

And in that defence Zabaleta continued a superb week, as did Vincent Kompany, in the end putting in a Messi-like performance of dribbling and attacking prowess. Maybe he's wasted in defence. He could certainly do a job once more as a defensive midfielder.

Playing against Arsenal in the past may have caused Samir Nasri to retreat into a metaphorical shell, but not the Samir Nasri of 2013/14. He was superb.
The attacking prowess right now though just takes the breath away. I keep saying it, but it needs repeating. I remember the pride a long time ago when a City goal made the shortlist of Match of The Day's "Goal of the Month" competition. It didn't win, a United goal did obviously, but I was still proud. Nowadays, we could fill

all the nominations, every month. It's a style that can leave gaps in front of the defence, but it an utter joy to behold.

There can be no doubt about the Man of the Match, Fernandinho reaching new heights. Even without the goals he was imperious and as beautiful as his first goal was I think I actually preferred the lovely dink for the second goal that sent Szczesny the wrong way.

James Milner has had a good week too and when he came on he once more excelled, quelling Arsenal's threat down his side, and winning another penalty.

Maybe the run-in is a worse period, but this is certainly not a good time for teams to lose players to injury with games coming thick and fast, so fingers crossed that Sergio Aguero's calf injury is not too serious. City have back up in this area so hopefully won't suffer too much, especially if Jovetic can now stay fit and get some playing time. I've been waiting three months to see him perform (Wigan in the cup isn't enough).

Arsenal's best spell came after Aguero departed and whilst a move to one striker upfront should have suited City as it meant more of a presence in midfield, they seemed to lose their shape for fifteen minutes and Arsenal came at City hard, culminating in their second goal. That's why for me the fourth goal was the most important of the day, as it was a nervy time prior to that and it repelled the potential comeback from the Gunners.

There seems to be a feeling though that Arsenal were hard-done by due to refereeing decisions, especially regarding offsides, but they were not. If you watched Match of the Day you would probably think it was an even game - but it was not. Arsenal were dead on their feet by 70 minutes and if City had been more ruthless they could have had three in the following ten minutes alone. At the end of normal time I think City were flagging too and Arsenal came back once more as City tried to coast over the finish line, but it was too little too late. Oh and by the way, Walcott was offside for his second goal (by about 5 centimetres) – but hey, that doesn't fit the narrative.

What's more, Negredo, whilst generally excellent once more, could and perhaps should have scored two in the first-half. This game could easily have ended 10-5.

Stat attack (sorry): It's now 35 goals in 8 home games, and Arsenal conceded more goals than all their previous away games combined. The game saw 34 shots (22 of which were City's), 13 of which were on target. City had 53% possession and a 83% pass success rate. City have now scored in 58 consecutive home league games.
(I once took a book to a City match under Stuart Pearce. I think it was The Secret History by Donna Tartt.)

I'm happy Theo Walcott is soon to become a father, he seems a lovely bloke, very grounded, but please spare me the baby-rocking celebration. It was quite sweet when Bebeto did it 20 years ago, but for some reason it really annoys me now. Well done Theo, you have a satisfactory sperm count. Still, it beats Osvaldo machine-gunning the crowd last week I guess. And Fernandinho can cut out that heart celebration too, it's crap and Gareth Bale will sue him if he persists.

On a similar note, if you sang "the baby's not yours" at Walcott or think it is remotely funny, just to let you know – you're a cretin. Still, they all earn £200,000 a week so should be able to take a bit of TOP BANTER eh?

No surprise at the graceless manner of Arsene Wenger after the game. As Daniel Taylor commented on Twitter, it is a trait of his not to ever compliment opposing teams. You could argue no managers do, but Wenger takes it further, the bitterness seeping out of every pore when things don't go his way. His comment about City being no better than Southampton or Everton was classic bull**it from a bad loser, as were the complaints prior to the match about the fixture list. So what if City had an extra day to prepare? It happens, and we'll play plenty of games when we haven't had as much rest as the opposition and Arsenal will play games against teams who themselves have had to travel round Europe in previous days and I'm sure Wenger won't be moaning on those occasions.

In City's first Champions League campaign they had an away match after every single Group Stage match, including games against Liverpool, Manchester United and Chelsea. No wonder we only put six past United.

Shaun Custis argued on the Sunday Supplement that the league should help teams in Europe by moving games to give ample rest time, as other leagues do sometimes. But with City playing on Tuesday, why should they have to play on a Sunday? Would it have made much difference if the game had been a normal 3pm kick-off, thus giving Arsenal an extra 135 minutes rest? When it boils down to it, the clubs are about to reap the rewards of a multi-billion pound TV deal, so if they are happy to take the cash, they have to take the consequences. So Arsene, would you be prepared to scrap the TV deal to give your pampered players a bit more rest? No, didn't think so.

As you may have noticed in the past, the lack of grace often extends to the supporters, and there were some magical comments below the Guardian match report:

"No shame for any side to lose away to a team that cost a billion."

"Arsenal were robbed, plain and simple, there was not one dubious Man City decision but five Arsenal ones… the FA want manure to win the league and are doing all they can to keep them in the hunt."

"Our money came from inside the club, years of careful growing and saving up. Not some bored dodgy oil baron."

Apropos of nothing, Arsenal are raising their ticket prices by an extra 3%. Doing things the right way, you see?

We scored from a corner!!! I take it ALL back….

Leicester City 1 Manchester 3. Capital One Cup Quarter Final.

Job done with a professional and efficient performance from City. Edin Dzeko scored twice as City booked their place in the Capital One Cup semi-finals.

Kolarov scored the opener with a fantastic 25-yard free-kick, before Dzeko headed in his first from James Milner's cross.

The Bosnian striker netted his side's third after the break when he side-footed in from another Milner ball.

Lloyd Dyer scored a late consolation. A two-legged semi-final awaits, the nerves of another cup draw exacerbated by the possibility of drawing United. In a way this seemed the best option, as it sure beat having to play them in the final instead, but as it turned out United were the gift that kept on giving.

Fulham 2 Manchester City 4: Some Thoughts

Well thank god for that. I don't think I could have mustered the desire to type a single word if City had contrived to mess that up.

The team-sheet was always going to be interesting. Firstly, as had been rumoured in the press, Joe Hart was recalled to the first team (league). I was happy to see this, though I have no idea why Pellegrini chose this game to do it. Then there was the problem of the right-back position. In the end it was Clichy who filled in and that made some sense to me. There were numerous calls for James Milner to play there as he would always put a shift in, but he hasn't played there for a long-time and has only done it in the past to fill-in as he would be doing now so it could be too risky to throw him in. At least Clichy is a full-back by trade with a competent right-foot so he knows about the demands of the position. As it turned out he didn't cover himself with glory, but for now he may be the best of a bad bunch and City will just have to hope Zabaleta is back soon. Clichy's display will only heighten calls for Milner to play there against Liverpool though. What surprised me also was that Milner wasn't picked to play in front of Clichy to offer extra protection.
Finally, Pellegrini surprised me further by playing Dzeko and Negredo up front. A bit more on that later.

Fulham started brightly and are clearly playing better since Jol's departure, though results haven't followed just yet. Thus, Toure's superb free-kick was very timely and City created plenty of chances thereafter. Negredo was fairly quiet away from the Etihad once more until Dzeko departed, and it was the Bosnian who had more chances and was quite wasteful.

Having said that, Negredo may not have seen much action in front of goal, but he worked his arse off. As always. Even when he isn't dominating proceedings he is working the opposition defence at all times.

The defence was not good enough either, a recurring theme every other game. Kompany's goal was a freak of course, something City are masters of on the road, but generally Fulham were given far too much room at times and you have to wonder if a high defensive line that has already cost one manager elsewhere his job is the way to go. Demichelis was rash once more, constantly diving in unsuccessfully for balls, but we all know the defence is not as it should be at the moment and needs some work on it. Another purchase is needed, and if the team could play with a settled defence for just a few weeks that would help. For all his faults though, Demichelis is a great header of the ball, cleared balls endlessly and is a threat at set-pieces as he demonstrated yesterday.

The defending for Fulham's first goal was especially shambolic and downright lazy by two players in particular. Demichelis dived in once more, then Clichy slips, but what was worse than that was Kolarov and Yaya Toure ambling back allowing Richardson all the space in the world to slot home the cross.

But this is the price perhaps of attacking football. As City attacked prior to that goal, Vincent Kompany was the only outfield City player in his own half. That attacking football has seen City average three goals per game over the opening 17 games of the season.

As for the own-goal, Kompany takes the prize for most ridiculous own-goal of all-time, nudging Jamie Pollock out of the way (some feat, all things considered).

But for all Fulham's chances, City had more and deserved the victory. It's just a shame the team didn't tighten up when two goals up, but they had plenty of opportunities to put the game to bed just after half-time and almost paid the price. For this reason I wondered about the decision to play two up front rather than a 4-5-1 formation (or 4-2-3-1 or however you want to describe it) that would have restricted Fulham's ball-playing skills – because they do pass the ball very well indeed. So credit to City for not letting the goals put them off-course. Some City teams of old would have gone on to lose that game. What's more, City are creating far more chances than they were earlier in the season in away games.

There's no putting it off any longer. Time to talk about Alan Hansen (get that paranoia klaxon ready). Hansen put his £50,000 fee to good use by dissecting City's defending and he couldn't wait to get stuck in. The thing is, he was right as I have already discussed. The defence was at sea at times and Demichelis, who I generally like, deserved criticism, but what craws is the fact that when City have just scored four away from home to go second in the league (and could easily have scored six or seven) I do not expect a five-minute diatribe about our defending, including a bizarre montage pointing out that we were appalling for a 10-minute period after their equalizer. No replay of a wonderful free-kick, no analysis of our striking prowess or Negredo's beautiful assist for the final goal. Nothing.

Still we all know that the punditry scene is one dominated by ex-reds, be it endless ex-Liverpool players, from Phil Thompson to Mark Lawrenson to Hansen to Michael Owen and Robbie Fowler and Steve McManaman and Jamie Carragher and Graeme Souness (and on and on and on) or the United cabal of Gary Neville, Dwight Yorke (dear god), Andy Cole (dear god again) and more. Still, we have Danny Mills and Niall Quinn to stick the boot in so be careful what you wish for.

So that is seven free-kicks scored this season. Remarkable.

I love Jesus Navas and I love his goal celebrations too. That is all.

Manchester City 2 Liverpool 1: Some Thoughts

A tense, nervy 90 minutes against a team who gave as good as they got, but in a hectic Xmas schedule where results count more than anything City held on for three points.

With Aguero out and Sturridge absent for Liverpool it always seemed likely to me that Pellegrini might just play one up front so as not to lose control of midfield, and that's how it turned out, though the rumour was he would have played Dzeko up front with Negredo if Demichelis hadn't injured himself in training, though I don't see the logic to that.

I was more anxious about this game than any other and my fears proved to be well-founded. Liverpool were everything I expected, with a skilful front-three that worked the City defence to the limit. Suarez might be a despicable cheat at times, but what a player he is, a world-class performer right now full of running, movement and exquisite ball-control. Coutinho and Sterling both ensured Sturridge wasn't missed, whilst Jordan Henderson continued improvement means Steven Gerrard isn't missed much either.

City's defence thus performed fairly well in my opinion considering the pressure they were put under, but no one covered themselves in glory. Kompany scored a vital goal but was, like those beside him, turned too many times by Suarez, Sterling et al. The team as a whole were dogged, resilient and had just enough quality without ever reaching the heights. Perhaps for once fatigue played a part.

Yet again City have beaten a rival and all the talk is about how hard-done the losers were. Brendan Rogers' comments about Lee Mason's place of residence were pathetic and showed a bizarre ignorance of how Greater Manchester allegiances lie. The fact is that that there was no disallowed goal as some claimed as the whistle went before Sterling shot, and Joe Hart stopped trying. Of course Sterling would definitely have scored, just like he did in the second half with an easier chance. Oh, hang on…

On top of that, the score was 0-0 at the time, so if Liverpool had scored, they would not have then scored the goal they actually did score in the game, as history would have changed and everything that happened thereafter would have been different. This fact will sail over many a numbskull's head.

Finally, it seems the distance he was onside has increased the wrath of some Liverpool fans and increased the sense of injustice at losing the game. If he had only been just onside we'd probably have less of an uproar, which is strange. It was bad officiating, but there are wrong offside calls in most games – this was no different.

As for the tugging of Suarez's shirt, it is a non-issue, because as many have already commented, Skrtel does that at every corner, including during previous games. He was all over Kompany for the captain's goal. Still, it was stupid of Lescott to be doing that when protecting a slim lead late in the game. Funny though how the tug on Suarez forced him seven feet into the air, and take on the appearance of a wounded soldier, but nothing should surprise us with him.

Stats are often meaningless, but for all of the opposition's whining, City had more possession and more shots on and off target. If you were watching Match of the Day (ah that old chestnut again), you'd think the second half was a wave of Liverpool pressure, which it certainly was not, as the editors once more misrepresented what happened on the pitch, even using the banner "red rampage" to show highlights during the analysis section. City may not have carved out guilt-edged chances in the second half but were on top for some periods before Liverpool came back strongly, and a highlights package should replicate the general patterns of play, not just show chances.

Negredo's goal was a strange one and took attention away from the superb link-up play that preceded it. To be honest he got it all wrong trying to curl it in the far corner with the outside of his foot and it curled the other way instead which is what probably did for the keeper.

Hart was excellent, saving City on more than one occasion. Maybe Pellegrini, renowned for his man-management, got this spot-on after all and we can but hope Hart can now maintain his form so that we don't have to discuss him on a weekly basis in the future. He has had the kick up the arse he needed and has responded excellently and with dignity and professionalism.

I still worry about the amount of space that opposition teams of quality sometimes get in midfield though. Before we all get cocky about facing Barcelona, let's remember how well they press and boy can they pass the ball.

But forget the performance, because Christmas is a strange time and a hectic one – the fact is that City won and the result is everything. December has been a superb month - City were the form team even before the last two victories and have put together an excellent run since the horror show against Sunderland, beating Bayern Munich, Arsenal and Liverpool in one month. They have scored as many goals in the first 18 league games as anyone in Premiership history (equalling our own record of two seasons ago), and have hauled themselves to the brink of the table summit as we approach the new year. The need now is to get two more victories this week with rotated sides and head into cup season near or at the top of the table.

There will be no need to go mad in the January transfer window, but eventually certain areas need ot be addressed, especially in defence. The priorities by the end of next August must surely be a left-back and a central defender. Maybe even another right-back will be required if Micah Richards cannot stay fit. With City still linked with various goalkeepers in the gossip columns it could be an area seeing considerable upheaval in the coming year.
Just think – Liverpool's excellence could be the deciding factor in whether United finish the season in the top four. Now that wouldn't go down well across the city.

Another 100% tackle success rate for Javi Garcia. Though to be fair he only touched the ball once.

Manchester City 1 Crystal Palace 0

Another important Edin Dzeko goal saw City go temporarily top of the table. It wasn't City's most inspiring of performances, but over the packed Christmas schedule, the result was the most important thing.

It was time to look back at another eventful year….

2013: A Review

2013 started with a hung-over nation watching the latest almost-daily football clashes through bleary, blood-shot eyes. So the same as every other year then.

Within days, Mario Balotelli was back in the news as he grappled with manager Roberto Mancini in training. It made headline news, but no one really cared any more. Wild speculation ensued that Balotelli's time at the club was over, and that Mancini was losing the plot. For once the speculation was right. Balotelli exited first to Milan and not surprisingly ended the year back on sale.

One Daily Mail commenter had strong views on the matter:

So the Arab 'benefactors' have brought shame and pity to football, an unflattering, unprofessional, nasty, pantomime, an embarrassing antics roadshow to Manchester.
Whatever words we chose, it's just not right. Like all human endeavour, sport should earn its awards through striving, consistency and dedication over a period of time. Sugardaddy demands for immediate, unearned purchase of success, brings nothing but embarrassment, shame and yes pity to a small but once decent club like City.

As the nation unwittingly chomped on horsemeat the issue of ticket prices was in the news as City returned some of their allocation for the match at Arsenal. City won at the Emirates, but with United defeating Liverpool earlier in the day, retaining the Premier League title was looking less likely by the week. Vincent

Kompany was once more sent off for a clean tackle, though amazingly this time the card was later rescinded.

Three days later Paul Scholes committed a far worse tackle against West Ham but there was no media outcry for the lovable, shy family-man despite his late lunge missing the ball by 5 yards and completely taking out an opposition player.

In the heart of the city Michael Johnson was photographed enjoying fried food rather too much for a supposed footballer, and it soon emerged that City had given up on the wayward star. Across town, a new star was born and of course hyped beyond all belief:

Daily Telegraph Article Header

Meet Crystal Palace striker Wilfried Zaha – as tough as Maradona and as skilful as George Best

He would soon be usurped by an even bigger talent as United's miraculous youth system churned another Busby Babe off the production line.

City continued to progress through the FA Cup once more – having defeated Watford, Pablo Zabaleta put Stoke City to the sword. Elsewhere, Eden Hazard was sent off for kicking a ball-boy in the ribs after the 17-year old had seemingly fallen asleep on top of the ball. The boy reacted much as Suarez would after being gently brushed on his thigh – i.e. as if he had just been shot at Ypres. Overnight he became a Twitter sensation because that's how the world works now until everyone moved on bored the next day when they realised 17-year-old ball-boys don't have much of interest to say (like 39-year-old bloggers in many ways).

A home draw against Liverpool pretty much extinguished City's title hopes, Aguero's magnificent equalizer soon forgotten. Worse was to follow though with a horror show at Southampton, Gareth Barry scoring the first of two emphatic City own-goals in the calendar year. In the cup however progress continued, as two championship sides from Yorkshire were easily defeated and another trip to Wembley was secured.

Thankfully the Champions League provided ample opportunity for bitter blues to have a good laugh at United's expense as they went out of the competition to Real Madrid. According to twitter it seemed the red card for Nani was one of the worst decisions ever made. Needless to say, it was nothing of the sort.
James Lawton at the Independent called it an assault on natural justice and I laughed myself to sleep.

Meanwhile, over at The Sun:
20th March 2013 – TOURE: GIVE ME A NEW CONTRACT BY SATURDAY OR I'M OFF

Two weeks later Yaya Toure signed a new 4-year contract.

City triumphed at Old Trafford, but it changed little and then the Iron Lady popped her clogs and half the country celebrated wildly, the other half, or less, mourned and got angry. This should have nothing to do with football, but inevitably there were calls, mostly from Tory donors such as Dave Whelan, for a minute's silence before Premier League matches – after all, what could possibly go wrong?

Soon a new joke was born.
A Manchester City fan walks into a bar near Wembley.
"The usual?" asks the barman.

City were back in London and progressed to another Cup Final with a 2-1 win over Chelsea. The latest hammer-blow through the collective heart of the English football fan came soon after with the announcement that the 2013 FA Cup final would kick off at 5:15pm. Guardian journalist Jacob Steinberg commented that it was hardly a surprise that some people now treat the FA Cup with indifference if the FA can't be bothered protecting it and fans.

A pitiful defeat at Spurs finally signalled the end of City's title campaign. No red Champ20ns t-shirts were being thrown in the bin this time round, as United clinched the title with time to spare.

And with the title secured, the time had finally arrived. Alex Ferguson was finally retiring, and he meant it this time. Half a city rejoiced and it helped buoy the mood further before a trip to Wembley for the FA Cup Final against Wigan. Everything was falling nicely into place.

And then of course City lost the FA Cup Final. The uncertainty over the manager's future seemed to deeply affect a team that barely turned up to contest the match. A torrential downpour on exiting the stadium just capped off the evening perfectly, and the night was spent drowning many sorrows.

And then Mancini exited stage left. Having alienated most of the people he worked with, he fell on his sword, the perfectionist at an imperfect club. The papers went to town on his autocratic reign, some of the allegations not far off the ones I made up below.

MANCINI'S REIGN OF TERROR

•BANNED ENGLISH IN THE DRESSING ROOM

• YOUTH PLAYER MADE TO WEAR CLOGS

• BALOTELLI ALLOWED TO KILL "AT WILL"

• PASTA HAD TO BE FIRM

By the end of the year though, I had heard from too many places that the rumours had all been true.

And so finally Norwich came to town. A limp home defeat, appalling defending, strange team selections, rumours of City's captain thumping another player – normal service for City had resumed.
Throw in a public spat between Kolarov and a whole stand, Kompany with a face like thunder and a mostly-empty stadium to greet the lap of (dis)honour, and it was a fittingly miserable end to the season. And that was that. The season over with a whimper.

The summer was long as it lacked football, bar the odd post-season friendly tour to the Big Apple, an Audi Cup, pre-season friendlies and the hugely entertaining Confederations Cup. Hey, City even created a new club just for the hell of it.

The appointment of Manuel Pellegrini was a "done deal" for almost a month, with the odd story coming out of Real Madrid wanting him, Barcelona wanting him, PSG wanting him, then Porto wanting him. In the end it was said to be a small contract dispute that delayed the inevitable, but eventually the announcement of City's new manager was made, though it was not until the first days of July that Pellegrini actually got his feet behind an Etihad Stadium desk.

City fans raised £7000 to put an advert in the Gazzetta Dello Sport thanking Roberto Mancini, a nice touch, but I had better things to spend my money on, like PPI payments and salt and pepper spare ribs.

Carlos Tevez moved on, signing for Juventus, the old lady, on a 3-year deal, whilst Wayne Rooney looked on in envy. Tevez's stay at City has seemed to run parallel with his old manager Roberto Mancini. Both seemed poised to leave as soon as they arrived (if you believed the press), both were successful but flawed, their baggage enough to incur a £10,000 surcharge with Ryanair.
Isco moved on also – to Real Madrid, and an entire fan base wailed long into the night after realising a 13,000 page thread on Bluemoon had all been for nothing.

City moved quickly (for once) and tied up the majority of their summer transfer business with six weeks of the window remaining, replacing two departed strikers with two new additions, whilst also bolstering the midfield with two other signings, all done in the nick of time as Manchester's once-in-a-decade hot-spell came to an end. Suckers!
But at the end of another tedious window, another unsung hero went for pastures new, as Gareth Barry moved to Everton on loan, effectively ending his City career.

Prior to that and City put on a pre-season party, namely City Live at Manchester Central. As with anything the club does it split the fans, with many not willing to pay £25 to see the players on a stage, so they didn't pay and others did and the others went and had a good night.

Jamie Oliver introduced his pukka bespoke pies and burgers to the Etihad, which taste much like the old ones but for more money. Nice chips though.

City somehow contrived to lose at Cardiff, the home side's red home shirts sending too powerful a force for City to resist as their buffoon of an owner looked on with his pants up to his shoulders and a moustached that shouted "bow before me mere mortals". Eat your heart out Simon Cowell. Sadly poor away form was to hamper the club for the rest of the year, further defeats to Aston Villa and Sunderland still yet to be explained by the planet's brightest boffins. At home though, City were an irresistible force, swatting away mid-table teams like Norwich City, Swansea City and Manchester United.

Mick Hucknall, Terry Christian, Eamonn Holmes, James Nesbitt, Mumford and (bloody) Sons, Terry Christian again, Zoe Ball, Paddy Crerand, Lou Macari, the chosen one, Clayton Blackmore, Terry Christian again, Mark Ogden, Usain Bolt, Gary Neville, Howard Webb, some bloke who used to present Play School, Terry Christian again. Your boys took one hell of a beating.

There was proof that Stevan Jovetic exists as City put five past Wigan in the Capital One Cup. Then Bayern Munich came to town and put City to the sword. It would seem revenge would be needed once more.

Elsewhere and Alex Ferguson released his latest instalment of his memoirs, a predictably myopic view of events that conveniently whitewashed the awkward moments in his career, omitting the Glazers' influence on the club, his fall out with the previous owners that led to the American takeover or his son's role as an agent. He even forgot to mention his speeding ticket and bowel evacuation caused by a dicky stomach. If you've ever had a session on Holts bitter, you'll understand his predicament.

The best bits were left for City though, which was nice. Of the 6-1 Old Trafford massacre, he commented:

"There was never a point where City looked superior to us."
"We battered them."

No one really cared about the past though, because it was all about the future. A new star had been born, a mix of Beckenbauer, Maradona, Duncan Edwards (obv) and Eusebio. Adnan Januzaj had arrived. And that wasn't the only good news across town. Unilever became United's 'personal care and laundry provider in SE Asia' and Mamee their official noodle partner in Oceania and beyond. Manda Fermentation Company become the club's 'Official Nutritional Supplements Partner'. On the downside, United launched an investigation into a "completely inappropriate" Nazi Swastika-style logo on their club email. People are so picky sometimes.

Harry Redknapp too released an autobiography, which needless to say was largely fabricated (allegedly). Apparently Spurs only had two points from eight games when he took over (news to me). Next you'll be telling me Dave Whelan once broke his leg in a cup final.

New figures released showed Sam Allardyce to be the 13th highest-paid manager in the world. Harry Redknapp is 26th (Pellegrini 10th).

The biggest scandal was yet to come though when two players were seen exchanging shirts at half-time. Oh, the humanity, and so soon after Flamini wore a long-sleeved shirt, urinating on over a century of Arsenal's history in the process.

City's away form slowly improved, and peaked as the team triumphed in Munich, finishing their Champions League campaign with three away victories. Sadly Manuel Pellegrini's rudimentary grasp of mathematics saw City fail to go for the jugular, namely a 4th goal that would have seen them top the group and as a result a tasty double-header against Barcelona awaits in late winter. West

Ham stand between City and another trip to Wembley in the Capital One Cup and Blackburn host 7,000 inebriated City fans in the New Year. A hectic month awaits after a year that has never been dull as City continue to write the headlines for Fleet Street's finest and worst.

And so a storm-ravaged country crept towards the end of the year, and with the Premier League title race closer than it has been for many a year, here's to another exciting year of football, England sweeping all before them in Brazil and on a more realistic note for David Moyes not to be sacked, as he is doing a great job.

Tweets of The Year

Eamonn Holmes, after the appointment of David Moyes – *THE LEGACY LIVES*

@footyaccums – *City buying Negredo for £24m is such a bad piece of business. So many better strikers out there for that price.*

Bob Cass – *Jones is again the play-anywhere diamond for England. When he finally gets a crack at central defence, he'll be one of the world's best.*

Rob Beasley – *Klopp n Lewandowski to Chelsea. Jose n CR7 to Utd*

Peter Spencer, MEN: *"You won't get me saying jones is the new duncan edwards - yet"*

Jones the new robbo?

Said Baines for utd 2 years ago...great to be right for once

Its Ronnie utd really want believe it

Fgkljhgfoigjhofgiigfo

(Pete hasn't quite mastered tweeting just yet, bless).

Stewart Gardner - *Makes a nice change for Kompany and Aguero to appear in front of a full house...*

Piers Moron - *And you know what @SamNasri19 ? Arteta's a better No8 for us than you ever were. #Arsenal*

Neil Ashton: *City 4 United 1. Could be the day English football died after City start with ten overseas outfield players.*

Joey Barton – *I'll just re-iterate for a lot of the buffoons tweeting me. I WILL NOT BE PLAYING IN THE CHAMPIONSHIP NEXT SEASON. Hope that clears that up!*

Favourite Quote

"A Marseille player, whose name I don't remember, speaks badly of Neymar, Brazilian football, Beckham and Ibra. As no one talks about him, maybe he thinks he'll drool over the big players so that we know he exists. It makes me want to win even more, to shut this Englishman up. What does he know about Brazilian football? I can't remember playing against him for the national team." –
Thiago Silva on Joey Barton

Other stuff

What Suarez said, what Terry said, was for private consumption, no matter how unpalatable. It was abuse, pure and simple. Horrid, racist abuse, **but ultimately meaningless.** – Martin Samuel column.

The index in Sven Goran Eriksson's autobiography:
Relationships with women 255, 267-8, 283-4.
See also Alam, Faria; Caprioglio, Deborah; Dell'Olio, Nancy; Jonsson, Ulrika; Mancinelli, Graziella; Pettersson, Ann-Christine 'Anki'; Yaniseth

2013/14 Predictions – Louise Taylor

League Winners

Tottenham. Europa League involvement and the potential loss of Gareth Bale are worries but Roberto Soldado and Paulinho look excellent signings and AVB is a class coach.

Player of The Season

Hatem Ben Arfa. Providing he stays fit, Ben Arfa belongs on a different planet to most mortals. Capable of eclipsing Rooney, Bale and even Suárez.

Signing Of The Summer

Paulinho. A sort of Brazilian Frank Lampard, his ability to score freely from midfield promises to transform Spurs.

Manager To Watch

Paolo Di Canio. The self-styled "revolutionary" is clever enough to confound his many critics and lead a reborn Sunderland into the top 10.

Swansea 2 Manchester City 3.

No match report for this as I watched the game through one eye, the previous nights' festivities still taking its toll. Yep, it was New Year's Day and another case of job done, City making us suffer once more by conceding a late goal that meant we couldn't relax until that full-time whistle went.

A great result though, especially considering the efforts of previous years. Fernandinho, Toure and Kolrov scored the goals and the fact that Bony's first goal as half-time approached was offside didn't seem to unduly concern the commentary team or media in general, Fancy that.

Never mind, this was a sign that City's away form was correcting itself, as it was the first time under Pellegrini that City had won two consecutive away games in the league.

Speaking of the media…

Yaya Toure – Manchester City's Liability

It is tradition for Manchester City fans to throw large objects at television screens when Match of the Day is on and on New Year's Day Dietmar Hamann kept that tradition alive and well as he almost melted Twitter by describing Yaya Toure as a liability in his analysis.
For once though my heartbeat didn't have me reaching for the pill cabinet as Hamann spoke a truth hiding somewhere within his garbled message.

Yaya Toure is not, has never been and never will be a liability. He is a world-class footballer who would walk into any team in the Premier League. What I would hope Hamann meant when he called him a liability is that how he is deployed in away games results in the game passing him by on occasion, on account of how deep he sits. Thus, the argument is not about how good Toure is, the worry over his position exacerbated against teams who like to press hard up high up the pitch. The criticism for me is not against the player, but the manager for deploying a two-man midfield that allows too much space to the opposition, something Swansea got plenty of on New Years' Day. Yaya Toure does not "track-back" consistently whilst Fernandinho for all his brilliance is not a natural holding midfielder. With these two playing together there is not that barrier in front of the defence, though it has rarely mattered at home so far, where opposition teams have been consistently overwhelmed.

Pellegrini has often changed the formation in second halves by bringing on Javi Garcia to plug the gap, a player oft-criticised but who does that simple task effectively. By doing this though, a top-class attacking player must be sacrificed and so perhaps Pellegrini considers it worth the risk keeping things as they are. City are the form team in the league and were even before their three recent victories so it is hardly cause for panic. The two elephants in the room are the Barcelona ties, a team apparently not at its peak but clearly still capable of ruthlessly exploiting space.

The city manager is no mug of course and must be aware of this. He is a proponent of attacking football and he may accept this as the price to pay, as for all the space it leaves it also means a greater attacking threat. The counter-argument is that if Yaya was freed to be even more attacking it would be even more devastating for the opposition.

The problem with Hamann was his bad choice of words. English may be his 2nd language but he speaks it perfectly well. It only takes one word to invoke rage.
The other cause of anger is that after every City victory the analysis seems to focus in on their faults. Perhaps a bit more praise for the record-breaking form team would be nice, but to be honest who cares anyway? As long as City keep winning, there's little to get angry about.

Football in 2014: Some Predictions

Resolutions

A stormy New Year saw an endless run of football continue unabated. Adnan Januzaj was booked for diving, a decision that David Moyes called scandalous. United were linked with Wesley Sneijder, obviously. They were also linked with various other players they had no intention of signing. The United-fed media PR campaign commenced, as £100m war-chests were announced, which soon rose to £150m then £200m. Unfortunately David Moyes and the Equalizer could still not find any value in the market.

Manchester City won 7-1 at Newcastle, but Alan Hansen was not happy with City's defending for the Newcastle goal. In the Match of the Day studio he spent 15 minutes pulling apart the positioning of Michael Demichelis, demonstrating his weaknesses with a life-size mock-up of the St. James Park penalty area and various inflatable dolls.
Words and phrases used included "sloppy","poor,poor defending", "got to do better than that", "amateur" and "capitulation". Alan Shearer called the score-line flattering.

Arsene Wenger took a bold and brave plunge into the market and purchased a new coat, which very much resembled his old one. He said: "I have never been afraid to spend when necessary. The old coat had developed a small tear in the hood."
Manchester United target Koke signed a new deal with Atletico Madrid. The Telegraph reported that United never submitted a bid as David Moyes and his coaching staff were not convinced about his upper body strength.

There were three weeks of riots in north London after Theo Walcott blew a kiss to Spurs fans when being substituted. Adnan Januzaj was booked for diving, a decision that an exasperated David Moyes called scandalous.

Joe Kinnear announces on a radio interview that Newcastle are looking to sign Luke Remmie and Patrick Ever and sell Joan Cabby and Shola Amoeba.

Manchester United signed a sponsorship deal with Autoglass. *"Love United, hate glaziers? Then come to Autoglass for all your cracked-screen needs."* *(T & Cs apply, policies not covered by acts of god or run-ins with the Men In Black)*

And then the news everyone dreaded. The news that blew a hole through England's excellent World Cup chances. Wayne Rooney broke his metatarsal once more chasing after a referee in a league match in late March. The diagnosis was bleak. Two months out.

"ROO META RIO KO," screamed The Sun.
"Wazza Disazza for Roy's Lions," said The Mirror.
"England To Suffer Wettest Summer in 50 Years," said the Express.

Vigils were held outside Rooney's house. A gaggle of reporters stood forlornly outside a hospital wall waiting for some news. Any news. Viewers were treated to aerial shots of the hospital roof. A nation prayed.

Manchester United signed a sponsorship deal with Durex, who became the club's exclusive pregnancy-avoiding partners in South Asia, Oceania and Peru.

After Newcastle lost to Sunderland a Newcastle fan was arrested at Knowsley Safari Park for punching an ostrich.

Manuel Pellegrini mistakenly celebrated a title win for Manchester City after thinking it was four points for a league win. In the end the title went to Chelsea after Jose Mourinho wore down his competitors with his mind-games, a win he celebrated, due to a touchline ban, from inside a laundry basket.

Manchester United and Liverpool went head-to-head for fourth place, the battle of the two teams with the most history, apart from all those teams formed before them. In the end United just prevailed, thanks to a trio of Ashley Young-won penalties in the final match against Southampton. Adnan Januzaj was booked for diving, a decision that a haggard-looking David Moyes called scandalous.

Alex Ferguson continued to look on from the stands, fiddling with his coat as the empire burned.

Bayern Munich won the Champions League once more to complete a quadruple, and celebrated by organically buying Borussia Dortmund's best two remaining players.

RACE FOR RIO

Wayne Rooney's race for fitness went to the wire. Roy Hodgson named him in his squad, but he wouldn't be fit for the first two group games.
Phil Jones' face went a colour previously unknown to man as he lolloped around the Amazon basin, and England's post-golden generation exited the competition with a whimper after a penalty shoot-out loss to Switzerland, who wrongly had two goals disallowed during normal time. Lee Cattermole was sent off after 17 minutes. Greg Dyke was seen mimicking a cut-throat gesture in the direction of Roy Hodgson close to the players' tunnel.
The following day the Sun replaced Hodgson's head with an aubergine. Ashley Cole later starred in a Pizza Hut advert, Phil Jones in a Dulux one.

The World Cup was eventually won by Argentina in dramatic circumstances as Sergio Aguero fired in a last-minute winner against hosts Brazil in what he later called "the second-best moment of his career". The final score was 4-3, though Alan Green called the match "poor" and the stadium "a disgrace and lacking atmosphere".

Off the pitch and an ITV panel of experts consisting of Alan Shearer, Michael Owen and Mark Lawrenson creates the biggest electricity surge in British history, leaving large swathes of the country without power for days.

Roy Hodgson resigned and the nation as one turned to Harry Redknapp, freshly acquitted after a 3-week trial where he was accused of using his deceased dog Rosie to claim widow's benefit. Redknapp claimed he couldn't read or write still so it couldn't have been him and anyway he leaves that sort of thing to the chairman. Redknapp offered to take the England job for free but the FA insisted on paying him a working wage. QPR reluctantly let him go after a plucky 7th place finish the previous seasons.

Pjanic On The Streets Of London

Headline writers whooped with glee as Miralem Pjanic signed for Spurs.
Manchester United target Ross Barkley signed a new deal with Everton. The Daily Mail reported that United never submitted a bid as David Moyes and his coaching staff were not convinced about his work-rate.
The new TV deal for Premier League clubs sees a glut of spending, even from traditionally smaller clubs. Diego Costa went to Fulham for an undisclosed fee, Thiago Silva made a shock move to Norwich City and Pedro was taken on loan by Crystal Palace.
A hectic transfer deadline day saw Peter Odemwingie ram-raiding the gates outside Fulham's ground and Harry Redknapp's failed attempt to sign Iniesta for England. Wesley Sneijder was linked with a move to Manchester United. Wayne Rooney handed in a transfer request before signing a lucrative new contract.

A new season brought new hope for all, hope that most had cruelly crushed within a fortnight.
Paul Scholes came out of re-retirement. "It's like a new signing for us," said David Moyes.
Sam Allardyce admitted that he ran the parody Twitter account in his name and that all the stories posted were true. This was not

enough to save him from the sack from relegated West Ham who moved quickly and hired Glenn Hoddle, who was forced to resign after only 2 months after attributing a Carlton Cole miss as punishment for him being a brothel-owner in a previous life.
Adnan Januzaj was booked for diving, a decision that a balding, red-eyed David Moyes called scandalous

Manchester United target Juan Mata signed a new deal with Chelsea. The Guardian reported that United never submitted a bid as David Moyes and his coaching staff were not convinced about his defensive work.

Mario Balotelli returned to England as Chelsea took him on loan, but he was soon in trouble again when a game of "fire-darts" went horribly wrong at Chelsea's training ground, resulting in 3rd degree burns for two youth players.
Luis Suarez was sent off after pouring a BBQ glaze over John Terry's (left) arm and lunging in at him prior to a corner at a league match at Stamford Bridge. A subsequent 6-match ban resulted in Liverpool players wearing T-shirts in support.
Adnan Januzaj was booked for diving, a decision that a wheezing David Moyes called scandalous.

The Dark Knight Rises

Adnan Januzaj was booked for diving, a decision that a sobbing David Moyes called scandalous.
Mark Clattenburg was dropped from his role at Total Hair Loss Solutions after he was seen wrestling with a Southampton player in the tunnel as the St. Mary's Stadium.
Over at the Daily Mail, Neil Ashton pens an article entitled *"The Day Football Died? Manchester City field eleven players wearing colourful boots."*
To protest against a refereeing decision in a game against West Brom, Jose Mourinho vows not to shave for 4 months. He was true to his word.
Adnan Januzaj was booked for diving. David Moyes was not available for comment.

Joe Kinnear reminisced on a radio interview about his honour at winning Time Magazine's Person of the Year. Three times.
Joey Barton called Neymar "a poncey pub-league player" on Twitter.

The traditional big teams were fighting it out for the title as Christmas approached. Promoted QPR were bottom under Harry Redknapp, who admitted his squad was down to the bare bones, adding that no manager could keep his team up.

The Qatar World Cup was finally abandoned due to concerns about the temperature in mid-summer. Sepp Blatter announced it would now be held in Canada, in the winter.

Adnan Januzaj was booked for diving, a decision that Manchester United manager Alex Ferguson called scandalous.

Blackburn Rovers 1 Manchester City 1: Some Thoughts (FA Cup Round 3)

So yet again – phew. The bottom line as always after a cup game irrespective of the performance is whether your team is still in the hat for the next round draw. And City are and should in theory progress easily to the next round.

And I will try and excuse the performance by pointing to City's Cup-winning run of three years ago, when Edin Dzeko had to salvage a draw at Notts County on the way to the final.

As I got off the train in Blackburn I thought to myself that this was all very nice but what I and my bank balance needed was more City games, as I felt like I had hardly seen them over the past few weeks. Thanks a lot City.

For the players, the ultimate punishment – a jaunt to Abu Dhabi canned for a replay in front of a half-empty stadium in wintry Manchester. The jaunt should never have happened anyway, so every cloud and that…

The team picked by Pellegrini was not unexpected, as significant changes were inevitable, but perhaps Pellegrini has not learned from previous poor performances when resting players, in that you cannot take out virtually all the key players in a team (and what's more, the spine of the team) and still expect a good performance. City cannot start a game without any of Zabaleta, Kompany, Toure or Aguero. Pellegrini had three of the four available.

And my opinion on the squad depth is this: we do have the strongest squad, but like any team, you cannot play a 2nd XI and still expect a top performance as they tend to play as strangers, as was witnessed yesterday. Outside the first XI, there are probably seven or eight players that could come in if not part of wholesale changes and the team quality would not dip noticeably. But there are still weak areas in the squad and areas therefore to strengthen, plus a few players who will either be forever injured or are simply not good enough.

And boy did the team play as strangers. The play was plodding, the counter-attacks slow, the passing often sideways and non-threatening, whilst intelligent off-the-ball running was scarce and when made never rewarded. Worst of the lot was probably James Milner, who had a nightmare. It was a bad way to mark his birthday, which seemed to distract him. Of course Milner is a model professional who would have approached the game in the same manner as any other, but you do wonder if some rum had been slipped into his birthday cake.

The thing with Milner is he always has a bad game in him, as was seen at Southampton, when everything seems to go against him. The nadir against Blackburn was the launch of a counter-attack when he kicked the ball straight out of touch. Away to Bayern Munich I was bemoaning him after 10 minutes, concluding he just wasn't good enough for where City wanted to be. By full-time I had completely changed my mind, and that is Milner for you. He has so many qualities and is a vital member of the squad but when he's bad…
Still, what can we expect from a player who seems destined to play out the rest of his career playing away from his preferred position?

There are certain partnerships that just don't work. Aguero and Negredo does, but I doubt Dzeko and Negredo ever will. What's more, Negredo seems untouchable for criticism when it has been Dzeko who has probably performed better in recent weeks. On the flip-side, Negredo has probably never had to play so many games in such a short space of time and is suffering as a result. The team's tika-taka approach doesn't help when you have two big lumps up front who would thrive on crosses yet you have two full-backs who can't whip a cross in, especially Clichy who repeatedly checks back when receiving the ball out wide. Once more, the team struggled against a team with men behind the ball and the play was all very congested.

The team as a whole looks tired though. It's a brave City fan who would moan about that of course as every team has the same problem and most of them have far fewer resources than us, but it shouldn't be a crime to point it out. The worrying aspect is that Pellegrini does not have a single youth player that he trusts to fill in – this week would have been the perfect time to play the likes of Guidetti or Lopes. And all the while we have a youth player out on loan captaining PSV.

I think the Blackburn goal ends the goalkeeping debate for now (hopefully).

And as for Dedryck Boyata – again a player out of position, but I think the kindest thing to say is that I will never think he is good enough and I will leave it at that.

The replay ticket prices had better be £15 at most.

And then of course there is the small matter of Joleon Lescott. As you probably know by now, Lescott went on to Twitter (minus his spellchecker, like me now) to apologise to City fans for not acknowledging them at the end of the match as he had been personally abused by a minority of City fans, presumably related to his appearance. It is saddening to hear such stories, but then hardly surprising, as with any club there are a minority that follow the club that are morons, cretins, buffoons and/or pin-headed semi-alcoholic self-pleasers. As a collective we have been so spoiled too that some can simply not handle a poor performance and thus react rather badly to it all. The away days around Lancashire towns also seems to attract a certain breed of young scrotes, so I am told. Apologies if you are one of them.

But. But. I am sorry Joleon, but the abuse is no excuse not to acknowledge the fans. The abuse will have come from a few people at most, or to put it another way – 99.9% of the away support didn't abuse you. These fans travel all over the country and many all over Europe following the team, at great expense, often forced under duress to consume vast quantities of alcohol. But seriously, many of us have been doing it for decades, home and away (less away for me nowadays) and it shouldn't be too much to ask to clap the fans that have sung your name or cheered you on, even if the atmosphere was rather flat yesterday and even if we are all fickle souls liable to moan if a player so much as misplaces a pass.

Now it doesn't matter to me whether players clap the fans and it doesn't matter to many others. But it DOES matter for huge numbers of fans and it is hardly putting yourself out to spend 5 seconds clapping. I went to a fans' forum at City a few months ago and someone suggested, as a discussion formed about how to improve the atmosphere, that the players should be told in no uncertain terms to clap the fans at the end of games, as a collective unit, as it would help bridge the gap between players and fans that clearly exists in the modern game. As is often the case, the example cited of a better world was from the Bundesliga, where players often link up and acknowledge the fans at the end of a match, in a league where there seems to be a far better connection between players ans fans (Borussia Dortmund being an obvious example). Now of course the players shouldn't have to be told to acknowledge the fans anyway, but it would be nice if they did so even if it is under duress. Show some bloody respect for the people who effectively pay your wages.

One final point away from yesterday. It's often pointed out that we shouldn't get upset at some of the drivel written in the media about our club, as it doesn't matter. Yesterday i was reminded how lies printed about our club does matter and does trickle into the psyche. I was sat in a pub in Manchester after the match when two Sheffield Wednesday fans came into the pub. Apart from one's laughable claim that Sheffield Wednesday should have been taken over not City as they were a bigger club and his obvious pride at missing the birth of his daughter because he was at a pre-season friendly against Bury, they tried to be complimentary about the four of us as we were "proper fans" who went to matches and that we were all alike as "we never sell out any games". There then followed a 20-minute argument about the excrement that was flowing out of his mouth and he was adamant that City never sell out any matches. I expect this sort of c**p from United fans, but when Sheffield Wednesday fans are parroting the same rubbish, then I realise why we as fans must correct the lies often spread about our club. You may still not care if people think such things, which is fair enough and probably the logical approach, but it will never cease to wind me up.

Onwards and upwards…onto the other domestic cup…

Manchester City 6 West Ham 0

Semi-finals are supposed to be difficult, but a pitiful performance from West Ham soon after their FA capitulation to Notts Forest resulted in a stroll in the park for City, for whom Alvaro Negredo scored a hattrick. With a second leg to come, City could prepare for another Wembley victory and I went into hiding from my bank manager.

Newcastle 0 Manchester City 2

Phew again - etc etc etc

City continue to live on the edge and grey the few remaining black hairs I have left, but the results continue to come. It is now over two months since City lost a game, a statistic all the more impressive as we seem to play every three days at the moment. With these two goals City have surpassed last season's tally with four months to spare.

It was attritional, messy, unruly but ultimately successful. Another key away result for the team that apparently can't travel, though admittedly the team continues to struggle to reach the heights on the road, bulldozing its way over the finish line.

The team line up contained few surprises. Kolarov is now the number one left - back and Pellegrini continues to pick two up front, after Dzeko and Negredo combined so well against an admittedly pitiful West Ham last week.

But yet again it was a formation that proved troublesome. It allowed too much space to the opposition and City struggled to retain the ball for much of the match. And once more, it curtailed Yaya Toure, made him look lazy and thus limited his authority on the game. A liability eh? Thus it was better to have Javi Garcia on the pitch, again, as he does his simple job effectively and shows small signs of becoming the player we had hoped for.

It was the defence that excelled however. Joe Hart was excellent, whilst Kompany and Demichelis made 25 clearances between them. Apart from one defensive mix-up the back-four copied admirably. It's about time the defence got some praise, especially when it has to work so hard in many away games and Kolarov added to the list of excellent defensive performances, especially with one late crucial block and of course an assist.

Sorry, my mistake – Alan Hansen knows the score: *"Hart's return to form is timely because if you are looking at the City defence all they have basically got is Vincent Kompany."*

City started brightly and scored an exquisite goal (as it went in I commented "what a move". I then realised it was about the 30th time I have said that this season. We really have been spoilt), but after that their play became scruffy and their crisp passing deserted them (recording their lowest pass completion rate of the season at 73% according to football365.com). Half-time couldn't some soon enough, but for all the home team's continued threat after the break, it was City who fashioned the better chances in the second half, Negredo at the centre of most of them with Fernandinho striking the bar.

Negredo again didn't sparkle quite as much away from home, though he was still a constant threat, even if not everything came of and even if his goal had an element of look to it.

So onto THAT goal. Or not, as it turned out. It was strange celebrating still being ahead in a game 30 seconds after being resigned to an equalizing goal. As for the fairness of it all, it merely highlights once more the ridiculous nature of the current rules. I don't think offside should be subjective, but that's how it is, not that the original rule was perfect either. I think it's fair to say that if the roles had been reversed we'd all be moaning about the injustice of it all, but it's hardly the worst decision of all time, though City have clearly benefited from a stroke of luck, which happens from time to time. The rules on calling offside were altered slightly in the summer and the new rules seem to back the opinion that a goal should have been awarded, though I've seen three different versions of that rule change online, but what is clear is that the player called offside was not in Joe Hart's line of vision and I very much doubt Hart was going to save the shot. However, the Newcastle player did swerve out of the way of the ball and it is possible he caused a distraction in that split moment. You can rule out the goal on a technicality and argue that case, but City were rather fortunate. Having said that, Newcastle had three players offside, and it's hard for our defence to play the game efficiently when the rules are so vague and everything is open to interpretation.

The other problem with the decision to disallow the goal is that it ended the referee's control of the game. I commented at the time that the referee might look to "even things up" thereafter, the general consensus being by awarding a soft penalty, but he took the alternative route of turning a blind eye to Newcastle's rough-house tactics, tactics that may well be linked to one of our best players this season missing the rest of the season and perhaps the World Cup. For all the whinging about the disallowed goal, the main talking point was the foul on Nasri by Mapou Yanga-Mbiwa, which on second viewing could easily have resulted in a red card, but elsewhere Newcastle could and should have had at least two players sent off, most notably Cabaye who was allowed to get away with two clear bookable offences whilst on a caution. (check out Nick Miller's article on football365.com, one of the few to point out that the talking point was not Tiote's disallowed goal).

Still, no media outrage at Swansea's offside equaliser the other week. Nor at Aston Villa's offside first goal or the second goal coming from a free kick that should never have been given. No comment that Walcott's second goal against City was just offside. No uproar at the fact Sunderland beat City with an illegal goal for the fourth season in a row. No uproar at the disallowed Negredo goal in the corresponding fixture. No rolling-news story for three days on any bad decisions against City at all in fact, no interviews with ex-referees on Sky Sports News, or condemnation of how City had been let down by poor refereeing decisions that could ultimately cost them the title. It all evens out over the season eh?

When you look at blog stats, you can see how people have been referred to your blog post. When I recently criticised the walking billboard that is Tony Pulis, my blog somehow ended up on a Crystal Palace forum, garnering considerable criticism. With that in mind, I think the criticisms are about to go up a notch or two, because it's time to talk about Newcastle's class-free manager, a buffoon of the highest order with form for buffoonery and a masters degree in advanced buffoonery from Oxford University.

"Shut your noise, you f*cking old c**t," shouted the grey-haired Newcastle manager as he continued his constant prowl around the technical area, ready to complain about any perceived injustice, from an incorrect throw-in call to a City player looking at him the wrong way. In the end, like a child who was sulking after not getting a PS4 for Xmas, he kicked the ball away from Zabaleta as he prepared to take a throw-in and a spat soon followed.

Here's a man with all the class of a dodgy east-end barrow-boy turned bad. Then he enhanced his "reputation" further, shouting towards Nasri as he lay badly injured on the floor, clearly insinuating he was play-acting. Still, at least he didn't push a linesman over this time, so every cloud and that….

Pardew waited for the referee at half-time, was back in his ear as the teams were led out for the second half and continued his whinging and moaning throughout the second half. It's not surprising that Pellegrini was tetchy when you see an opposition manager moaning for 90 minutes and trying to influence match officials. The graceless moron should be charged by the FA asap. An apology does not wipe the slate clean.

It's no surprise of course that Pardew has since apologised, a natural course of action once he realised he had been found out and with the threat of a(nother) FA charge looming. Needless to say it's not the first time he's had to apologise to a rival manager after a touchline spat.

(On a similar theme, I've never understood why managers (I'm looking at you Mr Wenger) feel the need to whinge and moan at 4th officials the whole match anyway, an official who has no bearing on the decision-making process. It's the act of a bully.)

I'm not sure I could have been as restrained about the whole affair as Manuel Pellegrini was. There's your holistic approach to matters right there, a gentleman who kept his cool in the face of provocation and doesn't allow the story to be about him.

In 2003, the BBC described Pardew as being a "dangerous and distant animal" in the media, referring to his public relations abilities. A bit harsh, but Arsene Wenger might agree, having two touchline spats with Pardew in 2006 alone.

And the sense of injustice spilled into the crowd, as you would expect – no different to how we would react I imagine. But a small point for Newcastle fans - at the moment that a player is being stretchered off with his leg in a brace whilst almost crying in agony – well that's probably the point where it should become apparent to you that he is not play-acting and didn't go down to try and get the opposition player booked/sent off. Booing him as he is taken off might just therefore be construed as the act of a bunch of pea-brained cretins. I hope this helps.

The most bizarre comments on my Twitter fans were the usual accusations of City "cheating". Just to clarify, a Newcastle player falling to the ground after no contact to win a free-kick outside the area, as happened in the 2nd half, is cheating. A referee disallowing a goal is not and had nothing to do with City, unless one or two City players talking to the referee (which after all has never happened before in the history of the game) is somehow construed in these deluded people's brains as influencing the referee. The decision had nothing to do with City. Slag off the referee all you want if it makes you feel better, but please stop boring us with these puerile claims of cheating and of buying the referee.

Since the match, Nasri has tweeted that he should be out for 8 weeks – a relief really, as it could have been much worse, but still a blow for City. This should mean more match-time for Milner and Navas, or even Rodwell (stop laughing at the back).

And so to the Emptyhad (ha!) on Wednesday, and what will surely be a weakened team. Expect run-outs for Clichy, Milner, Nastastic (if he is fit), Rodwell (if he is fit), Richards (if he is fit), Jovetic (if he is fit) and even Aguero (if he is fit).

Could This Be The Flukiest Title Win Of All Time?

It's officially on. The flukiest league title-winning campaign since football began is within a certain team's grasp. Week after week, Manchester City spawn win after win against all the odds and against all recognised logic and perceived ideas of fairness and justice. The team stops at nothing in its quest for three points. Referees are harassed until they overturn goals, opposition players are called offside should they venture within 40 yards of the City goal and any discretions by City players are conveniently ignored. Vincent Kompany only has to raise his arm and the referee immediately stops play.

Strange things happen with time to this narrative too. An offside decision against Raheem Sterling magically becomes a disallowed goal in dispatches, despite the whistle going before he even touched the ball. A shirt-pull on a Liverpool player is given greater coverage than 90 minutes of shirt-pulling on a variety of City players. A two-month injury caused by a cynical tackle that wasn't sufficiently cautioned is not factored into the luck debate. Cherry-picking has rarely been this precise.

But don't worry yourself either about the bad decisions that have gone against City. The offside goals against Aston Villa and Swansea. The free-kick that shouldn't have been at Villa too, leading to their 2nd goal. The wrongly disallowed goal at home to Newcastle, the illegal goal at Sunderland and the failure to send off one of their players. Don't waste time thinking about Chelsea's disgraceful equalizer at home to West Brom or Samuel Eto's carte blanche tackling policy against Liverpool, or Liverpool's own game-turning "Spanish penalty" against Stoke in the past week. Not important.
Focus instead on City's constant good fortune. We have a narrative, an angle, and it's been dictated by whinging managers and blinkered fans, as always.

At least this spectacular run of good fortune brings with it the opportunity for laughs. With each victory comes a spectacular breakdown from the opposing manager, the vanquished soul often displaying the grace of a horny <name removed for legal reasons> outside a closed massage parlour.

Brendan Rogers questioned the geographical roots of the referee, Tony Pulis bemoaned City's wealth (again) and Alan Pardew morphed into Michael Douglas in Falling Down. God help us all if a decision goes against Cardiff on Saturday, as Ole Gunnar Solskjaer will no doubt blame defeat on the Illuminati (Bavarian branch) or the Knights Templar. At least Pardew apologised, so no need for an FA charge there, something for Luis Suarez to consider the next time he resorts to cannibalism.

City are no longer ruining football by spending a billion on the team, now they are bribing referees and getting all the calls. This is the proof that the club has "arrived" and the next logical step is to form some sort of semi-secret cabal with other clubs (call it something snappy, like the G14), threaten a breakaway super-league, then watch the money and the trophies roll in. Mission duly accomplished.

#sarcasm

Manchester City 5 Blackburn 0

City eased into the 4th round fo the FA Cup with a brace from Negredo and Dzeko and a goal from Aguero a minute after he came on the pitch having recovered from a calf injury. The wrongs of the first game were put right.

What I Miss About Manchester City

I miss looking up the league table with false hope or down it with trepidation. I miss reading about fights on the training ground. I miss sitting in a stand without a roof.

I miss press reports about rifts in the dressing rooms and a lack of team morale. I miss the paparazzi sitting in trees at our training ground.

I miss my club spunking £3-£5m on a lower-league journeyman because he once scored against us. I miss the dead bird hanging from the Kippax roof to scare away the pigeons. I miss the abandoned games because of a waterlogged pitch.

I miss the outside toilets behind the Kippax stand. I miss the Football Pink at 6pm sharp. I miss the club paying four managers at the same time. I miss caretaker managers. I miss managers with moustaches and flat caps. I miss not seeing a goal for three months. I miss Joey Barton being our great hope. I miss the pride of a City player representing England, if only briefly and disastrously.

I miss a certain chairman's toupee. I miss queuing at the ground for five hours for a Wembley ticket. I miss play-offs. I miss terraces. I miss us playing in laser blue. I miss Buster Phillips, Ged Brannan and Kare Ingrebritsen. I miss relegation fights. I miss not winning away for a whole season. I miss our massive floodlights. I miss David Pleat skipping across the pitch. I miss paying on the gate. I miss guessing which match number the home fixture was that week.

I miss our nearest rivals hoovering up trophy after trophy. I miss us being everyone's 2nd team. I miss the frisson of excitement at the possibility of a City player being nominated (but never winning) the goal of the month competition. I miss enviously watching other fans travel to Wembley. I miss the rumours about debt and administration. I miss having to sell our one decent player to balance the books.

I miss surfing Ceefax for the latest football news. I miss playing at the Theatre of Base Comedy. I miss Eddie Large sitting on the bench. I miss him giving half-time team talks. I miss Curly Watts. I miss misshaped stands. I miss slagging off our right-back. I miss obstructed views. I miss City's season ending in January. I miss the pride at making a quarter-final. I miss the false hope of thinking that finally this might be "our year".

I miss being last on Match of the Day. Or not being on it at all. I miss barely appearing in Sky's Premier League Years, except when losing crucial matches. I miss teams beating us without having a shot on target. I miss that banner at Old Trafford.

But the truth is that apart from the Football Pink and terraces, I miss none of it. Smiley face.

But here is what I ACTUALLY miss.

I miss the walk through rows of terraces towards Maine Road. I miss it more for the night games, as I miss the lights rising up from behind the houses.

I miss standing. I miss paying on the gate.

I miss the cantilever roof on the main stand. I miss having a main stand. I miss laughing at the people in the Gene Kelly stand when the Manchester weather did what it does best.

I miss keeping the same kit for two years. I miss the Kappa kit. I miss wearing my City kit to watch the FA Cup final because it was a big occasion and kids can do stuff like that.

I miss having a season ticket book.

I miss City players with bushy moustaches (bearded Spaniards don't count).

I miss "it's a goal!" on Piccadilly 261. I miss "oh no!" less, unless it was United, which it usually wasn't.

I miss phoning premium rate numbers to get transfer gossip then denying everything when the bill came. I miss getting news off

Ceefax. I don't miss missing the page and having to wait for it to cycle round.

I miss Niall Quinn's disco pants. I miss inflatable bananas.

I miss football not being about money. I miss a world that didn't need 24-hour football news.

I miss waiting for the Football Pink to be issued. I miss the match reports sometimes cutting off the last five minutes of the match.

I miss a simple offside rule.

I miss the chippy near Maine Road. I miss chips wrapped in newspaper or in a cone. I miss that last chip.

I miss the friends I made who sat around me in the Kippax. I miss standing in the same area when I was too small to see anything. I miss that first walk down the terrace steps.

I miss good commentators on the telly. I miss John Motson being on top of his game. I miss Grandstand and Saint & Greavsie.

I miss Ali Bernarbia and Andy Morrison and Shaun Goater.

I miss local pre-season friendlies. I miss my maroon socks.

I miss going to away games when the result didn't really matter.

I miss the evening after we won the league, I miss losing a football match not feeling like the end of days.

I miss wanting City players to always represent their country.

I miss collecting football stickers, less so having seven Peter Beardsleys.

I miss being able to fit into my old football tops. I miss teams tossing a coin to decide which way to kick first half (if this ever happened).

I miss tackling. I miss not having to play United every season.

I miss our massive floodlights. I miss decent pubs near the ground.

I miss Subbuteo and my Wembley board game. I miss when scarves always showed just one team and I miss men at games listening to the wireless.

I rarely look back, but I miss it all. I lied about the bananas.

Manchester City 4 Cardiff City 2

City passed the 100-goal mark for the season as they saw off a determined Cardiff side to stay one point behind leaders Arsenal at the top of the Premier League.
City were given a stern test by bottom of the table Cardiff, but goals from Edin Dzeko, Jesus Navas, Yaya Toure and Sergio Aguero were enough to see City home.

The game also saw a first, as goal-line technology determined that Edin Dzeko's shot had crossed the line to opening the scoring.

West Ham 0 Manchester City 3

A routine game sending City to Wembley with a brace from Negredo and a goal from Aguero. A late injury to Negredo though proved costly for his season and almost as costly for City.

Manchester City 4 Watford 2: Some Thoughts

I'll be honest, at half-time I had consigned myself to an FA Cup exit. I reassured myself that at least my wallet wouldn't suffer further, as I couldn't see City coming back. Typical City was alive and well after all.

My pessimism was increased by the cold, hard fact that Watford fully deserved their lead. They counter-attacked superbly and played aggressively. Credit to them for pushing men forward and for their counter-attacks and swift interplay. They may only have one win in fourteen, but that was done mostly to the ex-manager and the Watford fans I watched the game with commented that this is technically a better side than last season, but without the results to justify that claim. That said, City should still have won comfortably of course.

But in the end, it was the senior players that dug City out of a hole, further evidence of what a superb first XI we have, a quality that decreases when you dig further into the squad.

Without spending too much time on a painful first half, there were some important lessons for Manuel Pellegrini once more. Like Blackburn away, when major changes are made to the team and partnerships are trialled for the first time, the result is catastrophic. Lescott and Demichelis can do a job alongside Vincent Kompany, but together they were a mess. Demichelis will rightly take the brunt of the criticism as he continues to commit too early, especially disastrous when he is too slow to recover. City cannot afford to play a game without a top-notch senior player in defence and unfortunately at the moment that man is Vincent Kompany, and only him. Whilst I don't want us spending big money on an ageing psychopath, it makes the constant overtures towards Pepe more understandable. Demichelis has the experience, but is just not good enough anymore to lead a defence.

But remember that like at Old Trafford, we have a new manager this season and should thus in theory be "in transition". Our two central defenders yesterday will probably not be there in 2 years(or even 1) so we will have to muddle along until reinforcements are brought in, presumably in the summer.

As for Pantilimon, further proof he is a back-up and nothing more, his effort to prevent the second goal rather pitiful for a man of such stature.

And then there's Micah Richards. Once more he appears to be the wrong weight, or build, and he was poor. He is simply not athletic enough right now (as has happened in the past) to cover for Zabaleta, even against a mid-table Championship side. It would be easy to write him off as we wait endlessly for the Richards of old, but until he plays a run of games, we can't really judge where the player is at right now. Will that ever happen though?

Likewise for Rodwell. I have no doubt there is a class player in there, but he spends so little time on the pitch he suffers when he does, not helped by a lethargic Toure (at first) and a youngster in front of him. Will he ever get a good run in the side though? I doubt it. He needs to play alongside the likes of Silva and Nasri, not in a weakened side.

In midfield the problems were confounded in the first half, with Lopes unable to influence proceedings, but he wasn't the only one. We can't read too much into the player from yesterday's showing.

At half-time, with goals needed, the obvious thought is to throw on some attacking players. That Pellegrini did the opposite may have baffled a few but soon made sense. City had enough up front to haul themselves back into the game, but it was a weak defence that had undermined everything in the first half. It was little surprise that City came at Watford strongly in the 2nd half and no surprise either that Watford retreated. Kompany drove the whole team forward and once more Zabaleta and Navas constantly probed down the right. City in the end got a deserved victory, but still left it late. With a goal pulled back within 12 minutes, the omens looked good.

But then I saw the 70 minute mark arrive and City were still losing. Then eighty minutes was fast approaching and I felt queasy. I would happily have taken a replay with 12 minutes to go. Thankfully that wasn't necessary and some praise is merited for City keeping going, something that wouldn't have happened three years ago and beyond and for Sergio Aguero for being, well, Sergio Aguero.

Special praise though should go to ITV for their highlights programme on Saturday night, the picture quality making me reach for the remote control to adjust my settings, reminiscent of the "Back In The Big Time" promotion video I have on VHS in a drawer somewhere. When Andy Gray's dulcet tones popped up during the Everton game, I knew it was time to turn off. Apparently the commentary for the Wigan game wasn't even by the guy who had originally done it for ITV, so who knows what went on there? Whatever, the channel continues to display ineptitude at covering the national sport.

The quadruple is on! Sorry.....

Tottenham Hotspur 1 Manchester City 5

Smiley face.

Another lucky victory, another three points bought from the officials – you know the stuck record by now.

This was the first of two difficult games that would test City's championship credentials once and for all, and the truth is that I wouldn't have been too disappointed with a draw going into the match.

The line up had few surprises, Clichy preferred over Kolarov, perhaps for his pace, something Spurs traditionally have in abundance. The rest of the side was as you might expect with Negredo not risked to start the match, though perhaps Dzeko would have been picked anyway, as has happened previously away from home.

For half an hour, City were simply majestic. They passed their way round Spurs with consummate ease, scored one, should have scored plenty more and the only concern was that we may pay for the profligacy. Spurs came back into the game in the last 15 minutes of the half, but once down to ten men there was little to worry about. City closed the match out after the Spurs goal with great professionalism.

For me, Spurs paid the price for being far too open. It's been City's downfall playing teams who pack midfield, press high and press hard and harry City's midfielders. Spurs did none of that and played right into Pellegrini's hands. City have turned around their away form in recent months to the point that people have almost stopped talking about it, but the performances have not come close to matching those at the Etihad and there have been some roller-coaster rises along the way. Against Spurs it was so refreshing to see such dominance on the road against a side with Top Four aspirations.

On the surface, Edin Dzeko had a terrible game, his second in succession after the FA Cup horror show, spurning chance after chance on a night when he could easily have equalled his four goal tally from two seasons ago. For much of the match I found myself exasperated by him and adult words were heard drifting towards the television screen on more than one occasion. But away from his shooting, he once more put in an excellent shift, worked his socks off and led the line well. He will continue to both exasperate and excite until the day he leaves.

Sergio Aguero was once more unplayable, making his injury all the more worrying. You would hope he was being very cautious by effectively taking himself off, but he could easily be out for over a month. City have coped admirably without Aguero, barely breaking stride, but Barcelona is a whole new ball game and City's chances of getting past the Spanish champions will be severely hindered without their talismanic front-man.

Great performances were littered throughout the side, Jesus Navas once more catching the eye (and Silva, obviously) whilst Martin Demichelis' shift in midfield was once again a success. Elsewhere and it is great to see Stevan Jovetic not only playing but scoring and he is quickly showing signs of becoming the player we hoped for.

Be thankful that the Spurs goal was not prevented by the hand of Fernandinho, otherwise we'd be another man down on Monday.

Where to start with BT? I mean, really, where?
It was clear that a narrative had been set from the moment the half-time whistle sounded, namely that Manchester City had once more got the benefit of decisions. A blatant handball was not deemed worthy of analysis, nor an Adebayor stamp or any other rough-house tactics, nor was there felt the need to mention that the free-kick that preceded the disallowed goal was won with a dive thus making everything thereafter utterly irrelevant. But why let these trifling little details get in the way of another Manchester City conspiracy theory. The BT team felt a goal correctly given offside was worthy of repeated analysis, for reasons that defeat me apart

from the obvious intent to create a story that wasn't there. Adebayor, a player who should not have stayed on the pitch for the duration of the game, was clearly offside, went for the ball and said ball shaved the top of his head. There ends the debate. In the end, the linesman gave offside against Dawson, incorrectly, but he made the right decision even if it was for the wrong reasons, the City player playing Dawson onside totally obscured by Adebayor to the linesman.

As for the penalty, another miscarriage of justice it was not. Rose got his foot on the ball, but this is irrelevant. It certainly looked a nailed on penalty when first viewed, and this is what the officials base their decisions on, not a super slo-mo replay from 3 different angles. I would argue it was a tad harsh, and if it had happened the other way round you would probably be agreeing with me, but contact on the ball does not matter if you foul the man as well, and Rose not only grabbed Dzeko's right hand but also made contact with the back of the Bosnian's legs -there is enough there to justify the decision. I've mentioned before that the double punishment for such an offence is unduly harsh in my opinion, but that's not City's fault, nor was it their concern last night.

And then there was the commentary…..brace yourselves.

Watching the game in the pub, the avalanche of drivel spewing out of Michael Owen's mouth eventually became too much for one patron, who proceeded to rip his own ears off before trying to flush them down a toilet. Thankfully a doctor was seated at the next table and helped sedate the man until the ambulance arrived. As he left on a stretcher, the pub rose as one and applauded him out of the building.
I hope you're happy with yourself BT Sport.

With that in mind, you don't need to hear anymore about the world's most banal co-commentator as you know it all already, though I particularly liked his inept attempts to dissect the disallowed goal for Spurs ("it's offside on the video replay, but clearly not offside for me") and his complete lack of ire when Adebayor stamped on Demichelis or when Benteleb juggled the ball.

But perhaps we've all been had here. It's occurred to me that Owen has played a decade-long trick on us all, having played the long-game and as a result it is he who is having the last laugh. From his tedious twitter account to his monotone commentary, this could be one big act to give him an "angle" in his post-playing media career. He's been pretty savvy as it happens, but thankfully I am intelligent enough to see through his act and thus will not be getting irate when next I hear his unique brand of analysis.

But time for praise outside of City. I half-expected Alan Hansen on the Match of the Day "sofa" to spend fifteen minutes dissecting the goal City conceded, but let's be glad that they actually showed Bentaleb's handball, that Hansen noted it should never have been a free-kick prior to the disallowed goal then pointed out that the offside call was correct. It is ridiculous that I should be praising a programme for pointing out the obvious, but this is what it's come to.

On a more positive note, some credit is merited towards Tim Sherwood for being honest in his post-match comments. No whinging, no blaming of officials or bemoaning their luck nor were there cries of great injustices, he just said it as we would. He has gone up in my estimation, a nice contract to the classless spiv that patrols the St. James' Park touchline.

And on a similar note, some credit too for Andre Marriner for a sterling attempt to deflect criticism away from Michael Owen's performance or that of the home side. He was inept from beginning to end, intent on not giving City a free kick all night, even for the most blatant of fouls, whilst booking Demichelis for being stamped on. Bravo, a promotion cannot be far away.

Unexpected draws for Arsenal and especially Chelsea have given City breathing space now. Chelsea cannot go ahead of the Citizens even with victory on Monday, and City will be there or thereabouts come-what-may. I'll settle for that, but victory on Monday would make a huge statement to the rest of the chasing pack and put City in a very strong position indeed.

Good to see Vincent Kompany move ahead of Adnan Januzaj in the goal-scoring charts.

The Bumper Bundle of City Slurs: The Journalist Files (Part 2)

In **Part two of City Slurs: The Journalist Files**, it's time to look at more recent years. City had re-educated many a journalist over the first couple of years of the Mansour reign, but there were still plenty of dissenters.

A good source was always the Sunday Supplement, a relaxed forum for croissant-eating ill-informed opinion and general prejudice. One episode in particular stands out:
In it, moral arbiters and Chelsea supporters Rob "Jose's my bessie mate" Beasley and Paul "Dracula" Smith went to town on classless City.
Smith: "£220 grand a week for Yaya Toure? . **Someone must be out of their mind there**. The thing is about Manchester City is…that whole structure there is an absolute load of nonsense."
Beasley: "They've got so much money, but **morally they are bankrupt**," said the Chelsea supporter.
Chelsea supporter Smith: "They've got a manager who is clearly arrogant in his ways..it's a typical example of a club who think they can go and buy success. You wouldn't have Mourinho, a good manager, doing this, buying left, right and centre," added the Chelsea supporter.
"I don't think they'll win anything under Mancini," added the Chelsea supporter Smith.
Chelsea supporter Beasley then added: "They're the richest club in the world, but for me they are morally bankrupt. **Any man who brings in the new manager, and sits him in the stand, while they've still got a manager, and any manager who agrees to that, to sit in the stands while they've still got a manager, knowing he's going to be unveiled after the match, it's just moral bankruptcy."**
"And I hope City pay the price," said the Chelsea supporter, "I've used this word two or three times – about DIGNITY," said the Chelsea supporter.
"There's no dignity there..the posters they put up..it's not dignified," added Chelsea supporter Beasley.
"They've got loads of cash, but no class, I hope it all implodes."

added Chelsea-supporting Beasley.

"Where is the structure there?" asked Smith

"There isn't," says Brian Woolnough.

Beasley added (Chelsea supporter): "Hughes knows he's up there..I mean, if that had been most people they'd have gone 'you can stick your job'..Hughes must have been absolutely fuming…"

"Football wants Fulham to win," added the Chelsea supporting Beasley.

Beasley was forced to apologise live on the show the next time he appeared for claiming that Roberto Mancini was in the stands during Mark Hughes' last game as City manager. Rob skilfully worked his apology to be under 5 seconds long.

Speaking of which, there was great criticism for City's owners at the disgraceful way they got rid of such a bright, promising young manager in Mark Hughes, who has since gone on to distinguish himself globally at various clubs. This prompted the Manchester Evening News' Pete Spencer to ask the questions none of us were asking, the best few of which are listed below:

Pete Spencer's 12 Questions To Garry Cook.

6: IF Mancini doesn't do as well as Hughes – and his appointment is a huge gamble as he has never worked as a manager in this country – will he go at the end of the season? Is he really a stop-gap until there is a better chance of landing Mourinho?

7: **ON reflection was it a mistake to sell Richard Dunne to aspiring rivals Villa?** I accept hindsight is a great thing but his replacements have hardly been on top of their game and, while I'm on this, how close were City – truthfully – to signing John Terry?

11: YOU want City to be a brand as well as a football club don't you? Well that brand is tarnished now so what can you do about it?

12: AND finally, the relationship that you have done so well to develop with the most important people of all, i.e. the fans, is now strained. What are you going to do to address this?

He had nothing on Michael Calvin though, who got a bit giddy after FCUM defeated Rochdale in the FA Cup.

By Michael Calvin

His Highness, Sheikh Mansour bin Zayed bin Sultan Al Nahyan, wooed the wrong noisy neighbour.

Instead of blowing £1billion on Manchester City, he should have **donated £1million to FC United**.

He wouldn't have been able to shape a club owned by the fans, for the fans.

But, for a relative pittance, he would have become **a folk hero**.

He would have helped expose the hypocrisy of the Glazers, the unfair burden of leveraged debt.

In so doing, football's richest man would have discovered **what football is all about**.

The empowerment of a community, rather than the enrichment of opportunists.

Faith, defiance, and the credibility of commitment.

Passion, unprocessed and deliciously unrefined.

Joy, rather than empty rhetoric, and massaged opinion.

You don't need advertising copywriters and simpering apologists to make a statement of intent.

Alienated Manchester United fans did that, when they formed a football club to give a human dimension to a protest movement.

Equally, the League pyramid cannot adequately measure the difference between City and FC United.

On paper it is seven Divisions. In essence the clubs are **separated by a chasm, which separates constructive outrage and graceless vulgarity.**

I defy anyone to watch a re-run of FC United's FA Cup win at Rochdale without a smile. Players were stripped to homemade Superman underpants by euphoric fans.

They cavorted for the cameras in the dressing room, and **promised not to turn up for work on Monday.**

Their manager was wide eyed, and about to be legless. "We'll have a couple of sherberts, here and there" he promised.

I'll take Karl Marginson, before Roberto Mancini, any day of the week.

The FC United boss does need a personal website that is beyond parody. "Roberto Mancini," it croons. "The football. The class. The champion."

Strange how it didn't mention the cautious coach, the closet politician, and the **cry baby**.

Marginson used to be a milkman, reliant on boot money from the likes of Salford City and Bacup Borough.

You wouldn't catch him posing for soft-focus photos, like a 10th-rate George Clooney.

Blue Moon Rising?

I prefer **the red flares of class warriors**, which illuminated Spotland's Willbutts Lane Stand.

Money has siphoned innocence from football.

City's purchasing power is intimidating, and intoxicating to outsiders.

I came across a caricature of a marketing executive late on Friday night.

He was worried my views would compromise his commercial relationship with Eastlands.

His type – swivel-eyed networkers who couldn't spell the word integrity, let alone grasp its meaning – are everywhere.

I loathe what they represent, why they genuflect at the feet of the City hierarchy.

They are prepared to overlook the positive aspects of City's problems.

Three successive defeats remind us that wealth is worthless, if used unwisely.

Briefings, and counter briefings, tell a cautionary tale of **unchecked egos** and unseemly ambition.

But, with apologies to the vast majority of City fans **who will understand my disillusion**, let's light the bonfire of the vanities.

I hope Mancini crashes and burns.

I pray FC United realise their impossible dream, a third round tie at Old Trafford. And that someone, somewhere, **has the courage to inform His Highness that he needs to act. Now!**

Apropos of nothing, Mike too has his own website – check it out at michaelcalvin.com. This is ok though, as Mike has had a far more illustrious career than Roberto Mancini, as you are about to find

out.
His biography reads:

Hello.

*I could go all corporate on you, and describe myself as an **award-winning sportswriter who developed a significant secondary career in performance management, strategic communications and socially-responsive sports programming.***

*But, truth be told, I'm a hack, down to my scuffed trainers. I've been lucky, **working in more than 80 countries**, watching the great, and not-so great, events of world sport.*

That's propelled me the wrong way around the planet, as a crew member on a global yacht race against prevailing winds and tides. It has pitched me into politically incorrect car rallies, around the Amazon basin and Arctic circle.

*My Mum will tell you I've **twice been named Sports Reporter of the Year, and have collected the Sportswriter and Sports Journalist of the Year award**. I've featured at the British Press awards on seven occasions, and been honoured for my coverage of sport for the disabled.*

Back to City though.

Mario Balotelli was back in the news as he grappled with manager Roberto Mancini in training. It made headline news, but no one really cared any more. Wild speculation ensued that Balotelli's time at the club was over, and that Mancini was losing the plot. For once the speculation was right. Balotelli exited first to Milan and not surprisingly ended the year back on sale.

One Daily Mail commenter had strong views on the matter:

So the Arab 'benefactors' have brought shame and pity to football, an unflattering, unprofessional, nasty, pantomime, an embarrassing antics roadshow to Manchester.

Whatever words we chose, it's just not right. Like all human endeavour, sport should earn its awards through striving, consistency and dedication over a period of time. Sugardaddy demands for immediate, unearned purchase of success, brings nothing but embarrassment, shame and yes pity to a small but once decent club like City.

Last season though, the club did something unspeakably bad. Something so appalling, so pathetic, so cowardly, that they deserved all the criticism that came their way.
What did they do I hear you ask? Change the club name? Change the kit colour? Move the stadium to a new town? No, much worse than any of that. They failed to retain their Premiership crown. Here's what James Lawton thought of it all over at The Independent:

Has the Premier League title ever been surrendered so pathetically?

In the long and not always glorious history of football there may have been more **disgracefully gutless performances** than the one put in by the champions of England at Southampton on Saturday. There may also have been a more bizarre series of utterances than those which came from the mouth of the man who carried the most direct responsibility, the Manchester City manager, Roberto Mancini, but if compelling comparisons are somewhat elusive there is one thing about which we can be certain.

It is that never before can such **a miserable example of broken down professionalism, of abandoned self-respect** and a total failure to deliver a sliver of value for money (the transfer value of City's starters was approximately £206m, with substitutes James Milner, Aleksandar Kolarov and Maicon representing another £48m), have provoked less in the way of red-blooded outrage. Another truth was much easier to grasp this last weekend. It is that City have become **a parody of a club** who might be anywhere near taking their place at the heart of European football.

Their dismissal from the Champions League was one shocking development. The tolerance of the Mario Balotelli situation was an affront to professional standards. The reinstatement of Tevez after his Munich mutiny was another compromise to **make the flesh crawl**.

When Gareth Barry scored his tragi-comic own goal at Southampton he displayed **the body language of a zombie**. It was also a reasonable way of defining the performance of most of his team-mates. It wasn't a defeat. It was a submission. It was a terrible statement about what happens when a team is **separated from any sense that it can still achieve its most basic ambitions**. For many, it was almost entirely the fault of players grossly overpaid and seriously under-motivated…..

To be fair, he was right about that Southampton performance….

To be honest, there was something EVEN WORSE that City had done prior to that – changed the name of their new ground. As sure as night following day or a Phil Jones gurn, Ollie Holt tweeted his disgust:

There are many ways in which the current owners of Manchester City have shown class. Renaming the stadium after a sponsor isn't one of them.

I know part of the answer is FFP but if City have got so much cash, why do they have to sell a piece of their soul for stadium naming rights?

Many City fans saying they don't care about stadium renaming because new stadium never had an identity anyway. Sad comment on the game.

Is it acceptable then to change name of team too? Presumably all in favour of Etihad Stadium would be fine with Etihad City as name of team.

If you defile the stadium by prostituting its name, you destroy part of the experience.

I said this at the time: *Last night I watched a documentary on the Formula One racing driver Ayrton Senna. When Senna crashed his car and died at Imola in 1994, as the helicopter carried him away from the track, Jeremy Clarkson commented (in a rare moment of sensitivity) that it really illustrated Senna's soul departing. A nation mourned over a lost soul. It has never mourned over the name of a stadium or the wages of a football player.*

But of course we have to leave the best to last. You all know it, you've all read it, you've all sent him an abusive e-mail. So put your hands together and give a warm welcome to the one and only Brian Reade!

Take it away Brian:

(ah f**k it, the whole lot's going in bold)

How Barca reserve Yaya Toure was seduced by the whore of world football

I've read many frightening stories about footballers in the Sunday papers.

But no tale has scared me as much as the one I read in a sniffy broadsheet, last Sunday, which could have come from the business pages:

"Manchester City's new £24m signing from Barcelona, Yaya Toure, is being paid £220,000-a-week. His initial wage of £185,000 will rise to £221,000 when the 50% tax rate comes in next April. He is due to receive £4.1m a year after tax, an image rights payment of £1.65m a year and a bonus of £823,000 each time City qualify for the Champions League and £412,000 if they win the competition. He will also get bonuses if the club win the Premier League and the FA Cup. The deal including his transfer fee, wages and bonuses, totals £79.6m."

Holy. Mother. Of. Jesus. Where will that leave the price of everyone's season ticket in five years time?

Even more frightening was what that report didn't say. Toure is not actually that great. He's not a creative genius who will get backsides off seats but a defensive midfielder who stops players who can.

He wasn't even a regular at Barcelona, having lost his place to Sergi Busquets. He may not even get a game for City, who already have four highly-rated players to fill that role – Patrick Vieira, Gareth Barry, Nigel de Jong and Vincent Kompany.

And scariest of all, Toure says he only joined City because his agent "told me I had to leave Barcelona". To add insult to injury the best he could say about his move was "it's an honour to be playing with my brother Kolo," before telling Barca that he'd love to go back there if they'll have him.

If you're a City fan, I'm guessing you'll have no problems with the story. It's proof the Sheikh is more determined than ever to land you the big prizes, and after all those years in United's shade who could blame you licking your lips at the prospect.

But how do outsiders begin to describe how depressing the implications of this transfer are? I can understand luring the sought-after David Silva to Eastlands for £140,000-a-week, but giving a quarter-of-a-million quid every seven days to a defensive squad player who no other club would have touched for that kind of money and whose name won't sell shirts, is insanity on a previously unimagined scale.

See how those figures play with Carlos Tevez and Emmanuel Adebayor's agents, or the leeway it gives Fernando Torres's and Didier Drogba's advisors if they decide to listen to a City offer. What do you reckon, half-a-million-a-week minimum? See how it impacts on other clubs trying to keep pace with wage demands.

See the shaking of parents' heads when City scouts ask to let their little fella join their academy. See the disillusion on the faces of the City youngsters who won the Youth Cup two years ago.

City aren't alone. Most Premier League clubs will invest the bulk of their summer spending abroad. They're just the most extreme example of why England's national side continue to fare so badly at the big tournaments.

Our clubs sent 106 players to South Africa, and the number has already soared past 110 while the contest is still on. Serie A sent 75, La Liga 57.

Spot the link with England's woeful performances which showed the lack of quality throughout the squad. We just don't have the players. Mainly because they've had their way blocked by average, over-paid foreign mercenaries.

An objective outsider would look at the obscene amount paid to seduce Toure to England, look at the country's lamentable showing in the World Cup, and conclude we deserve our misery because we've become the whores of world football.

THE END

A Letter In Football365.com

As Vincent Kompany wheeled away in delight after his goal against Spurs, I was reminded of the token Spanish kid I went to school with.

Jose, his name. He wasn't very good at football, but boy did he try. When we had a kick-around, he wouldn't get much of a touch. But if the keeper rolled it to his feet, he would smash it straight back in the goal and celebrate maniacally. Any kind of unsporting or unworthy goal subsequently became known as 'doing a jose'. eg. Kanu was guilty of 'doing a jose' for Arsenal against Sheff Utd that time in the cup.

Which brings me back to Kompany.

To celebrate wildly after scoring a fifth goal isn't classy at all. It was 'doing a Jose'. To do it after scoring a fifth goal against a ten-man team who had already given up any hope of scoring, from 3 yards out no less, for a billionaire club that are scoring 5 goals a game anyway, well that goes beyond 'doing a Jose'. That was simply pathetic.

The experiment is done. We've seen what would happen to a football club if you gave them unlimited resources; they score 5 goals a game. It's time for the experiment to end. It won't, and as this season wears on, the idea of this being a competitive season at the top end of the EPL will dissipate, replaced with the realisation that City have done a Sim City instead; typed in 'CASH' 50 times and built whatever they liked. To see them garner some sort of sense of achievement from it worthy of exuberant celebration is wholly depressing. I found it tasteless, classless and frankly embarrassing.

Rich Phippen

Football In The Bible

Genesis

1. In the beginning God created the Premiership and BSkyB
2. And God said, Let there be light entertainment: and there was light entertainment.
3. And God saw the light entertainment, that *it was* good: and God divided the light (Division 1) from the darkness (Divisions 2-4).
4. And God called the light THE PREMIER LEAGUE TM, and the darkness he called THE FOOTBALL LEAGUE. And the evening and the morning were the first day.
5. And God said, Let the earth bring forth grass, synthetic and real and also creosote markings.
6. And God said, Let there be floodlights in the firmament of the heaven to divide the day from the night. And let them be to give light upon the pitch: and it was so. And let not Malaysian betting syndicates remove this light; but it was not always so.
7. And God created in his own image Richard Keys and Andy Gray, though he made Richard with great hair, even on his hands.
   Andy, less so.
   For many years the two reigned in paradise, but wisdom was gained through disobedience at severe cost. And the lord saw that misogyny was their forbidden fruit and their downfall was a snake.
8. But before all could progress, new laws were set in place for the citizens and the devils and the pensioners and the toffees and the canaries and the Geordie tribe and the Mackems from the north and the gunners and their neighbours the spurs and more.
9. And God spoke all these words, to all, but mostly to the citizens:
10. **The Eight Commandments**
11. I am the Lord your God, who brought you out of Moss Side, out of the land of debt.

12. You shall have no other gods before me, not even David Silva.
13. You shall not murder Sloop John B songs, even if the city is yours.
14. You shall not commit adultery, unless you are a footballer or Russell Brand.
15. You shall not steal, unless it's a leverage scheme and a loose Fit & Proper test has been passed.
16. You shall not give false testimony against your neighbour by pretending they have lots of empty seats.
17. You shall not covet your neighbour's house. You shall not covet your neighbour's wife unless you are Ryan Giggs, or his male or female servant unless you are Ryan Giggs, his ox or donkey unless you are Ryan Giggs, or anything that belongs to your neighbour, unless you are Ryan Giggs.

---

1. Then hear thou in heaven, and of thy people Manchester, that thou teach them the good way wherein they should walk (with a swagger), and give rain upon thy land, which thou hast given to thy people for an inheritance and also as a curse. And a great plague was sent down on Manchester, and it rained for 40 days and 40 nights, and then another 40 days and 40 nights, and so on and so forth for all of eternity. And yet still when the rain did relent the lord said until his people that there would be a hosepipe ban. And further plagues were sent down on the people, first swarms of glory-hunters then Monday night football then Jim White.
2. But before all this came a man with false hair to rule over the Citizens. And at first all was well and Peter (Swales) doth say this is easy, but it was not easy.
3. The people did lose heart and rebelled, refusing to enter Maine Road and crying for a new leader who would take them back to the promised land.
4. During these years of wandering in the wilderness, Swales' patience was continually tested by the murmurings,

grumblings, and complaints of the people. At one point, Swales' patience reached its breaking point and he sinned against the Lord, in anger against the people, by signing Steve Daley.

5. When hence he did depart, their saviour arrived, but nothing was well still.

6. The citizens turned and took a journey into the wilderness by the way of Division 2, as the LORD spake unto them: and they compassed administration many days and many months. And the LORD spake unto them, saying, "Ye have compassed this mountain long enough: turn you northward."

7. Now rise up, and get you over the black burn. And they went over the black burn.

8. And the space in which they came from York, until they were come over the black burn was two years;

---

1. And Jesus provided many miracles, not least the return to the Premiership. And he did feed the 5000 (Fulham (H)), yet still they did run out of chicken balti pies by half-time. And Jesus said: "I have compassion for these people: they have already been with me 90 minutes and have nothing to eat, and they have been with Stuart Pearce for three years and have no goals to see."

2. And Jesus expelled the money changers from the temple, accusing them of turning the temple into a den of thieves, especially those ***** at Viagogo.

3. Thaksin was expelled into the wilderness, and he fled to the east. And all the while Sven begat Ulrika and Nancy and Faria and begat anyone who moved.

4. And the LORD said, I have surely seen the affliction of my people which were in Moss Side and now Beswick, and have heard their cry by reason of their taskmasters; for I know their sorrows;

5. And I am come down to deliver them out of the hand of the Shinawatras, and to bring them up out of that land unto a

good land and a large, unto a land flowing with milk and honey; unto the place of the Mansours, and the Sheikhs, and the snazzy F1 race, and the desert, and that appalling Michael Owen helicopter video on Youtube.

6. Seriously, look it up. It's terrible.

7. If thy people go out to battle against their enemy, whithersoever thou shalt send them, and shall pray unto the LORD toward the Citeh which thou hast chosen, and toward the council house that I have built for thy name. And my followers will not care about defeat, both now and the previous week, because of inebriation. And that shall be OK.

8. And so it was noted in Leviticus (19:27): " You shall not round off the side growth of your heads nor harm the edges of your beard, and to maintain the strength of your bitterness and lies your moustache should never diminish."

---

1. Now the Philistines gathered together their armies to battle, and were gathered together at the theatre of dreams, which belongeth to Trafford, and was pitched between Manchester and Salford, in the north.

2. And there went out a champion out of the camp of the Philistines, named Alex, of Govan, whose height was six cubits and a span.

3. And he had an helmet of brass upon his head, and he was armed with a nose as red as the blood of the citizens of Bethlehem;

4. And he had by him Wayne of Rooney. And Wayne had greaves of brass upon his legs, and a target of brass between his shoulders. And this brass was as old as the hills of Mezualeb.

5. When Graham Poll and all referees heard those words of the Philistine, they were dismayed, and greatly afraid. And all the men of the FA, when they saw the man, fled from him, and were sore afraid.

6. Now Roberto was the son of that Aldo and Marianna; and he had two sons, who he placed in the reserves. And he asked what shall be done to the man that defeateth this Philistine, and doth knock him off his perch?

7. And the people answered him after this manner, saying, so shall it be done to the man that killeth him, thou shall be inducted by Garry Cook into the Manchester United hall of fame.

8. And Roberto put his hand in his bag, and took thence a billion petrodollars, and slang it, and smote the Philistine in his forehead, that the stone sunk into his forehead; and he fell upon his face to the earth.

9. So Roberto prevailed over the Philistine with silva and more, and smote the Philistine, and slew him; but there was no sword in the hand of Roberto. And during this period did all witness the Exodus.

10. And so it was only 3-1, but the crowds did depart. It was only 4-1, yet more had left. It was only 5-1, yet the empty seats were plentiful. And then it was 6-1, and the land was bare. And so it came to pass that it should have been 10. And they did thank themselves that it was not 10, and considered the good fortune of the illegitimate.

11. And it came to pass in the eighteenth year after the children of England were come out of the land of the football league, in the fourth year of Mansour's reign over the Citizens, in the month May, which is the fifth month, that Roberto finished building the house of the champions*.

12. And the City had no need of the sun, neither of the blue moon, to shine in it: for the glory of petrodollars did lighten it. And the people did say Agueroooooo. And the word of the citizens came to Roberto, saying, "Blessed are the owners, and may all their teas be chippy teas".

13. And the lord did say "Drink it in. Go forth and celebrate, for you will never see anything like this again." And they did drink it in and they continued to drink it in and some are still drinking it in.

14. But the rejoicing did wane as a great curse returned on the team. Roberto was betrayed by one of his apostles,

probably the kit-man, who did travel to the Sun and tell of his master's tyrannical ways.

15. And so from a cold land came a holistic man who brought with him many goals.

16. And the knight finally departed, not only because he was of great years and his powers had waned, but also because he transgresseth by wine. But the fear of his followers, who numbered three billion and ten, were assured not to worry, as on the mountain of Sinai in the summer of the 14th year of the millennium the chalice which no one yet knew was poisoned was passed to the chosen one: David from the town of Glasgow in the north. And they did proclaim that the legacy did live on.

17. And so it came to pass. But they couldn't, because they were English, so the chosen one led his followers back into the wilderness. But behold! There was great rejoicing in the west as it came to be that they now had an official drinks partner for America and Asia.

18. And a star rose in the east, and the Lord called him Adnan. And he came from the land of Albania and the land of Belgium and the land of Kosovo and the land of the English. And he told the Lord that he did not know from whence he had come. But the Lord and all around him saw that he shone brighter than any other star, and he guided the wise men to Bethlehem and beyond, into the realm of the cusp of the Europa Cup.

19. Blessed is the war chest for it shall break open and restore the power of those in red. And the growth begins and it shall be organic, both through history and success, in the west and especially in the east, where their star shines brightest. And it will be so as is it is in their DNA. And the chosen one went forth once more and he proclaimed "we are back!"

20. But then they were defeated at home to Swansea.

21. And David did proclaim (Psalms 3:6): "I will not be afraid of many thousands of people who have set themselves against me all around." And he had by him the holy trinity, so all was well in the kingdom.

22. But more support was coming in the dark. For, lo, David did raise up the Men In Black, that bitter and hasty nation, which shall march through the breadth of the land, to possess the dwelling places that are not theirs. They are terrible and dreadful: their judgment and their dignity shall proceed of themselves.
23. They shall come all for violence: their faces shall sup up as the east wind, and they shall gather the captivity as the sand. And they shall force Rio Ferdinand to sign a new contract. But they shall not force Nemanja Vidic to stay as he leaves the chosen ones.
24. And having slain some families on Wembley Way they doth proclaim: our work is done. And it had to be so, as they did not return to the land of the twin towers for a long time.
25. **Numbers**
26. But the blue tribe had become too powerful, and the other tribes doth protest at this power, which had not been earned how they wanted it to be. And thus Michel pushed for new laws, for he was angry as he had a woman's name.
27. And one man who protested hard was Arsene Wenger, but to no avail, as in the land of the blind, the one-eyed man is king. And the weight of Arsene's coat was five thousand shekels of gold.
28. The special one did also speak, and he did speak some more, then some more and the lord said to the people "please shut up this interminable bore" but the special one was not for shutting up and he doth speak some more.
29. Jesus, crosses, blah blah…..

The heavens descended on Manchester, and rightly the Sunderland home match was called off. It was quite handy at the time as City were in a run of congested fixtures and with the odd injury niggle to deal with too, but it was typical city that later in the season a documentary would be aired on the club (Inside City) that decided to focus on the run up to this game.

An Ode To Garry Cook

This week, City's ex-CEO Garry Cook gave a fascinating insight into his time at the club, a time that cost him much in his personal life but which he clearly still holds dear.

Cook was never a popular man outside the club. Seen as prone to gaffes and keen on management-speak, his departure gained little sympathy. Journalists resented the fact that he had lied to them about finding a successor to Mark Hughes - they obviously expected him to openly tell them City were looking for a new man.

Cook was certainly high-profile, sometimes unwittingly, high-profile CEOs being the epitome of modern football. Overseeing one of the most talked about football stories of our time, he brought unprecedented growth in the club and its profile. You might recoil at the thought that football is all about money, but it has been that way for decades - that's not Cook's fault, and with the dawn of Financial Fair Play, Cook and the owners knew that City had to expand their profile and increase marketing in order to compete. He did his job, and he did it well.
But Cook offered something else too that you won't see mentioned. Most people know only half the story.
As Oliver Kay of The Times tweeted after his dismissal: *What I found endearing about Cook was that he cared about the fans. Very few do.*

And he did care. There are endless stories of how Cook has helped City fans - sorting out tickets for games, spending hours chatting to fans and listening to their opinions, doing impromptu ground tours for visitors and generally putting himself out. Most CEOs wouldn't. He clearly lived for the job, and took his role seriously, to the extent of it costing him his marriage. I recently went on one of the club tours accompanied by a "city legend" who mentioned how Cook is still sorely missed by everyone at the club.

The ridiculous overreaction by a minority of City fans to Cook's slip of the tongue when he introduced Uwe Rosler into the Manchester United Hall of Fame was symptomatic of modern fandom and the shrieking hysteria and mock outrage felt by some at any little thing. It was the worst time possible for a faux pas on Cook's part, but it was just a simple mistake at the end of the day, a slip of the tongue, hardly our CEO walking out in a full United kit then urinating on the front table.

(And for the record, Kaka did bottle it. So there. When the press are taking the side of Silvio Berlusconi, then you know there are agendas at play and you can't win.)

In the end Cook dug his own grave over the furore with Nedum Onuoha's mother, an unfortunate end to a successful period at the club, but in recent years City fans have been spoilt and Cook helped make it all happen, leaving a wonderful legacy for the club. So once more, thank you.

Manchester City 0 Chelsea 1

Ouch. The frustration of a Monday night match was exacerbated by a poor home defeat and a deserved victory for Chelsea, as the press lauded the master tactician that is Jose Mourinho.

It was the first time City had failed to score in a home league match since November 2010 as the Premier League's most potent attack, with 68 goals, was kept out by the best defence - the visitors have conceded just 20.

A goal from Ivanovic in the first half was enough, but City were not at the races and couldn't complain. For once Pellegrini got the formation wrong and City were overrun in midfield. By the time he changed things around, it was too late, though in his defence there are few better teams at defending a lead than Mourinho's Chelsea. With defeat, City spurned the chance to go top and brought Chelsea back into the title race. It looked like a three-horse race as the season took another dramatic twist.

Norwich City 0 Manchester City 0

With the need to get their title challenge back on track, this result was all the more frustrating as City failed to score for the second successive match and loosened their grip further on the title race. What's more, they again spurned the chance to go to the top of the table. Clearly City are intent on doing this the hard way, as ever. The truth was that as against Chelsea, City deserved little, struggling to create apart from a Negredo header against the bar. In fact, Norwich could easily have taken all three points near the end. And so a lull for City that needs to be ended soon before they lose touch,. In a title race involving at least three teams, there is little room for error, as you cannot rely on multiple teams losing form.

Manchester City 2 Chelsea 0: Some Thoughts

Now that was better. An utter transformation from the game of 12 days previous, the roles were reversed at the Etihad as City won comfortably and the special one made failure his speciality for the day as City inflicted Chelsea's second FA Cup defeat in open play since 2008 – the other also being City of course.

With Daily Mirror exclusives warning us during the week that both managers were to play weakened teams, needless to say they were completely wrong as per usual as two strong teams were fielded. Thankfully, on the premise that Jovetic is not a specialised front man, Pellegrini chose a 5-man midfield in a bid to restrict the acres of space that the likes of Hazard had enjoyed in the league game.

And I felt a rush of confidence from seeing Lescott back in the team. For all his faults I still feel more at ease when he partners Kompany, at least until Nastastic can find his form of old (or more to the point, stay fit for more than a week at a time). I will be truly sad to see him go in the summer, but it has been coming for some time.

And it worked a treat. Pellegrini has commented numerous times that he will not betray his ideals and formations due to the opposition, a worrying thought with Barcelona on the horizon, but it seems he learnt from his mistake and made the relevant changes.

In the end, it was comfortable. Chelsea never threatened, with no shots on target and no real chances of note, some achievement by the City team, a team who were clearly out for revenge. With the midfield tight, it was City who fashioned enough in the opposition penalty area to come out on top. Apart from the goals, City went close on a few other occasions and had a goal disallowed.

The second goal may have been marginally offside, it depends when you stop the replay, but as Chelsea didn't have a chance all match, it was hardly match-defining. Perhaps a second yellow card for Luiz rugby-tackling Dzeko ten minutes into the second half may have had a greater impact.

Phil Dowd was rubbish.

It's hard to pick out a man-of-the-match when the whole team did its job. Jovetic continues to flourish now he has kept his fitness and is an excellent link between midfield and attack, though he clearly needs to eradicate the play-acting – let's leave that to Moyes' Marvels and his holy trinity. Silva and Toure were superb and Kompany and Lescott majestic. What's more, Javi Garcia also shone, a player who may never get a fair crack of the whip at City, but who once more did his job effectively.

(it's sadly predictable that Garcia gets more stick for a couple of bad performances than Mario Balotelli ever did after half a season of half-arsed performances prior to leaving City. And yet still some fans want him back)

And what a joy to see Nasri back on the pitch, his influence immediate. This is what man-management can do. He's like a new signing and all that….

And as was seen with Nasri, Pellegrini managed the substitutions perfectly. Silva was taken off to rest before Tuesday, Jovetic too may have been brought off for the same reason, or perhaps because he does still not have 90 minutes in him, but City had the luxury of bringing on Navas and Nasri thus not significantly weakening the team. Mourinho made three substitutions but none of them had an impact on the game, not even Oscar.

So, after the Mourinho love-in following the league defeat, when we were told of his tactical master class and how he had once more out-witted Pellegrini, I expect the same will be said in reverse today, yes? There was a ridiculous overreaction to Chelsea's victory at the Etihad last week, especially as it came off the back of a goalless draw at home to West Ham. A draw and a defeat since should bring a bit more perspective. City were slated for a league defeat in which they had 65% possession and 24 shots. Yesterday, Chelsea had 3 shots, none of which were on target.

This victory also had a few extra benefits elsewhere. History shows that a team going for trophies on multiple fronts can often end up empty-handed and the pursuit can often unravel in one bad week. Thankfully the prospect of two cup exits in a week (a comfortable home defeat to Barcelona is effectively an exit even at the half-way stage) is no more and what's more for now the oft-quoted subtext about Mourinho having a hoodoo over Pellegrini can also be put to rest, for now.

And so to Chelsea, a master class in nastiness off the pitch. I can excuse the odd fan from not obeying a minutes' silence if they are just entering the stadium and may not know about it, but to my ears the singing was a tad more extensive than that – I can't say I'm that surprised, nor by their fighting at the end with the odd monkey chant aimed at a steward. Classy as always.

And then there is Mourinho, lovely, cuddly Jose Mourinho. By talking about him I have no doubt most journalists would tell me that I have simply fallen into his trap and what he says has thus worked. Whatever – I don't need lessons in psychology and mind-games from anyone thank you very much.

There is no doubt that Mourinho does foster a resolute, strong, "us-against-them" spirit in his squads and the drivel that regularly spews out of his mouth is often attributed as a factor in this spirit. To me it is all rubbish. I doubt the players pay much attention to little spats with other managers and it is his relationship with them in the dressing room and on the training ground that is more important. As I have mentioned, you will often see journalists say that Mourinho's tactics have worked as soon as a manager dares respond to his bile, but allow me to let you into a little secret – they are talking b***ocks. If another manager hits back it does not mean Mourinho has "won", it means they are doing what Mourinho has done himself, so why there is a winner in all of this eludes me. There is no evidence that what Mourinho does has won his team a single point in a football match, so spare me the lecture on what a master he is in the dark arts. He is simply a classless, spiteful man quite prepared to gouge an opposition coach in the eye, so his reverence amongst the press pack is merely because he provides easy copy for them and creates a story, which is exactly what they want. This whole situation would not exist if journalists actually asked more sensible questions on conferences rather than try and create a story (and I am not referring to all journalists of course – it is a select few that are ruining it for everyone, and their sub-editors who create hysterical, sensational and often false headlines to the accompanying story). Mourinho has been shown to contradict himself on an almost daily basis and we all know that he is full of crap, so let's try and ignore him from now on.

But I HAVE just written a thesis on him, so he has won after all. Damn you Mourinho!

And now for the really big match….a game we dreamt about for decades. So let's try and enjoy it.

I have rarely been as nervous as when I approached Tom Finney to get his autograph at a City do a few years ago. Very few carry that aura or truly deserve a legend status. R.I.P.

Manchester City 0 Barcelona: 2 Many Thoughts

The biggest match of a generation? The moment we had all been waiting for, had always dreamt of a mere 5477 days previous when we had lined up against Macclesfield? Well whatever, the hyperbole for this match was off the scale, the giddiness hard to restrain.

Clearly this was not our biggest match in decades. A first-leg tie in the last 16 of the Champions League does not compare to that day against QPR, or the Newcastle match that preceded it, nor the derby before that or the FA Cup final against Stoke and not even the semi-final against United. Our owners may see it slightly different of course. But it's what it symbolised that is important. This was not our first game against a European superpower, but it was out first game in the knock-out stage and perhaps Barcelona carry a slightly different aura to those that we have played already. It was a match in the knockout stage of the Champions League against Barcelona and some of us struggled to get our heads round the fact that this was happening when we considered what had gone before.

So, caught up in the excitement from others, I spent yesterday with a churning stomach, worried and also expectant about what lay ahead. I have always been negative about City and remain so against the top sides as I can't shake it our of my system after decades of disappointment, and I felt stupid for adopting a similar mind-set as when we used to play United as massive underdogs – namely, please don't concede early and don't get walloped. I just wanted us to be competitive over these two legs, as it would be another step forward for the club. As I said, rather negative, but hopefully one day my glass will always be half-full.

But to be honest, I was still not THAT bothered. The Champions League has not yet captured my imagination, as domestic honours still mean more to me. Let's look at it from a clinical point of view. Should we get past Barcelona, we then have the likes of Bayern Munich, PSG, Atletico Madrid, Chelsea, Real Madrid and Borussia Dortmund to beat to the cup. Domestically, we are 3-1 to win the treble. United fans argued with a friend on Facebook last night wondering how we could not see the Champions League as a priority, but it's just being realistic. If City win the league and a cup (or two), there's not a City fan on earth who would give a damn about our exit to Barcelona.

Terrorizing Europe? All in good time….

Nevertheless, Manuel Pellegrini had a huge dilemma for the match. Should he stick to his mantra of never conceding to the opposition when picking his side, or should he be pragmatic and try and negate Barcelona's multi-pronged threats? He would have been praised and criticised in equal measures whichever route he took, but thankfully for me he took the latter route and was pragmatic. It was not a total success, sadly.

But as I said, it's what I would have done, the Bayern rout fresh in the mind still. We don't quite have the team yet to play our strongest XI against any team. Not yet. Not quite – and as Jonathan Wilson explained in his match report – you HAVE to take special measures against Barcelona.

The surprise came with the selection of Kolarov in left-midfield to nullify the threat of Alves and Sanchez and whilst City's two left-backs did not have great games, the pairing did work to an extent. With Kolarov off the pitch, Barcelona's threat down their right increased rapidly.

Typical City lives on – the mosaic piece our section had to hold up fell to pieces as soon as I touched it, and left I and many others covered in black pieces that took the rest of the evening to scrape off our hands, faces and phones. Thanks.For.That.

Barcelona hogged the ball for 20 minutes, but perhaps City were happy with this. I was slightly concerned if this was setting the pattern for the rest of the game, but I wasn't worried about Barcelona's immediate threat as there wasn't one. City retained a tight shape, were disciplined and there were no chances for the visitors. After that, City grew into the game more and saw more of the ball.

And possession does not win games. We all remember the Mourinho master class that was administered to us the other week, all done with minimal possession. When Bayern Munich beat Barcelona 4-0 last season, they had 34% possession. Pellegrini may well have been fine with City not seeing much of the ball.

Those who have watched Barcelona say they are weakest in defence and are vulnerable from wide and clearly Pellegrini included Navas and Kolarov with the intention of getting plenty of balls into the box from wide to test Barcelona's defence. The biggest disappointment of the night for me was that we just didn't get into enough good positions to do this. Alba stayed deep to negate Navas and Kolarov was simply unable to get past his full-back.

And yes, up to the red card, Demichelis had played well. His distribution out of defence was occasionally wayward, but he wasn't the only one. His experience was put to good use prior to his dismissal, with interception after interception, and the trio of him, Kompany and Fernandinho kept Messi super-quiet. But the fact is, City are currently deficient in one of their central defence slots, and whoever Pellegrini had picked would have proved troublesome and a potential weak link. Lescott hardly covered himself in glory once he was introduced.

Then of course came the turning point of the game. It was probably a foul on Navas, especially in the context of a fussy referee, but not getting a free kick in the opposition half is not worthy of great debate. Demichelis is understandably the focus of huge criticism today, but Kompany did not help by playing Messi onside. With hindsight, Demichelis should have let Messi through and then if he scores, he scores. But he had a split second decision to make and was probably aware of how bad it would look if he didn't make a challenge. Sadly, he was never getting the ball and the rest is history.
As for it being outside the area – as Micah Richards showed in a pitiful 2-0 defeat to Everton a few years ago, a foul by holding a player that starts outside the area but continues into the area is a penalty, but I am not sure it applies to a tackle also. The foul as we

all know happened outside the area, but I hold little blame to the officials as at full speed it looked like a penalty to me and plenty around me.

After that it was damage limitation and City almost did their job. I may have low expectations, but I was proud of how they coped for the final half-hour, after a small post-goal surge from Barcelona. What a shame that they threw away all the good work at the death.

There really has been a huge disparity of opinion on how well City played however. Men against boys said some, a good display until one crucial turning-point said I and others.

As I have said all along – we are not as good as Barcelona yet. Critics will moan about how we have spent billions of pounds, but this is clearly not the complete side or squad yet and it will take time and it will take a successful academy to reach where Barcelona are. Barcelona themselves went through this same process a decade ago, revolutionizing their whole approach to how they were run and City are playing catch-up now. We also have a new manager, and like all managers, he will truly make his mark in the transfer market in his second summer transfer window. We need a top class central defender (perhaps two), we need a top class left-back and we need a top class defensive midfielder. If we make the academy produce just one good player a year, the future is brighter than we could ever imagine. Perhaps PSG are showing you can spend and be the finished article quickly, but as long as we continue to move forward there's little to complain about.

As for the referee, it is all part of the learning curve for mastering European competitions that you have to put up with such displays. As is often the case, having replayed the match he wasn't quite as bad as I had first thought, but he was ridiculously fussy, his protection of Valdes was ridiculous, his handing out of yellow cards unnecessary and he failed to let the game flow. Apart from that he was fine.

Jamie Jackson of the Guardian's Five Talking Points included the following:

David Silva sparkles only sporadically
....after Messi's penalty – and Demichelis's sending off ...he became an ever more peripheral figure as City engaged in damage limitation.
Yaya Touré struggles to make an impact

Elsewhere, the Telegraph gave Kompany 6/10.

As for after the match, I was very disappointed with Pellegrini, something I never expected to say. I thought he was above such tirades. Perhaps he is now trying some of these amazing mind-games that deflect attention away from the team, or was trying to paint a story of bad luck in front of the club's owners or maybe he just lost his cool. Either way it was stupid, he will now be banned and he has not helped the side in any shape or form. Please leave that sort of stuff to the likes of Mourinho in the future.

So Pellegrini must now decide how to approach the second leg. There is an imperative to keep it tight of course once more, at least in the early stages. But goals are required, which surely merits the obvious return of Aguero, but also Nasro and Jovetic. Keep the shield in front of the back four, play Nastastic, and then pray.

Still at least the defeat proved a nice season-highlight for United fans. That and the claim that their stadium tour sold out yesterday. In times of hardship, as we well know, you take what you can....

Manchester City 1 Stoke City 0

Relief all round as City secured three points due to a Yaya Toure goal. The performance was nothing to write home about, but City got away with it
The game was noticeable for Dzeko's amazing miss from four yards, but thankfully it didn't cost City dear, which was just as well after Chelsea defeated Everton earlier in the day.

Manchester City 3 Sunderland 1: Some Thoughts

So there it is – a domestic treble completed in three years, another trophy that would have seemed so unlikely just a few years ago. City did not excel but showed two moments of such quality that we won't forget the match for a long time. A first League Cup win in my years of supporting the team but defeat for Sunderland in their first Wembley visit in 16 years and first final in 22 years. At half-time it seemed like another no-show was on the cards, another day where the underdog triumphed and the City of old returned, another miserable journey home followed by a week of recriminations, but in the end individual quality prevailed.

This blog is mostly not about football but instead I thought I would focus on trains. Boarding the first train of the day to London, the driver soon informed us of a one-hour delay due to engineering works overrunning. My long run of good luck on trains had run out and it wasn't the best start to the day, especially with the bar soon running out of alcohol.

But as expected, once in London it was nice to have a stress-free day with little fear of trouble. Thank the lord for David De Gea's late fumble in the other semi-final.

City fans have been spoilt in recent years and will continue to be, but the walk down Wembley Way never fails to stir this ageing heart, even if it resembles a war-zone. Everyone in red and blue was in good spirits, as it should be.

As for the team, the good news was that Sergio Aguero was passed fit and started, though doubts would remain over just how match-fit he would be. Kolarov got the nod over Clichy, and Demichelis unsurprisingly started alongside Kompany.

And then of course there was Joe Hart benched. We'll all have our own opinions on this, but I believe there is little room for sentiment when picking a cup-final team and the manager should play his strongest side. If he is picking a specific Capital One Cup side then why not pick Lescott?

So how big an occasion was this? Big enough. When United were hoovering up trophies, I always pithily dismissed a League Cup trophy as nothing to get upset about as it wasn't the biggest of trophies and they were competing for bigger prizes so this was nothing to get het up about. I will now contradict myself by saying this was not the case for City. In fifteen years' time it may be, but for now it held significant importance for me for a number of reasons. Firstly, it would be a first trophy for Pellegrini, at the earliest opportunity, putting to rest the argument that he has never won anything (apart from those times that he did win stuff, but as we all know if it is not in Europe then it is irrelevant). Secondly, a trophy takes a small amount of pressure off the players as they compete for the other bigger prizes – this will not be a trophy-less season and thus is already an improvement on last season. Finally, City are not at the stage to be disregarding trophies, but are at the stage where trophies need to be accumulated – only then can we claim to have a history, eh?

As for the game, it was the most exciting spectacle I have seen yet at Wembley with plenty of goal-mouth action, at least compared to previous tight affairs. But depressingly City once more struggled against a team that packed the midfield and crowded central areas. Pellegrini picked a narrow team himself when width was needed, with two wide players in Silva and Nasri who naturally will drift infield and crowd things further. Now few managers would have the nerve to drop either Nasri and Silva to accommodate the opposition, but it played into Sunderland's hands, who countered dangerously and soon reaped the rewards. Pellegrini realised this eventually but reacted too late, though again it is a brave manager who makes a tactical substitution in the first half of a cup final (or any game for that matter).

You could also argue of course that the formation was toothless because in addition to the above problems, City's full-backs couldn't get forward enough to provide that width.

What didn't help was endless aimless punts upfield from Pantilimon that lost us possession time after time rather than the better option of us playing the ball out of defence. My argument is undermined somewhat by the punt upfield that led to City's second goal.

As for Sunderland's goal, it provided a handy occasion to criticise City's resident scapegoats, namely Martin Demichelis and Costel Pantilimon. I am amazed Pantilimon has had some criticism on forums considering he did nothing wrong, his positioning not particularly out. Sometime you just have to acknowledge a great finish, which it undoubtedly was. Demichelis is always going to be a scapegoat and we just have to accept it now, not that he had a great game, but then he wasn't alone in that respect and did plenty of good things during the match (especially clearing headers) that will receive scant coverage in many areas. He was outpaced by Borini and could have had the forethought to cover behind Kompany, but the captain must surely take the blame for the goal, his decision to try and clear the ball rather than shepherd Borini proving to be disastrous.

Which brings me to the excellent Michael Cox of Zonal Marking and Guardian podcast fame. Michael is a rare beast in that I don't know which football team he supports because he always comments without any bias or prejudice and has a superb tactical awareness of the sport. What he says goes for me. He thought Poyet won the game tactically, which is a fair point as City won the game through two moments of sublime skill rather than through their overall performance. One other thing of note though was a twitter discussion I and others had with him today in which he commented on how he thinks Vincent Kompany is overrated as a defender and makes a glaring mistake at least once a game and is pretty poor positionally. I disagreed strongly (thus doubting him for the first time ever perhaps). It is true that a lot of Kompany's status in the game and for City comes not through just how well he may play but through leadership qualities and his effect on the team – he is undoubtedly a driving force for the team, a team that lacks something when he is not there. He is not perfect however, but I argued on Twitter that he needs a consistent partner beside him as a settled defence is a godsend, and City's defence has chopped and changed week after week for a variety of reasons. Defenders don't get away with mistakes like attacking players do and Kompany and the other defenders suffer somewhat due to Pellegrini's attacking ideals, which can leave them exposed especially if there is no Garcia on the pitch. If Kompany was playing under a defensive manager (or an Italian!) there would probably be no discussion to have. No defender is perfect anyway.

But back to the match and there can be few better feelings than that minute or two of football that saw City go from losing to leading the match. Not only was there the joy of turning the match around, but also in the wonder of witnessing two of the greatest strikes of the ball you could ever wish to see. Both goals were simply magnificent. As Toure hit the ball I shouted out in exasperation at what he was doing before the ball hit the back of the net. As Navas wrapped up the game I had just spent two seconds screaming at Toure for not passing to his left. What do I know, eh? Toure is an amazing footballer, one who can be terrible in defensive areas as seen by him not tracking Fletcher late on as he messed up a good opportunity, but we all know he is at his best going forward and is wasted somewhat in a deeper role. In the first half he was average at best once more as he was shackled and he cannot prosper in a packed midfield.

So having got it initially wrong with team selection (in my opinion and with hindsight, a wonderful tool not available to managers) Pellegrini at least did react during the match by bringing on Navas for width and Garcia to secure the game as Sunderland reacted well to going behind.

City held on after Sunderland came back strongly, and the third goal helped settle the nerves and saved us counting down the four minutes of injury time and whistling frantically at the referee.

Yaya Toure certainly likes that goal at Wembley. With three goals scored in it, does he now get to keep the net?

Dzeko was beyond awful and I am officially giving up on him (until next week). He had a run of great form over the New Year, but has regressed spectacularly since then. He is not good enough, but that is an argument that depends on where you place him in City's pecking order. Players like him and Demichelis have had far more time on the pitch than may have been originally intended when the season kicked off. I still maintain that Demichelis, bought cheaply on low wages, is more than good enough as a backup defender, but nothing more. Likewise, Dzeko as a fourth choice striker would be one of the best backups going, but I would prefer a rising star in that position rather than him. Eventually he will leave City and score a bucketful of goals for another team.

PARANOIA KLAXZON. You know what is coming. The narrative was clear, from Martin Tyler, to John Dillon's Express opinion piece to numerous other reports – money won the day. We all know of course that money brings success, we all know that it did before City come along, we all know this. What continues to exasperate, though I should rise above it, is that no other team gets this treatment. If Chelsea has beaten Sunderland yesterday, there would have been no mention of the disparity in team costs and we all know that Manchester United's team cost has never been mentioned by any commentator or in any match report. Chelsea spent big before City came along and yet it is City that fascinates the envious out there, perhaps because we are conceived as having been transformed by money more than Chelsea, but we finished in the top half of the table before the takeover and Chelsea were close to going bust before Abramovich came along (as were City). There is little difference. As Arsenal slowly start splashing the cash in a desperate attempt to win a trophy, any trophy, then their boorish fans' arguments will slowly become even more desperate than now. As for United, organic growth is of course fine, even if the way the club helped create a closed shop is more odious than a rich owner spending his own money and removing debt from a club.

But enough of the moaning. What a wonderful day, what a wonderful atmosphere, and the Sunderland fans did themselves proud. Drink it all in, you could be back there twice in the next couple of months, along with City.

Oh hang on, more moaning. The trains back were "dry", causing much consternation. I will take the alternative view however and state that I can understand the reasoning, even if as usual the sensible, well-behaved majority are punished for the actions of a vocal and drunk minority. I am clearly getting old by choosing to comment on such matters, but all train journeys (and those of friends elsewhere yesterday) back from Wembley and other parts have been uncomfortable affairs due to the actions of a few morons who act a certain way under the influence. We can hardly be surprised therefore that train companies don't want their vehicles trashed or treated with contempt. Banning alcohol just creates more tension though, but as I said, it might be wrong, but I can understand why it happens. Having said that, we all know that football fans are considered as the scum of society much of the time, when people acting inappropriately after drinking is common in all walks of life, not just on a football train. God I'm getting old.

My decision to take the Monday off rates up there as one of my best.

I bet Nasri still bitterly regrets leaving Arsenal.

Three Wembley Goals: The Holy Trinity

Yaya Toure

Not again, surely? All the hope, the giddiness, the expectation extinguished. Another no-show, another loss to an underdog. Another long, painful journey home as another hangover kicks in. Another week of avoiding all newspapers, social media and the inevitable recriminations that will continue for some time. Another week of ridicule at moneybags City "coming a cropper". And we can't complain as the team hasn't played well enough, hasn't created. Again. It was a miserable time in the concourse at half-time.

But we are playing a bit better in the second half, but still no chances.

That was a terrible free-kick, for ****'s sake. Still got the ball though, small consolation. Come on City. Get it wide! No, not there. Too narrow still. Oh Yaya what is that for…oh my god! Oh my god! YES! YES! WHAT THE…?!!! What a goal! WHAT A GOAL!

Hug someone! Punch the air! You beauty! Back in it! Thank you!

Samir Nasri

Phew, calm down. What a goal. WHAT A GOAL. We're level, and in the cup all that matters is not losing, you're still in it if you're not losing. Now please kick on City, please. I hope the Sunderland players' heads drop, but I doubt it.

Oh, everyone's doing the Toure song, I feel awkward doing that. I'll make a token gesture, waggle my hands a bit.

Right, good header back Kolarov. He's working hard.

Oh not another long punt from Pantilimon! Pass it out for god's sake! All bloody match. Blimey, good control by Sergio though. Come on, attack them!

Good chance of a cross here. A deflection, and where's it going, it'…..BLOODY HELL!

BLOODY HELL!! OH MY WORD!! We're winning!!! How, why, what?!!! What a two minutes!!!!! Hug someone! Punch the air! Come on City! You beauties! They turned it around, never in doubt!

Jesus Navas

Don't look at the clock, Howard. It goes slower when you do that. A quick glance, not long to go. I bet there's four minutes of injury time though. There's always four minutes and Edin took an hour to leave the pitch. Wouldn't surprise me if there was five. Bloody referee, he's been awful and he hates us. I hope Sergio's not injured.

I feel really tense all of a sudden. My sixth Wembley visit and every injury time has been torture. I hope we coast to victory here one day.

Ooh, was that a foul (?), he's bound to…oh no, he's played on, Yaya is free. Come on, come on. He's still going. Still going. Left, Yaya, left! Man free on the left! No, not right, left! Oh Navas is running on to it, player in the way though, got the shot in, keeper has got his hand to it, it's in the net!!!! YESSSSSSS!!!!

WE'VE WON THE CUP!!!

THANK YOU (NON-EXISTENT) GOD!! JURASSIC PARK! Hug someone! Punch the air! We're gonna win the cup! Ha ha ha!Oh this feels so good, the joy and the smiles, are everywhere around.

And relax.

The A-Z of Manchester City Villains

Antic, Raddy. The first on this list and the first villain of my City-supporting life. A mere year into my bumpy journey with City and up popped Antic to condemn City to relegation and make me question if I had made the right allegiance, something I continued to question for a couple of decades. He was also responsible for David Pleat's inclusion on the list, as you will see.

Ball, Alan. Where to start? A terrible, terrible manager and it seems that telling players you once won the World Cup doesn't guarantee better performances. Who knew? A flat-cap on the touchline is not a great look either, if I'm honest. There have been so many poor managerial appointments in City's history (yes, we do have one), but Ball stands out for me.

Crerand, Paddy. There is a cast of thousands, and it would be easy to choose Eamonn Holmes, Clayton Blackmore, Lou Macari, Terry Christian, Mumford & Sons and many more, but if you were to choose one United sycophant who sees everything through red-tinted glasses, can never see any fault in their club and drones on repeatedly about history and the DNA/soul of their club, a DNA and soul that makes them more special than any other club, then this is your man, the man for all occasions.

Danny Mills. Need I say more? Well I will anyway. Happy to leech off the club for years and seems even happier to slate the club at every possible opportunity. I don't know what he has against the club and I don't care, but how the guy gets endless media jobs and onto an FA Commission is baffling.

Everton. Bogey club, c*ap restricted view, poor quality 100-year-old seats, a crowd baying for blood, with every decision that goes against them portrayed as a miscarriage of justice (see their booing of Lloris as he lay partially-unconscious on the pitch this season), and older fans will tell you what thugs a sizeable minority of them were in the 80's, and thus their hatred for them. And then there was the CHOSEN ONE's bleating over the Joleon Lescott transfer. For that alone they are on the list.

(and we lost 9-1 to them in 1906).

Ferguson, Alex. David Moyes or Alex Ferguson? A ruthless dictator who got more out of his teams than seemed feasible, the day of his retirement was a good day for City, Chelsea, Arsenal et al. In every sense of the word(s), good riddance. Check out his autobiography's mentions of City if you are ever down, it will cheer you up no end (don't buy it,obviously, just find the extracts).

Gene Kelly stand. Always amusing to watch other people dressed in cheap mackintoshes getting drenched, but come on – what a ridiculous addition to the old ground. An embarrassment, if truth be known.

Halsey, Mark. Yeah, that's right, Mark Halsey. Please spare me how he was a hero for the added time amount in the play-off final. The amount added on was correct, and merely him doing his job. Since then he seemed to go out of his way to give us nothing. Now he is whoring himself around in the pursuit of money and fame. So sod him.

Ian Rush – yes, City did what City do best by holding the ball in the corner when drawing a match they needed to win to avoid relegation, but if Liverpool had done their job and not put any effort in, as morally they should have done in a meaningless game for them (ahem), then perhaps the king of all cock-ups may never have occurred. Rush scored that day so I hold him especially responsible, in one of those irrational hatred things we all have. (Don't we?)

Jon Macken – for scoring one outrageous goal against City on a rainy day in Preston, thus convincing our profligate manager that you were worth spending £5m on. If only it had bounced wide.

Karl-Heinz Rummenigge. Ah, the pied piper of the city-are-evil-and-are-killing-football-you-can't-disrupt-the-status-quo-we-do-things-the-right-way-and-intend-to-keep-squashing-anyone-who-gets-in-our-way-and-we'll-go-crying-to-UEFA-if-you-try-and-stop-us-or-perhaps-start-a-European-super-league brigade.
As Bayern Munich chief executive, Rummenigge likes nothing more than to bleat about City and not meeting financial fair play rules. Thankfully his bleating seems to have been in vain whilst his own club do things the right way, organically backed by huge corporations.
The Bundesliga is all that is good in football of course and you only have to mention the league to David Conn and a change of pants is required but the likes of Ruminegge have got their way and domestic and European domination has come to fruition for Bayern now. Mission accomplished.

League, Champions. Little known fact klaxon – in 1929, a young George Orwell wrote a book that was never published called 1992. In it, the anti-hero James Grimble was conditioned to like a "brave new world" by a constant stream of propaganda that was communicated through big screens (Orwell was a visionary). This new world had shiny balls, evocative opera-lite music blasted through huge speakers 24/7, and money. Lots and lots of money. Orwell called it the Champions League, a league for champions and all their powerful friends who weren't champions but needed to stay powerful so they could keep trying to be champions along with their select group of friends. There was no resistence to this world that Orwell painted so evocatively and hauntingly. Resistance was, after all, futile.

And thus City, and so many other clubs, never had a chance of success anymore without a benefactor. The beautiful game.

Michel Platini. The devil himself, in human form. The greatest trick Platini ever pulled….

I don't know if Platini is angry because he has a woman's name or he genuinely thinks Financial Fair Play is a good thing, but the fact is it addresses few of the issues in the modern game (it would not have prevented Portsmouth's woes, for example), helps maintain a status quo and was introduced only after pressure was applied from Europe's most powerful clubs, which tells you all you need to know.Any footballing great is diminished in my eyes when he becomes a politican, and that is all he is now, the rights and wrongs of the game of little concern as long as he gets along in life.

Newspapers. They all have it in for City, right? Well not really, but they sure make life difficult for City, as with any other sporting institution. From the stupid press conference questions, the agendas, the lies, the appalling agent-led transfer gossip to the pitiful opinion pieces from the likes of Harry Redknapp, Brian Reade or Ian Wright, we really would be better off without a swathe (but not all) of our football press.

Office, ticket (Maine Road). Only City could have an outside ticket office in the rainiest City in the country. The night the League Cup match v Ipswich was abandoned due to Paul Dickov almost drowning, I queued for my ticket outside a portakabin for 30 minutes, and have been dryer than I was that night when submerged in a bath. I haven't been the same since.

Pleat, David. Faster than a kerb-crawling car, David skipped across the Maine Road pitch in his loafers and one of the first memories of my City-supporting life was etched indelibly on my brain. He hugged Brian Horton on his travels that day, but Brian's a lovely bloke so I'll let him off. The previously mentioned 1-0 home defeat to Luton in 1983, condemning City to relegation from the top flight was a perfect example of what was to come. I've always held an irrational grudge against Pleat ever since, probably fortified by the opinion that he is a terrible co-commentator who can't pronounce the simplest of names.

Quinn, Niall. Another player that makes it onto the Heroes & Villains list, once I realised this is a stupid way to compile a list (wait until you see the Z entry!). Quinn gets in for his new role as simpleton-sidekick to Martin Tyler, his inane ramblings and his ability to talk drivel about City never a joy to behold. Where United have ex-pros scattered throughout the media ready to fight their corner with ludicrous levels of prejudice and bias, here is yet another ex-player all too eager to stick the boot in. I'm not saying pundits should be biased towards old teams, but everyone else's ex-players seem to be, so why not ours? How have we managed to scar every single one of them?
(don't answer that)

Revolving door. A metaphorical one. City's inability to keep one manager for any considerable period of time added to their many woes for decades and prevented any chance of stability at the club. Many managers should never have got the job in the first place of course, but the odd diamond in the faecal matter rarely stayed for too long anyway.

Swales, Peter. City's own pantomime villain. He meant well, he was after all a blue, but it's fair to say there were some terrible decisions along the way, and the Granada TV documentary that followed him around makes for some painful (and I'll admit, hilarious) viewing. The footage of John Bond's interview for the manager's job stands out. Swales' reign was never going to end well and it turned out the grass wasn't greener on the other side after all. A sad time for the club and for all concerned.

Tony Coton. Yes he is on the heroes list as well, but he left us for United, so big boos all round to him. Judas!

United, Manchester. Boo, hiss (see C,F and X for further details).

Villa, Ricky. Judging by the number of times I am subjected to it, it seems Villa scored the only great goal in the history of the FA Cup. None of us will ever be allowed to forget it. The magic of the FA Cup,eh?

Weah, George. It's stretching the definition somewhat to call Weah a villain, but he is symbolic of City's buying policy for much of the dark days of decades past. Purchasing players who used to be good was something City specialised in and Weah fit the bill perfectly, bringing with him a large pay packet (£30k a week). In the end, Weah played 3 full games for City, but at least he didn't hang around for too long and thus cost the club that much money. By purchasing players in the twilight of their career the odd gem was acquired this way (Ali Bernarbia springs to mind), but plenty of duffers passed through also. I'm looking at you Steve McManaman.

X-rated tackles. Martin Buchan, Roy Keane. There's a pattern developing here.

Yeboah, Tony. His wonder-strike (you know the one) stopped the miraculous possibility of a City player actually winning goal of the season. That's all I've got. If you think that's bad….

Z – the letter Z in the club shop printing section. Hear me out, it's the biggest villain of all. Because of City's influx of Georgian players, namely Georgi Kinkladze, Kakha Tskhadadze and Murtaz Shelia, the club shop ran out of the letter Z for the back of shirts. This caused a slump in sales of shirts in the shop as Mr Kinkladze especially was the most popular name and as the club charged by the letter, was a money-spinner for the club at a time when money was scarce (hence Joe Royle's suggestion to the board to sign the enigmatic Bulgarian playmaker Vladivar Romavaronichinov). Anyway, this slump in income was crucial in City's failure to remain competitive. A succession of poor players bought on the cheap as a result of the failure to sell shirts eventually resulted in two relegations and put the club back over a decade, brought near bankruptcy and the exit from Maine Road. Few realise it was all little Georgi Kinkladze's fault.

Manchester City 1 Wigan Athletic 2: Angry Thoughts

There's little worse than waking up after fitful sleep and immediately realising that the terrible performance you had hoped was just a bad dream actually happened the day before. That was how I started the day, due to an embarrassing defeat, something I had hoped the team had resigned to history. Silly me.

A review of the match can be found elsewhere. What is gnawing away at me is the team that Pellegrini put out, the excuses, the ridiculous prioritisation of the wrong competition and not only the throwing away of a great chance of a domestic Cup double but also virtually handing Arsenal a trophy on a plate. They won't repeat our mistakes. What gnaws away more than any one defeat though is the concern that our manager is not tactically aware enough to adapt to different situations.

The whole build up to the game was wrong, though hindsight is a wonderful thing and we fans fell into the same trap. The feeling was clear - we only had to turn up to win, tricky as the opposition were, especially with the front five we were playing. The sun was out, everyone was in good spirits, and Wembley beckoned once more. And yet every fan will have seen it, the elephant in the room - Lescott and Demichelis in defence once more.

I can excuse our manager making mistakes. He is human after all, and as a new manager in a new country, should be allowed the same transition phase as other managers get, especially considering the job the guy down the road is doing.
The thing is, I expect our manager to learn from mistakes. And yet yesterday Pellegrini seemed to fall into a trap for the third time in

the same competition. Why can't he not see what was staring everyone else in the face? Lescott is a fine defender who has served the club admirably, whilst Demichelis, for all his faults, has been harshly singled out at times, but we already know that the two alongside Kompany can do a job (sometimes), but together they are simply an accident waiting to happen. Pellegrini made it worse by throwing in reserve full-backs and a reserve keeper and the rest is history. This was a defence which arguably may all start next season elsewhere. And why does Joe Hart need resting? Did that one block he made against Denmark tire him out?

Without Kompany or Zabaleta, the team loses its drive - it happens every time we don't play both of them, and it reasserts the theory that this squad does not have the depth many claim, and is reliant on a core of players. So why do it? Why?

When you narrow it down, the team put out at home to a championship side should have won with considerable ease, whatever our concerns. Pellegrini's gamble should have had few repercussions and left him with super-fit key players for the midweek game. The front five should have had a field day. But a weak defence undermines a whole team, especially when the attackers are impotent for various reasons and a couple of your big players don't play with any intensity or desire against "lesser" teams, not helped by yet another opposition manager being tactically aware and shackling City's attacking players, Pellegrini being slow to react yet again, playing wide players against a back five, which suited Wigan perfectly. With three central defenders and wing-backs restricting Richards and Clichy, City created nothing for an hour, a statistic as damming as any defensive howlers.

City strikers have now not scored between them in their last 900 minutes on the pitch. Negredo is a shadow of his former self, Aguero has not hit the ground running post-injury this time whilst Dzeko cannot even hit the target with over 90 percent of his last 35+ shots. Damning.

The annoying thing is that it was clear after ten minutes that the shape was wrong.

To state the blindingly obvious, this was an FA Cup quarter final. It should have been the undisputed priority of the week. Sadly, the only people who seem to disagree with this is our manager and our owners. The owners have earned the right to prioritise as they see fit, though it is merely speculation anyway, along with the far-fetched conspiracy theories that they are dictating line ups to the manager. Whatever, City should have fielded their strongest side, whoever the opposition was. Can Pellegrini not remember as far back as Blackburn and Watford? Did he learn nothing? To prioritise a mid-week competition that City are as good as out of over being overwhelming favourites to reach an FA Cup semi-final and another trip to Wembley is unacceptable, and he even admitted post-match to underestimating Wigan, which is staggering and poses questions not only about him but his coaching staff. The second goal in the first leg against Barcelona should have been the moment that priorities switched exclusively to domestic affairs.

And make no mistake, prioritising the Champions League is what happened. For all Pellegrini's claims that he rested players due to mid-week internationals four days before, that is what happened. To claim Kompany and Zabaleta couldn't play because of that sounds like a poor excuse to me, especially as Aguero was on the pitch. And now Pellegrini has placed enormous pressure on himself to get something from the Nou Camp, whereas a victory over Wigan could have seen us travel with relatively low pressure on the players' shoulders.

Having said all that, City should have won, with Wigan's second goal probably a foul and numerous chances spurned on a day when the ball rarely dropped in the right place as it bounced off posts or the goalkeeper's hands. The unintended bonus is not only to my bank balance but also to the fact that we will wake up on Thursday morning with City only in one competition (thoughts of beating Barcelona are the stuff of fantasy). The team need to re-focus and go for the league, though I feel that slipping away too. This is hardly all Pellegrini's fault either. The players must take responsibility, and when fighting on four fronts there is always going to be rotation, but it all comes back to what should be prioritised and playing THAT defence.

The sad and worrying thing is that whatever your think about Pellegrini's tactics yesterday, wherever you lay the blame, from perusing online yesterday evening it is clear that this result has tarnished the reputation of the Chilean. Predictable calls have emanated from a small section of spoilt reactionary fans calling for a new manager. This is par for the course with every City manager for the past 30 years or so it seems.

A minority have never truly accepted him anyway because of the man-love they still hold for his predecessor, but this surrender of a very winnable trophy has cut deep. Like any manager, as already mentioned, he has made mistakes - his poor mathematics skills in Munich was no laughing matter, his poor tactics in the home tie likewise. He has struggled to adapt at times to opposition teams that swamp midfield and shackle our team and his outburst after the Barcelona game was ill-advised. Then there was the home league game against Chelsea, where his tactics could have decided the title race. It's a learning curve, but he lost supporters yesterday. It's his job now to win them back, be flexible and adapt. A league title should do for starters.

Barcelona 2 Manchester City 1: Thoughts

So that is that – the end of City's cup competition involvement for the season, as City unsurprisingly failed to overturn a two-goal deficit from the first leg. It was always asking for a near-miracle, the history books show that, but the players couldn't have done much more. It wasn't to be.

To watch their team in the Nou Camp in the Champions League knockout stage was what many City fans had waited a lifetime for. Being stuck up in the gods in a crumbling ground may have slightly dampened the experience, but my Facebook wall and Twitter feed suggests everyone had a rather good time. Some may never come back.

The line-up was precisely what I had hoped for. With no in-form strikers there was little point playing two upfront especially considering its failure previously against the European elite. Milner would help raise the work-rate and the harrying when out of possession and he deserved a chance after his Munich heroics. The defence picked itself, as there were no other options.

With Manuel Pellegrini on the naughty step, I am ashamed to admit I wasn't aware of the name of our assistant manager. In fact, I've already forgotten it again.

City started brightly. It soon became clear they were going to threaten more than in the home leg. But Barcelona were soon looking dangerous and finding gaps. We were lucky not to concede in the period that followed.

In a nutshell, the game told us what we already knew – we are a couple of players away from competing at the highest level. There is little point lamenting the contribution of Joleon Lescott. He has performed admirably for the club and was as good as Kompany in our title-winning season, but he has never been world-class and he was always going to struggle against the likes of Messi (who wouldn't?). I admire City's resolve not to be ripped off in the transfer market from now on and thus to walk away from deals, but the failure to shore up our defence and find a top-quality partner for Kompany could cost us dear this season.

Lescott was woeful and wonderful. He could have been sent off quite easily for fouls, should have conceded a penalty, got his legs tied up in knots to gift Barcelona their first goal, but also recovered from the shakiest of starts to grow in the game and was excellent much of the time.

Much of the time isn't good enough, sadly.

There can be no complaints about the end result, as both sides missed chances, but there is still a slight frustration because City got into excellent positions on many occasions during the first half, but wasted the final pass, whilst David Silva once more displayed his Achilles Heel, namely shooting. Then to frustrate further in the second half, Valdes saved excellently and Zabaleta missed a sitter. But as I said, no complaints.

Well there is one. The referee gave one of the worst performances I have witnessed in 30 years of watching the game. It would take a well-researched thesis to pick apart what he got wrong, or even to work out which side was hardest done to, suffice to say he was staggeringly bad but certainly wasn't the reason City went out of the competition, getting decisions wrong for Barcelona early in the game that would have ended the tie as a contest, before turning his boss-eyed attention to City.

Inevitably thoughts will return to the first leg, where the tie was effectively lost. I supported the tactic of restricting Barcelona rather than being aggressive and attacking. One moment ruined that plan, but perhaps with hindsight, with Barcelona's struggles domestically and the slight bruising of their aura, Pellegrini might regret the approach at the Etihad. But hindsight is a wonderful thing, as I tend to say in every match report.

Here's a C & P of a paragraph from the match report of the first leg: nothing has changed:
As I have said all along – we are not as good as Barcelona yet. Critics will moan about how we have spent billions of pounds, but this is clearly not the complete side or squad yet and it will take time and it will take a successful academy to reach where Barcelona are. Barcelona themselves went through this same process a decade ago, revolutionizing their whole approach to how they were run and City are playing catch-up now. We also have a new manager, and like all managers, he will truly make his mark in the transfer market in his second summer transfer window. We need a top class central defender (perhaps two), we need a top class left-back and we need a top class defensive midfielder. If we make the academy produce just one good player a year, the future is brighter than we could ever imagine. Perhaps PSG are showing you can spend and be the finished article quickly, but as long as we continue to move forward there's little to complain about.

What did for City in the end was not just the deficiency in central defence, but the opposition having Messi and us having Aguero injured or semi-fit. His injuries are becoming a big concern now though. Aguero and Kompany, our two most important players, both miss too much game time, and we have suffered as a result. This is the truly frustrating aspect of the two ties for me – we never got to see how Aguero could affect proceedings. Imagine if we had got to play Barcelona without Messi – our chances of progression would have sky-rocketed. Aguero is no Messi, but his absence has hit us hard.

As for Pablo Zabaleta, I can understand his frustration, but it wasn't very professional getting himself sent off in that manner. It's going to be a weakened team for the first Champions League game next season, with all three players who started the match one card away from a suspension booked within the first half-hour.

But still the FA Cup exit hurts more than this ever could. I have written before about how the Champions League has never captivated me since we first qualified three years ago and I wrote after the first leg how we have to get used to playing these sort of games. This is not me being a bad loser. After ticket prices, the next thing that could turn me away from football in the modern game is the absolute acceptance that cheating is part of the game, that "winning" fouls is ok, that writhing around on the floor and trying to get opposition players sent off is all part of this sport we so love. I am not singling out particular teams, I am not claiming City are cleaner than others, but if this is European football then good riddance, give me domestic football any day – flawed and with some of the same problems, but nothing on the scale of what you can see abroad. The frustration is that, like when watching El Clasico, you are watching world-class players who have the ability to dazzle and entertain beyond your imagination, but who ultimately resort to cheating and histrionics in order to gain the upper hand. So, so frustrating, and sometimes football is little more than basketball with your feet.

And so the decision to rest players for the FA Cup game on Sunday has proved to be a fruitless exercise, something I could have told you on Saturday.

And now there is only one thing to fight for and the game last night may have unwittingly scuppered that fight too. Aguero's loss will be felt dearly, but what could hit the club harder this weekend is the ridiculous situation of having to play Barcelona on a Wednesday night then Hull on a Saturday lunch-time. Have no doubt – it WILL be a tired performance from City that we will do well to win. It does not matter if a player is paid £10 a week or £300,000 a week, various studies have shown the human body needs three days to recover between football matches. A fluky 1-0 win will do me just fine.

Naturally I ABHOR violence, but if hypothetically there was a player right now that I'd like to hypothetically repeatedly slam a car door against his head, hypothetically in a movie-scene-way like Vinnie Jones did, then hypothetically it would be Dani Alves. Hypothetically of course.

It's been a good week to be a United fan – your best week of the season in fact. I wonder if any of our matches will make it onto their season review DVD?

Hull City 0 Manchester City 2: Some Thoughts

What a difference seven hours can make. From feeling the title campaign was slipping away to thinking we may be favourites. A wonderful, stressful day.

What made the Hull match so important for me was that it removed many of the doubts that have festered in the minds of many City fans this week. Doubts about mentality, about the manager, about the energy levels, form and much more. Fears that the season was melting away have disappeared for the time being.

The line-up was well-received, the decision to play one man upfront surely a no-brainer. Garcia's inclusion would hopefully free Toure to be more destructive upfield.

But as I said after the Barcelona game, all I wanted was a win. Under three days after an energy-sapping game in the Camp Nou that had left Kompany and his troops' tanks empty, nothing else really mattered. And how nice to be proved wrong about how tired City would be. If they were, they certainly didn't show it, and created more chances at the end of the match than at its beginning.

The start wasn't too promising, but the first major incident could be one that defines City's whole season and perhaps bizarrely prove to be a positive. More on why that would be shortly. And so to yet another Manchester City red card, and the worse possible start to a vital game.

Despite the drivel that Shearer and Savage spouted on the Match of the Day sofa, or Neil Warnock on the pitch at half-time, it was a clear foul on Kompany by Jelavic. Kompany semi-trips himself up, but that doesn't change the fact that Jelavic quite clearly rakes his foot down his leg and is clambering all over him. Why Lee Mason suddenly thought this was acceptable considering that a hand on a player's shoulder was enough to concede free-kicks elsewhere during the match, as it always is, is a mystery. But this was just the second incompetent refereeing display of the week and little surprises anymore. The lucky City narrative was rubbish beforehand, now it seems utterly ridiculous, especially when you consider the yellow card handed out for a potential leg-breaker on David Silva later in the half, an incident by the way that Match of the Day <sigh> didn't seem worthy of showing.

Having said all that, Kompany's next action was really stupid. It is impulse of course, but surely it is better to let a player bear down on goal than get yourself sent off. Once play had been allowed to continue, there was only one outcome as soon as he tugged at Jelavic's shirt. He also dwelled on the ball for too long, strengthening Michael Cox of Zonal Marking's assertion that he always has a mistake in him, in contrast to his master-class in the Camp Nou.

At this precise moment, I had given up on the season, being the negative man I am. Everything had gone to pot, we had little chance of three points, the season was falling apart, Bluemoon was out of bounds until August. But the City team suddenly woke up and decided that this was not the end, but a rallying call. Silva's response was immediate, a beautiful curling shot. His teammates responded too and City were superb thereafter – committed, organised and resilient. The response from the two teams was the exact opposite of what you may have expected.

With the lead gained so quickly after the red card, City did not have to take risks and they did not create many chances, but almost went further ahead through Zabaleta. Only in the second half did they frustrate, namely through two huge misses from Fernandinho and Dzeko and the fear crept in that those misses would be rued. Thankfully Dzeko didn't mess up second time round.

One man gets special praise and rightly so, but let's put our hands together for the emergency defensive pairing of Demichelis and Garcia. They were both excellent, Robbie Savage pointing out that in the absence of Kompany, Demichelis stood up to be counted and marshalled the team superbly.

And one result of this was one of the best applications of the offside trap I have seen from City in many a year. Time after time the flag was raised, every decision correct.

The stats will show Hull to have had more shots on and off target and the majority of possession, but they threatened sporadically, Hart not having to make any spectacular saves.

We must of course talk about David Silva. This is rightly being lauded as one of the great performances in a City shirt, and when the team needed players to stand up and be counted, he was there, dictating play, always threatening, starting with a beautiful goal and finishing with an exquisite assist. He was mesmerising and this was the 20th time in succession that City won a game in which he scored.

And a note also about Joe Hart. I haven't mentioned him in match reports for some time, which is a good thing as it means he hasn't made any mistakes, but he deserves praise for a sustained period of consistent performances. He was strong against Hull, patrolling his area, mopping up where necessary and doing all that could be asked of him.

Speaking of which, it's only fair that after Boyd dived to try and win a penalty then spat at Joe Hart that Hart should be booked. I mean, he shouldn't have antagonized Boyd. Sections of the media will try and create a head-butt controversy now, naturally, but Hart was booked and that is that. Better luck next time guys. And just for the record, two players squaring up after a contentious moment is not the same as a manger head-butting a player on the touchline. It's not difficult to understand the difference, if you have a functioning brain.

As for the spit, I am not convinced myself that it was a deliberate act, nor am I convinced it wasn't. Slo-motion replays prove nothing and are utterly useless in such situations. Likewise, when deciding how bad a tackle is.

As for the other players, it was committed, and they gave their all, but with mixed results. As I have already said though, after the week they have had I can for once excuse any drop-off of performance. The result was everything. As an added bonus, Dzeko managed to score after 10 hours of trying.

I don't expect us all to know all the rules and regulations of the modern game (i don't), but I do expect football journalists to know that a "professional foul" carries a one-match ban, whilst only violent conduct carries a three-match penalty. Stu Brennan and the ever-neutral Mark Ogden were just two immediately reporting a three-match ban for City's captain. For a brief moment, a selection of United fans were getting giddy at the thought of him missing the derby. Hard luck. He would have missed the match if he had been previously dismissed in the league this season, as it would have meant a two-match ban. As it is, he should be nice and fresh for the match, providing he didn't break his foot destroying the Hull City tunnel.

BT Sport tried their best to create a controversy, bless them. Firstly Jake Humphrey tried to suggest an inappropriate gesture from Kompany as he left the pitch, Warnock having none of it, wisely mentioning that people would try and make an issue of it though, whilst after the match, the Joe Hart "head-butt" got the full treatment.

This was the first victory at Hull since 1909. Thanks must go to the wonderful Gary James for the link to the Daily Mail match report for that day, entitled: HULL CITY RUN UP AGAINST SOMETHING : A SALUTARY RESULT.
City are described as a strong and capable lot, and the report suggests Hull were a little excited at meeting a team with City's history.
Oh the irony.
I wonder if elsewhere a columnist previously called the Citizens the whores of world football for paying Billy Meredith 3 pence a week?
(Meredith had defected to United by this time).

Don't be rude. I said defected.

And then the bonus of a Chelsea defeat and the total breakdown of their discipline, a good day becoming one of those wonderful days where everything goes your way.

Another masterstroke from Mourinho. Obviously as the master of mind-games, where everything he does is pre-planned, the whole shambles at Aston Villa was pre-planned. The red cards and subsequent defeat takes the pressure off his team and puts it back on City, whilst by deliberately walking on the pitch he gets himself sent off, taking more pressure and focus off his team. Clever, very clever.

And now to support United. <SHUDDERS>. I think I'm going to be sick.

Sadly, and predictably, United failed to help City and succumbed 3-0 to Liverpool in a limp, pathetic display, whilst Arsenal triumphed in the north London derby, so City were still playing catch-up, though had been installed once more as favourites for the title by the bookies (just).

Harry Potter & The Theatre of Dreams

Little Eric Remi Jesper Busby Choccy Charlton Jones lay in bed, waiting for his father to say goodnight.

A Pete Boyle CD played softly in the background, containing all his favourite terrace anthems. His Phil Jones curtains had been drawn.

"To keep the monsters away," his dad joked as he ruffled his hair.

His bag was packed for school the next day. He had his Tom Cleverley pencil case, containing his Wayne Rooney rubber, Vidic pencil set and Van Persie fountain pen.

He snuggled up under his Ryan Giggs reversible duvet. His dad set the alarm on his Alex Ferguson clock.

"What time is it daddy?"

He looked at the clock.

"Anytime you want, son."

"Can you read me a story please?"

"Of course I can son. Now, which one would you like? We've got *Harry Potter and the Theatre of Dreams.* Or maybe *The Day Eric Cantona Saved The World.* Or this one, *Remi Moses: 1997 Annual* ?

The little boy looked pensive for a moment.

"Harry Potter and The Theatre of Dreams please!"

"OK, son. Though I should point out for copyright reasons, there is no mention of Harry Potter or spells or Hogwarts or invisibility cloaks in this book. It's full of magic though…"

He cleared his throat, and began……

Once upon a time, in a stadium far, far away….

The boy Potter entered the stadium, wide-eyed in amazement at the sights before him. His dad had managed to get him a ticket! They were like gold-dust, but thankfully his father had managed to get a couple off Bobby Charlton. What a nice man.

Fans hurried to their seats. Tourists took photos. Supporters threw down their pre-match noodles, thanks to Mamee, United's official noodles partner for Asia, Oceania and the Middle East.

His dad took a long swig of the nectar-like liquid in the bottle in his hand.

"Hmm, nice," said his dad. "The cool, refreshing taste of Singha, Manchester United's official beer."

"Here son, have a Mister Potato snack – they are the official savoury snack partner of Manchester United."

"What time is it daddy?"

"It's 3:52 and 30 seconds," said his dad.

"That's very precise dad!"

"I can be that precise, thanks to Bulova, United's official timekeeping partner." His dad shook his wrist to accentuate his shiny watch.

It was time to squeeze into their seats. Soon the game began. The passionate crowd swayed from side to side, the noise incredible. The opposition team looked petrified. It was an honour for them to be playing in this cathedral of football, but for now their only concern was repelling wave after wave of incessant attacks from the red-shirted heroes.

They couldn't resist for long though. No one ever could.

Rio Ferdinand swept the ball majestically out of defence. It landed perfectly at the feet of Ryan Giggs. The crowd gasped in anticipation. You could hear a pin drop.

Giggsy shimmied inside, passed it to Clevs, who fizzed an inch-perfect pass to Wellsy, who back-heeled it to the rampaging "little pea". He dinked a delightful reverse ball into the box, which was headed on by Roo. The crowd knew what was coming next.

He rose like a salmon. A manicured, tanned salmon, with gel in its gills. Some say he was on the edge of the area. Others say he was 30 yards out. Many will swear that on that fateful day, he headed the ball in from his own half.

The crowd rose as one. Cameras flashed, badges were kissed. The ball hit the back of the goal with such force that the netting was ripped from its moorings, the woodwork close to collapse.

The stadium announcer was close to tears.

"Van Persieeeeeeeee!!!!"

Two minutes later, more of the same.

Ashley Young soared beautifully, ten feet into the air, before crashing back down to earth. A triple pike. Forward roll. Reverse somersault. Full salko.

Penalty. No doubt about that.
Rooney took the ball. The opposition keeper tried to save it, but he knew it was a futile gesture. 2-0.

The crowd rose as one to salute the best-player-in-the-world-except-Messi as he milked the adoration flowing down from the capacity crowd inside this majestic theatre of football.
The ball was zipped around the pitch with a mystical majesty. The opposition players couldn't get close. They huffed and they puffed, but all in vain. They knew they couldn't compete with this amazing collection of players. Some of them couldn't even see the ball, such was the speed it was moved from player to player, from flank to flank. This was how the team always played, as it was in their DNA, part of their glorious history, some other guff, blah blah.

Wayne Rooney was given offside, and he joked with the linesman's assistant as he politely enquired as to whether he thought he had made the correct decision. The linesman's assistant replied that he thought he had, everyone laughed and continued about their business.
The United fans sang songs for the full 90 minutes, and for many hours after too. They were songs about their proud history, and their great players, and that night in Barcelona, and none about ManchesterCity because they were irrelevant and City fans sang songs about United on the rare occasion they made a noise because they were all obsessed and liars.

The vanquished manager David Moyes walked meekly into Sir Alex's office. A glass of Chateauneuf du Pape awaited him.
"Sorry I am late, was just doing some interviews."
"I don't. They disrespected me once. Get that wee drink down ya, make the day feel a bit better."
SIR Alex laughed heartily.
Moyes took a sip.
"You were magnificent today. We were lucky to only concede eight. You're definitely the best team I have ever seen, you will dominate the game for many years to come. I also love the way you give youth a chance and play football in the right way. You are

everything that is right about football."

"Aye, that's kind words indeed, We try our best. I like to stick to my Socialist principles."

"I'm just glad we only have to play you twice a season!"

Both managers laughed until their noses went purple, and agreed that United really were the best team ever…

"David, I'm sorry I had to put your fine Everton team through such an ordeal. I need a wee favour though."

"Anything sir. Just name it."

"You see, I want to be remembered as the best."

"No danger of that not being the case!" exclaimed Moyes, as he looked on with awe.

"Hold on, son. I want more than the trophies. I want my achievements to be realised AFTER I leave. For them to be rammed home to everyone, week by week. I want everyone to realise just how good I was and teach a few that are still here a damn good lesson."

"I see. And how do I come into all of this?"

"Well, it's funny you should say that. How do you fancy a change of scenery?"

And so it began…

Little Eric had a huge smile on his face.

"That's a great story, dad. I hope I can play for United one day!"

His father forced a smile.

"To be honest son, that shouldn't be too difficult…"

"So what happened after that. Did the legacy live on, like the big man Eamonn Holmes said?"

"Well that's a story for another time son. Maybe when you're a bit older, eh?"

"Ok dad!"

The father kissed his son on his forehead and tucked him into bed. He would sleep well with his head full of tales of derring-do. As he slipped out of the room, he turned off the light. But as he went to put the book away, he felt the need to see what did happen after that.

He sat down in his favourite chair with a single malt and opened the book.

EPILOGUE

It had been a tough six months for David Moyes. Another Monday morning had drawn round and he had no intention of reading the papers after United's gritty 1-1 draw at home to Hull City. Reluctantly he dragged himself out of bed and went downstairs. There was a solitary letter on the doormat. He opened it tentatively. It was from Sir Alex Ferguson. His heart skipped a beat. There was no message, but simply a poem, on the finest quality paper. As he wandered, dazed, into the kitchen, he began to read.

If you can keep your head when all about you
Are losing theirs and blaming it on you,
If you can trust yourself when all men doubt you,
But make allowance for their doubting too;
If you can wait for three points and not be tired by waiting,
Or being lied about, don't deal in lies,
Or being hated, don't give way to hating,
And yet don't look any good, nor talk too wise:

If you can dream of 4th place—and not make dreams your master;
If you can think of winning a game—and not make thoughts of winning two your aim;
If you can meet with Young and Anderson
And treat those two impostors just the same;
If you can bear to hear the inspirational team-talks you've spoken
Twisted by the press to make a trap for fools,
Or watch the things you gave your life to, broken,
And stoop and build 'em up with worn-out tools:

If you can make one heap of all your 6th place winnings
And risk it on one turn of cross-and-head,
And lose (of course), and start again at your beginnings
And never breathe a word about your losses;
If you can force your heart and nerve and sinew

To serve your owners long after they are gone,
And so hold on when there is nothing in you
Except Phil Neville who says to them: 'Hold on!'

If you can talk with dwindling crowds and keep your virtue,
Or walk with Glazers—nor lose the common touch,
If neither City nor every other visiting team can hurt you,
If all men count the crosses with you, but none too much;
If you can fill the unforgiving, depressing final minute
With sixty seconds' worth of distance run,
Yours is the Earth and every sponsorship deal that's in it,
And—which is more—you'll be a Man United manager, my son!

David rested his head against the fridge door. A solitary tear rolled down his cheek and dropped to the floor.
With only the sound of the fridge buzzing and his own heavy breath, he whispered;
"You b**ard Alex. You b***ard."

Manchester City 5 Fulham 0

Job done for City, who once more started slowly, but eventually turned the screw and could have had many more goals by the end.

A hat-trick for Yaya Toure meant he became the side's top league scorer for the season, the third goal a real collectors item, to add to two super-cool penalties.

Elsewhere Chelsea thrashed Arsenal 6-0 meaning City moved into third place. Was it now a three-horse race?

Manchester United 0 Manchester City 3

Oh boy, that felt good.

Another gut-wrenching, nerve-shredding, migraine-inducing derby day. God I hate them with such a passion.

And yet without them and the rivalry we would not have some of this club's finest moments in their recent history (what little we have of course). No 6-1, no "why always me?", no title campaign-turning 1-0 victory in April 2012, no Wembley victory on the way to our first trophy in a generation, no Aguero moment, and no cartwheeling into the office as I did this morning, grinning like the proverbial Cheshire cat. Again.
God bless derby day.

The line-up was mainly as expected, but as is often the case, with the odd curveball. Clichy was preferred over Kolarov, presumably for pace and to try and limit crosses into the box, whilst Navas was picked when many predicted Milner to start

So how to calm the nerves? Well scoring the quickest ever goal by an opposition team at Old Trafford is one way.

So City scored after 43 seconds with their third chance of the match. This was reminiscent of the Navas goal against Spurs that came after they had kicked off and Aguero had already had a shot.

And for 15 minutes City were simply untouchable. Sublime passing, interplay and control of the ball, United could barely get out of their half. The only concern was that City did not capitalise on this domination to put the game to bed.

As is often the case, the opposition got back into the game and for the rest of the half City lost the initiative, with United spurning a couple of fairly good chances.

Part of the problem was Zabaleta being battered around the pitch. I was incredulous that he managed to continue and thought it was merely a matter of time until he was substituted, as for ten minutes or so he was limping and out-of-sorts and United were finding space as a result. But this is Pablo Zabaleta of course, a man for whom no superlatives are sufficient and he soon pulled through and continued as normal, an elbow in the face little more than a slight inconvenience.

As for the two possible red cards for United: Welbeck's was a pure accident, slipping and kicking himself as he approached Zabaleta, sending himself crashing into the Argentinean. In the modern game even that is a yellow card though. Fellaini's elbow was nothing of the sort and was a clear cop-out from the referee. He had a clear view of a clear red-card offence, but decided to bottle it and award a yellow. The booking means Fellaini cannot be retrospectively punished, which I guess is even worse news for United. As it turns out, I am glad he wasn't dismissed as it is far more gratifying to win against eleven men rather than the opposition having an excuse for defeat.

Onto the second half, and it all went as well as could be expected. As soon as the second goal went in, United were a spent force. City did not go for the jugular but were sensible and protected a lead before striking a final blow near the end. It was the right thing to do, because this match was not about humiliating the opposition, but about gaining three points.

It is once more difficult to pick out players when so many perform admirably, but Silva was of course magnificent, as was Fernadinho as usual. Then there was Zabaleta, Toure and a 5th consecutive clean sheet for Demichelis. In summary, there were no weak links in the side.

Textbook from Dzeko, textbook. Having finally and unequivocally written him off a fortnight ago, he then scores a brace in a derby. With hindsight, it was inevitable.

Some stats: City now have a bigger goal difference than United have points. Norwich City have a better home record than United. Vincent Kompany won all three headers, made 4 interceptions and 3 clearances. This is the first time City have kept 5 consecutive clean sheets in the top flight since 1915. Despite me always assuming them to be consistently poor, City have scored 11 goals from corners this season, more than any other team. And for the first time in their history, four City players have scored 20+ goals in a season.

Paranoia klaxon. Well there always has to be a paranoia section after all. Martin Tyler is always unbiased, oh yes, no doubt about that. Funny then when Fellaini had a chance he screamed as if the league title was on the line, yet was strangely silent when Dzeko should have put City two up. #paranoia

Elsewhere, there was another balanced line-up in the studio and commentary box with Gary Neville and Paul Scholes in attendance. Seeing their faces afterwards made it all worthwhile (think two competitors in the finals of the World Slapped Arse Competition) and to be fair Scholes was pretty good, pulling no punches when discussing United and Arsenal.

But my, what a master class in bitterness from our red brethren on Facebook post-match. It wasn't long before a message appeared commenting on the money we have spent, and how our trophy haul was pretty poor all things considered. The "no history" tag was also attached, as expected. Funnily enough there was no further comment after I pointed out that their mid-table team cost more than City's.

You see, you could argue it's all a bit classless to be rubbing it in when United have their first bad season, but the fact is a significant section of their fans have brought all this on themselves. THAT banner, the endless City songs, the belief spread that we don't matter, the tags of bitters and liars and so much more. It would be rude not to pass comment when things don't go their way for once, because so many of them are utterly incapable of handling it well, or even dealing with the odd joke or two. The fact that I post a picture of the chosen one banner every time United mess up hasn't helped matters, but that banner is the ultimate irony for the present-day club. After counting year-after-year the lack of City success, they have now set themselves up for ridicule by displaying it, to the extent that stewards now have to protect it at the end of matches to stop it being torn down.

(Or as Bill Borrows commented," *they are haunted by a banner of their own construction that hangs at Old Trafford and mocks them every time they go to the ground or watch the game on TV. And they can't take it down…"*)

 I didn't mind that other banner, it was quite funny to be honest. Now we'll see how well they can take a joke. Or a hundred.

And if they can't take some ribbing, then tough. We've had 30 years of it and have waited a long time for this moment. Drink it in, drink in every last f***ing drop

.

As for Moyes and United, some comment is required. Well not required per se, but I'm going to enjoy wading in anyway with my penny's worth. Here is a man clearly out of his depth, but the United board/owners/fan base have got themselves into a moral quandary by perpetuating the myth that they always give managers a chance. Moyes simply isn't up to it. He is overawed by the job, is far too cautious and has not gained the respect of the players, whilst not displaying sufficient tactical nous to change things around. In press conferences he is utterly uninspiring, seemingly bereft of any fighting spirit. To say United aspire to be like City was a terrible thing for any United manager to utter, because you just don't say that, however true it may be. This comment will be another stick to beat him with until the day he departs from Old Trafford (I'll make sure of that).

This season and the summer beyond will damage United and their fan base because it will remove all the fragments of their arguments that they use to attain moral superiority and to boast about bringing through youth and doing things the right way and developing players. Of course we all know it was rubbish anyway, as they have repeatedly broken transfer records, but I will leave it to football365.com's Mediawatch section to say what we've been thinking for some while:

Mediawatch is intrigued by all this talk of Manchester United spending big in the summer. When Manchester City won the league in 2012, United still claimed a moral victory, having spent a fraction of their rival's total on transfer fees.

During the race to sign Eden Hazard that summer, Sir Alex Ferguson played up to the fans' claims, saying: "We know that City are going to spend a fortune, pay stupid money, pay silly salaries and all that. We know that happens. We can't do anything about that."

But now the champions are struggling, all that morality has suddenly been forgotten.

"This club has got spending power too," said David Moyes on Monday.

"City have got that. But I've not been told at any time that we don't have that and I do think that the club will compete (with City)."

So to recap: when United are on top, other clubs should be derided for shelling out big sums in the transfer market. But when they can't offer Champions League football and have to pay the big bucks, there isn't a problem.

At least that's cleared up.

Spot on.

The bad news is that this result, with Bayern Munich on the horizon, ensures that the chosen one's job is once more on the line – and no-one wants that. Give the man a chance!

And then another one, and then another one…

As for City, another huge, huge game looms on the horizon. At least now the team has a tiny amount of breathing space. Arsenal's title campaign has fallen to pieces, but they will surely be up for Saturday's game, and if, IF, City can repeat their performance of last night, they will have taken a huge step towards a league title I thought had gone just eleven days ago…and in City's favour, here is a squad that has clearly got its belief back.

Arsenal 1 Manchester City 1

And so to the Emirates and no match thoughts due to a vicious hangover. Opinion was divided as to whether this represented a good result, especially after City had taken the lead and controlled the game during the first half. For me it was fine, leaving us in the title race with another of our trickiest games out of the way. A victory though would have meant us being in pole position for the title, but as it turned out, there is still everything to play for.
It was the same story as ever – City spurned a chance to go top, but it was no disaster.

Manchester City 4 Southampton 1: Some Thoughts

Job done. The hardest home game remaining this season and a 3-goal victory procured, though not without difficulty and controversy. But three points was all that mattered to be honest.

A miserable day and the frustration of an early kick-off to go with it. There was little to surprise with the line-up though, except perhaps Jesus Navas once more being preferred over James Milner or even Jovetic, who seems condemned to the bench for the rest of this season.

And with the dull weather came a dull atmosphere, not helped by the underwhelming first-half performance and the time of day. I'm hardly the most vociferous of people so am not one to criticise, this is Premiership football nowadays.

City started very brightly, and helped settled the nerves with an early goal from the penalty spot. It was a penalty, but one of that are just accepted in the modern game without thought of how times have changed.

Nasri could easily have made it two and City looked in charge. But then they lost their control of the game and Southampton excelled with a wonderful exhibition of passing football that put us to shame for a while. We've been here before with Southampton of course, City once more struggling against a passing team that harries the City players, a worrying sign for next week at Anfield.

Thus when the equalizer came, also from the penalty spot, there could be few complaints. Though having said that, it was a rare shot on target for the visitors.

The second goal was clearly an illegal one, David Silva so far offside you wonder if the linesman was even watching the game. I must presume he did not see Dzeko's flick-on, but clearly City got lucky and it was a good time to do so. The flick-on completely changed the direction of the ball though, so it was a bizarre one to miss.

Still, the narrative of City being lucky/buying referees blah blah can now continue unabated. The Southampton manager claimed that it changed the course of the game, whilst the ever-neutral Mark Ogden reported that City were clinging on at the time. As already mentioned it was certainly well-timed as it came close to the break, but to say it changed the course of the game is simply unprovable. We have seen time and time again insipid first-half performance from City, followed by the team turning the screw in the second half. I have little doubt that this game would have followed the same pattern with or without the goal. For all Southampton's possession and pressure, they created few chances in either half. Away from the goals, City created all the best chances.

More to the point, City won by three goals. To claim one wrongly allowed goal has somehow handed us the game is frankly ridiculous.

And such relief to get another goal before half-time, the cross from an off-the-boil Kolarov outstanding.

And so to the second-half, where City dominated and created numerous chances, though Mark Ogden couldn't bring himself to describe any of them in his MATCH REPORT, still fuming from the incorrectly awarded goal. Apart from one half-chance for Lambert, City were rarely threatened and should have added more than one goal to their tally.

Credit once more to Javi Garcia, who came on and once more did his job, stifling Southampton's attacking intent and allowing City a greater foothold in the game. Like Demichelis, who only made one rash dive-in this time round, he improves like a fine wine week-by-week. Thankfully for the whingers amongst us, there is another play to direct our ire at.

Oh boy does ~Negredo need a goal. Any goal, off his arse, head, knee, it doesn't matter. His confidence seems shot and it is baffling how much he has gone off the boil since he came back from his shoulder injury.
But for David Silva, the opposite is the case. He is simply untouchable at the moment, another magical display from the diminutive Spaniard.

Less so from his countryman Navas. I did not think he was as bad as some others have said and I felt he was much more involved and lively in the second half, like most of the team, but the lightning-fast dashes down the wing followed by a pin-point cross have been rather less frequent than I had hoped for. He is a frustrating player but still a great player and a hard worker.

Does Yaya Toure not want to play against Liverpool? His histrionics at the end of the game were bizarre and rather stupid for a player who had already been booked for a pitiful dive. He did not cover himself with glory yesterday all-in-all, though take a mean penalty.

I didn't see clearly the first of Toure's two penalty-area falls, but a friend who sits at that end said it was a clear penalty. Sadly Match of the Day didn't deem it worthy of any coverage.

And so to the big one. By the time many of you have read this Liverpool will undoubtedly have defeated West Ham and the race for the title will remain as tight as ever. It may be defeatist of me, but a draw at Anfield will be no disaster.

Kudos to the Sun for putting Wayne Rooney in their team of the day, despite him not playing. Still, if you read The Sun, you get what you deserve.

A Look At The Title Run-In

It's the worst phrase in the English language (unless we consider "banter-bus"), but it appears it is squeaky bum time once more in the race for the Premier League title.

It also seems that some of the City fans' bums have already gone past the squeaking phase, despite what was a good week for the team. Chelsea imploded for the second away match in a row, so in comparison to them the week has been overwhelmingly positive. After all, which of us City fans would not have taken four points from two tough away games? I would have bitten off your hand for that and perhaps the odd extra limb too.

The reason for negativity in some quarters is of course Liverpool, the juggernaut rolling on fuelled by their history and destiny and the Kop sucking the ball in the net and all that. City can't compete (#sarcasm). The thing is, their week has been much, much easier. They had two home games, one against a team utterly out of form near the foot of the table and one against the most shambolic team in the league right now, a team whose league position could not be more deceptive. It is no surprise that Liverpool gained on City this week, nor is it a disaster. In fact, it could have been much worse. Liverpool fans seem to think it's in the bag, bravely singing about winning the league without fear of superstition/jinxes/other occult occurrences derailing their bid by predicting they may win something. City fans have been rather more negative, never wanting to express the possibility of a league title via the medium of group songs. Even when City won the league, I was horrified at the Champions scarves being proudly adorned by many outside the ground prior to the QPR game. This was a level of cockiness and bravado in fans that I had not witnessed before and I will admit – I didn't like it. As it turned out, it was their fault we almost messed it up. Liverpool fans would do well to take this on board.

But back to the run-in. The fact is that City have got through two of their really tricky four away games remaining resulting in the situation that they will go clear at the top if they win their two highly winnable games in hand at home to Sunderland and Aston Villa. The problem is that City are always playing catch-up. Some might argue it is better to have the points on the board and what's more, Liverpool are certainly on a roll.

But for defeat at Anfield to be really disastrous there is the assumption that Liverpool are to continue winning every game until the season-end. They are capable of this, but it would mean pulling off the longest run of consecutive victories in Premier League history, fourteen in total. If they do that, then good luck to them, they deserve the title, especially as it will include defeating their two title rivals along the way. It only takes an injury to the likes of Suarez though for the whole picture to change once more. The bookies see things rather differently to the pessimistic minority of Citizens. City are still odds-on to win the title, with Liverpool 15/8 and remarkably Chelsea can be backed at 8/1 despite the fact that yesterday afternoon they headed the table. The most important factor of all though is that you can't predict these things, thus making this whole article redundant. No one could have envisaged that Chelsea would sandwich a 6-0 hammering of Arsenal with defeats to Aston Villa and Crystal Palace.

You can over-analyse too. At the weekend I found myself considering how Crystal Palace's victory over Chelsea was a double bonus as it could mean they are safe from relegation by the time they play City, thus meaning they may not try as hard. Likewise, if West Ham could somehow defeat Liverpool next week. By defeating Sunderland this week ,West Ham are virtually safe from relegation and thus can play with more freedom and less pressure, which by my calculations makes them 7% more likely to defeat Liverpool. When looking at City's fixtures though, by worrying about the "big" games like Liverpool and Everton away, there is a danger of overlooking the threat posed by the aforementioned Crystal Palace or a dangerous Southampton next week.

This race to the line was fairly predictable. It was widely acknowledged at the beginning of the season that this could be a very interesting season indeed. City and United would be title-contenders once more (ahem), Spurs had spent £100m strengthening the side after the departure of Gareth Bale, Arsenal and Chelsea would fight for the title as always, whilst Liverpool and Everton would be looking to push on and challenge for the Top Four. It hasn't panned out quite as we all probably expected, but it has certainly been a fierce fight for the title and there will be further twists – that is guaranteed.

So in conclusion, let's take it one game at a time, try and remain calm about something over which none of us has any influence over and enjoy the ride. Simple eh?

And so onto the trickiest of all tricky away games - Liverpool. Here's a Q & A I did for Redmen TV prior to the game:

Do you see Sunday's meeting at Anfield as the title decider, or is it more complicated than that?

The media and especially Sky Sports will portray it as that, but no, it is not. The result can heavily weight the odds in favour of one team, but it is not over whatever happens. It is not a title decider, especially with Liverpool yet to play Chelsea. For Liverpool though, winning is fairly important. For City, not losing would be seen as a good result and a draw for example would leave them as favourites, just, for the title.

City started slowly, amidst a tight table back in autumn, but you must be delighted by your side's emphatic return to form after last season's meagre title defence?
Indeed. The problem last season was the mood around the place as much as the results – that is why Mancini went, because he had alienated virtually every member of staff. With Pellegrini in charge, the focus is merely on the football and not fights on the training ground. I am of course happy with the form. It has not been perfect and there are certain types of sides that City struggle against, but all in all it has been a big step forward this season.

You both seemed to be enjoying the new approach under Manuel Pellegrini back in December – nearly a full season in now, what are your thoughts on the impact of his system of individual expression being preferred to systematic constraint?
Well it is certainly easier on the eye. Every fan wants their team to play attractive football, so in that respect it is very pleasing indeed and it has led to some of the best movement, approach play and

goals I have ever witnessed. I still have small concerns over the defence, namely that the system allows chances for the opposition, due to City's attacking instincts and the lack of a true defensive midfielder on the pitch when the unfairly maligned Javi Garcia isn't on the pitch (i.e. most of the time).

A potential quadruple was reduced to a treble and then a double during February and March – what are your reflections on your Club's departure from the FA Cup and the Champions League?

Talk of a quadruple was ridiculous and certainly wasn't coming from City fans. The squad was never good enough to compete on all fronts and the odds of it happening were longer than Tom Cleverley winning PFA Player of the Year. The FA Cup defeat was the only hard one to take, and it was very hard to take. City had a golden chance to win another trophy and they blew it, the line up against Wigan easily strong enough to win, but the feeling prevailed that Pellegrini and the players had prioritised the much more difficult task of beating Barcelona away in the following week. For me, the FA Cup should have been the overriding priority.

The Champions League exit naturally directed more criticism City's way and perhaps Pellegrini was a bit too cautious and gave Barcelona too much respect, but hindsight is a wonderful thing and I agreed with his approach at the time. Without the red card and penalty, things may have panned out differently. Either way, the campaign was an improvement on previous years and the competition is yet to capture my imagination yet anyway, so I lost little sleep over our exit.

Whilst the signs were encouraging, the jury was still out on your summer signings when we last met – what are your thoughts, nearly four months on, and do you have any regrets about not picking anybody up in January?

The signings have overall been a success, and certainly a huge improvement on the previous summer's panic acquisitions. Fernandinho has been the jewel in the crown, whilst Alvaro Negredo was superb for five months but has completely lost his form recently. I love Jesus Navas and he has contributed greatly, but he can frustrate and with his pace should be destroying more full-backs than he does. Martin Demichelis was a cheap purchase intended as backup who has probably played far more than expected and has been the subject of widespread criticism, but he has improved immeasurably recently and contributed to five consecutive clean sheets in March. The big disappointment has been Stevan Jovetic merely because he has been injured, but what little I have seen of him makes me think he will be world-class if he stays fit.

We've dropped just 7 points apiece since last meeting – any particular highs and lows during that period that you consider pivotal?
If City don't win the league the pivotal losses were mostly in the first half of the season. The away losses to Cardiff, Sunderland and Aston Villa have left City playing catch-up all season, not helped my Joe Hart's mad dash out of his area in the last minute at Stamford Bridge. The only pivotal loss this year was the home defeat to Chelsea, at a time when I thought they were the true contenders for the title. The pivotal loss may still be to come of course.

It seems unnecessary to ask about your hopes, so what are your expectations for the remaining seven league matches?
To win the league - that would be nice. To actually go to Merseyside and put in two good performances would be a good start, and quite a novelty. I hope United can qualify for the Europa League too – their fans deserve a few Thursday night matches.

Are there any stories around the Club/amongst the fanbase that the mainstream may have missed out on?
There's one about our owners you definitely won't know about. In conjunction with the city council, the club are helping with the construction of housing for 7000 people in a stretch of rather derelict and down-trodden land lying between the club and the city centre. The fact is that for all the criticism of City's owners, the investment in players is just a small part of their total investment in the city as a whole.

What have you made of Liverpool under Brendan Rodgers this season?
You cannot be anything but impressed. To have Liverpool challenging for a title this season is some achievement and the style of play is very easy on the eye. Liverpool have been helped by having few other distractions but few would have predicted this scenario, especially as I felt pre-season this was going to be one of the strongest leagues in many a year with the likes of Spurs and Everton challenging the traditional order. This has hardly been done on a shoestring budget as some have suggested, but nevertheless it bodes well for a brighter future whatever happens this season. I also realise how much it would mean in the same year you hopefully get "justice".

Turning attention to Sunday – how do you expect the sides to approach the game, how do you see it playing out, and would you care to offer a prediction?
I would expect City to play with a solitary striker up front with Silva in the hole. Milner may get a call-up for his work rate and to protect Zabaleta, whilst Clichy will probably start ahead of Kolarov. Aguero may start, but I fear he will be on the bench. Liverpool will come at us hard and if City can weather the early storm and our defenders can keep their hands behind their back when defending the penalty area, then I am quite confident. I've no idea how the game will go though – anything could happen. I will plump for 2-2.

Liverpool 3 Manchester City 2: Some Thoughts

Ah, that horrible feeling waking up the day after an important defeat. A Monday morning and a league title slipping away. Wonderful.

I had tried my hardest to stay off the internet last week, the tidal wave of Liverpool sycophancy from the media unbearable. It barely seemed worth City turning up. My work colleague said he watched the hour leading up to the match on Sky Sports and you wouldn't have known who Liverpool were playing. City were gate-crashers to a private party. And as much as the title may have slipped away, it grates me almost as much at missing out on stopping this avalanche of sentimental, mawkish bull****. Oh I wanted a win SO much.
(and just to make it absolutely clear, as sadly it is necessary nowadays, all the above is not an attack on Liverpool fans, but media coverage).
Eventually the day was here though, with the accompanying butterflies. This was not the title decider being portrayed by many, but it could tilt the race hugely in one team 's favour.

The club had done well to keep out of the media spotlight in the days preceding the match, as Brendan Rogers speed his usual pseudo-bollocks. Let the football do the talking and all that.

Unfortunately mini-hysteria erupted the day before the match as Vincent Kompany limped off the training ground. Bullets were sent in the post to Micah Richards (u r waste off space Micah please go now #gudriddance). Why do things like this never happen to the opposition?
The negative 93% of me thought this was just part of the Liverpool story that would see them sweep to glory. No injuries, everyone fit, on a roll. Meanwhile we are sweating as usual over key players. I was right.

The team line-up was announced, late, no doubt due to a coin-toss over whether Kompany played, and as it turned out he did, though the elation at this was in the end misguided, his inclusion proving decisive for all the wrong reasons. Just as decisive was the inclusion of Navas over Milner, something every fan in the land could see was risky if not outright wrong. This was not Navas' type of game. It was certainly Milner's. It was one of those team selections that just seemed obviously wrong.

The minute's silence was impeccably observed, as I knew it would be. A time to remember is often tainted by the anxiety that someone will break the silence and there has been a recent trend to clap instead of remaining silent. For many occasions this is fine, but I think silence is appropriate for the anniversary of the Hillsborough tragedy.

There is of course a rivalry between Manchester and Liverpool which often crosses a line. Football is also tribal and we basically hate each other for whatever spurious reasons we settle on. We portray scousers as over-sentimental souls who would lay a wreath next to a dead chicken (true story).

The Hillsborough tragedy transcends all rivalries. What happened that day should never be forgotten by any football fan. For any match-going fan over 35 or so, it could have been you or me that day. Liverpool fans' persistent references to that day in 1989 ever since is not only acceptable but necessary, because as tragic as the day itself was, what happened afterwards is despicable beyond words and crucial to why coverage is on-going. To see your loved-ones never return from a football match (including many children) is unbearable on its own, but to then have their names smeared for years afterwards is beyond the pale. Until the reputation of every one of the 96 Liverpool fans is totally clean and the whole truth about what the authorities did thereafter, then the fight must continue. If you want to moan about the lack of coverage of Heysel or the Bradford fire then I cannot stop you, but the Hillsborough story is not just about the tragedy itself but about justice.

And so to the match. The supporters were "unleashed", which basically meant booing every time City got the ball. How twee. This seems to have wound up a lot of City supporters, but I didn't have a problem myself, though it all seemed a tad pointless. It was hardly intimidating, but the fans were trying to ram home the advantage of playing at Anfield, so they can do as they see fit.

All week the tactic seemed obvious - see out the first twenty minutes or so and we would be in a great position to win the match. That went well. Quite simply, City were appalling for the first half hour. The defence was all over the place, players being pulled out of position at will, the team could not keep hold of the ball and all the best-laid plans went out of the window. It was frustrating to see the team succumb to what was an obvious tactic from Liverpool (not that I have all the answers on how to combat it), and City were soon two goals down, and it could have been more. Kompany and Hart share blame for the first goal, Kompany for the second. At a crucial time our captain had a nightmare day, making you wonder if he was fit to be on the pitch. You need runners, stamina and work-rate to combat Liverpool, not a player running on a jarred knee.

To add to the woes Yaya Toure limped off, possibly ending his season. Everything that could go wrong was going wrong. In a way it could have helped us as that first half was not "his type of game" and at least Garcia could help protect the back four, but he could have had such an influence in that second half. The only question is why Milner didn't come on then and when he did come on, why was it four minutes into the second half? Very strange.

After half-an hour I was ready to go home and hibernate until the World Cup. But City edged their way back into the game and should have reduced the deficit before the break. A blatant penalty was of course ignored by Clattenburg, Fernandinho's weak shot was well-saved and a ball was cleared off the line.

And that trend continued into the second half. City's first goal was the goal of the day, and whilst the equalizer was rather fortuitous, it was reward for City's dominance. There and then, City were in control. Liverpool were as shambolic as we were at the start and control of the title race was there to be grasped.
And then…

I can always excuse a shanked clearance or an individual mistake. It happens, and it happened for City at the worst possible time. But the key moment was what should have been an easy pass to David Silva to complete a remarkable comeback and put City 20 minutes away from a glorious victory. Silva stabbed the ball wide when it seemed easier to score, not helped by an over-hit pass from Aguero and the rest is history.

Soon after City were behind to complete Kompany's misery and sadly could not come back strongly and exert any significant pressure, though Skrtel still found time to get two players in a headlock and punch the ball away. We were never going to get a penalty.

As for Suarez, he did what he did best, which is basically cheat, dive and fake injury. If he ever signs for City I will be in a very difficult position about supporting him in a blue shirt. His dive behind Demichelis' back was pathetic, only outdone by him writhing around on the floor, and then berating the referee, who of course was never going to hand out a second yellow card. I haven't seen 100 replays and have seen it claimed there was contact or that he was just evading the lunging Demichelis, but for pretending he was seriously injured alone he is a cheat so deserves no sympathy. I haven't seen a single replay of his later penalty appeal, but perhaps that was one penalty that Liverpool themselves should have had. I wasn't sure at the time, and am not now.

With defeat though comes so many annoyances.
 We all knew how Liverpool would fly out of the block, so why weren't the team prepared?
Why allow Kompany to play if not 100%? You can't carry players in games like this.
Why Navas over Milner?
Why is Skrtel allowed to do what he wants at corners?
Why has the Premier League's worst diver never been booked for diving?
(maybe he has?)
How did we lose a game we were in complete control of?

But at least we know for sure that this City team has pedigree. Few teams from the past would have had the fight, skill and nous to come back into this game and take control.

The decision to bench Aguero proved correct. He did little once on and would have struggled even more from the start.

For a team that has been widely labelled as lucky we got none in the biggest game of the season. From our captain injuring himself the day before the game, to our powerhouse midfielder going off injured early on, to Aguero not being match fit, to the refereeing performance and so on.

The result opens the Pellegrini debate again. It seems only other managers are allowed transition periods, but those early away defeats always looked likely to come back and bite us on the behind. Greater criticism is directed his way for some of his team selections, one in particular this weekend. I have been happy with what Pellegrini has brought to the club, but he has been far from perfect. Let's hope he grows with time. Many have opined that with Mourinho we would be winning the treble this season, but the argument is irrelevant. Our owners ditched Mancini and hired Pellegrini for very clear reasons that some seem still tot his day incapable of grasping and our owners who have invested over a billion in the club do not want "his sort" as the club's figurehead. They made the club what it is, so it is their call – they are not just concerned about results.

This is what Matt Stanger over at football365.com has to say about him:
There appears to be a consensus that City will have underachieved should that prove to be the case, but I would vehemently disagree with that position.
Firstly, there has been enormous improvement across the board at the Etihad - notably in the club mounting a much more convincing league challenge than last year, winning silverware, and progressing to the knock-out rounds of the Champions League for the first time - which included beating Bayern Munich at the Allianz Arena in the group stage. Were it not for City's investment in the summer, it would be agreed that the club have enjoyed an excellent campaign.

However, just because City spent significant funds in the summer, it doesn't mean we should have expected them to walk the title. It takes time to build a team and fashion a playing style - especially one so different to the previous regime - and Pellegrini has taken huge strides in this regard. When City play at their peak, there is no-one better in the Premier League, and the frequency of their top performances is only going to increase as the manager has more time with the squad.

Perhaps the most telling aspect of Pellegrini's tenure is that the biggest problems for City - namely the lack of back-up in defence and a significant drop in quality from Sergio Aguero to Edin Dzeko - are now more apparent than ever before. With City forced to play at their attacking limits - which wasn't always the case under Roberto Mancini - theses issue have become more obvious. The first is likely to be solved by further recruitment in the summer; while Stevan Jovetic and Alvaro Negredo will offer more variety in attack if they can remain fit for a full campaign. Demichelis was superb. Just remember that.

And so onwards. This title race feels lost, but it far from being so. City must now just take stock and concentrate on two highly winnable home games. And pray.

Too harsh over the Liverpool love-in? Over to you Ian Herbert (Telegraph):
"It felt like the triumph of a development club over a spending club. Millionaires over billionaires."

The week didn't get much better, sadly….

Manchester City 2 Sunderland 2: Some Thoughts

How painful was that? For all the talk of bogey teams and teams fighting for their lives, I did not foresee significant problems with last night's match, even less two minutes into the game. In the end,

City had to scrape a draw due to a keeper howler and the title campaign appears to be on its last legs.

And so to the team-line up on a balmy sunny evening, which saw a return of Aguero and Negredo upfront and Milner in place of the semi-injured David Silva. As is always the case when we underperform against "lower" teams, the team put out was more than good enough to win the game comfortably.

One beautiful dummy by Negredo later and City gained an early lead via Fernandinho and we all sat back to enjoy a feast of football.

Which never transpired of course. Sunderland should have been level within a quarter of an hour as City laboured for virtually the rest of the match. The whole team looked jaded, the passing was always a yard out and the fight was lacking. The second half brought little improvement and it was little surprise really when Sunderland scored two quick goals. That Nasri miss at the end is another key moment in throwing this title away, but as the equalizer was rather fortunate and Sunderland had spurned good chances themselves, no one could really argue with the result.

Still, as the crowd didn't seem arsed by the match, many not even bothering to turn up, it seems harsh to criticise the team. I'm no better so include myself in all of this, but it cannot help to have such apathy flowing down from the stands. We just expect to see the team win then go home happy it seems. Of course the players are paid rather well to do a job come-what-may.

James Milner, who I and many others would have been happy to have in the team was the poorest of the lot. He dovetails beautifully with Silva, less so without him and now with hindsight is there an argument that Navas and Milner were selected for the past two games the wrong way round? It's easy this management lark, but City missed pace last night against a dogged deep-lying opposition. Again.
(though I presume Navas was injured? I have heard nothing about his exclusion)

What has really done for this team is that at the crucial stage of the season the team resembles a bunch of hung-over Sunday League players. The fitness of too many players has deserted them at the worst possible time and the squad depth is not sufficient to paper over the cracks. Pellegrini deserves criticism for many things, but he hasn't had many breaks either. Losing your world-class striker for half a season does not help, and the other absentees are too many to mention. Every team has injuries of course, but City seemed to have timed theirs badly, and the resultant fall-off thus resembles your average Arsenal season.

To add to all of this, City are still over reliant on a key spine of players and seem incapable of functioning without them.

Psychology:. Manuel Pellegrini admitted after the game that the players were mentally tired after the Liverpool game. This isn't really good enough and will predictably attract much ire from City fans. We had hoped that the defeat at Anfield would bolster a fighting spirit in the squad, whereas the opposite seems to have happened. The players must take some responsibility for this, they are paid well to overcome adversity, but Pellegrini too is responsible for firing this team up and on this occasion he failed. The accusations will continue to fly that he is "too nice" etc...
The other angle is that the team on a roll in the league and looking like clinching their first title on a generation sought help to deal with such matters. Ronnie O' Sullivan, a man with many demons, successfully sought help from the same man. That man is the psychologist Steve Peters. No doubt many will dismiss using such avenues as lunacy, the sort of thing needed for people with serious problems, but other sports have already realised the importance of psychology and if our manager cannot fire up the players then he needs to hire staff as he would in other areas to help himself out. There is no stigma involved in hiring a psychologist, it should be the first signing of the summer. Of course the odd red-top may see it differently as Roy Hodgson found to his cost recently, but who cares?

It needs repeating, but this title challenge was essentially lost in the early months of the season, not now, when City suffered a number of away defeats as the new manager bedded in. City's form since then has been Championship-winning form, but the early defeats have left little room for error. Chelsea on the other hand can lose at Crystal Palace and Aston Villa within a fortnight and still be in the race.

What really grates is the now daily harking back to our glorious leader Roberto Mancini. I am disappointed and down about the team's performance last night and the week as a whole, but what is actually frustrating me more is some of our fans, not the players or manager. We all let off steam and say stupid things after a poor result and we all have the same right to an opinion. If you are a regular on social media you will be used to sifting through some ridiculous viewpoints by now, so it is hardly worth regurgitating some of them. What I cannot stay silent on though is Roberto Mancini.

The claims that Mancini would have done better this season or would have won two trophies by now or whatever is speculation that cannot be proven and has little basis in fact anyway. It is an argument that conveniently ignores last season and more to the point ignores the rather important fact that a year later some City fans still have trouble grasping – Roberto Mancini was not sacked due to results, so what he would or would not have done this season is irrelevant. And if you still pine for the Italian, do you not think it's time to move on, because he is gone now, he isn't coming back and our owners who put a billion pounds into the club and made all this possible did not want him at the club anymore. He will always have a place in our hearts, but what is done is done. If you are a City supporter, then support the new manager-he deserves time to bring more trophies to this club. If next season follows a similar trend then I will admit we have real problems.

There is one thing worse of course – and that is the tedious calls from a minority for Pellegrini to go now. It feels like I've spent the majority of the past five years defending whoever our current manager was. Looking back through the archives, I found three articles defending Mancini against the "out brigade" from his first two years in office, including this time two years ago of course. Nothing changes. There is clearly a section of our fan-base so utterly spoilt by the last few years they now think we have a divine right to win multiple trophies each season. They have learnt nothing from history and think changing the manager will fix everything, and will then start moaning once more when the new manager doesn't start playing perfect football within six months. Anything less than capturing the big trophies is abject failure, fuelled by the media-led myth that our squad is so much better than everyone else's and heads must roll and serious questions must now be asked.

Football thankfully doesn't work like that. If the best team always won then no one would watch the games. I'm not trying to argue that this means criticism is not allowed, that's ridiculous, just that the reaction when things don't go our way is absurd from a select few. We're no better than THEM.

To be honest, the lines are too fine in football to write-off Pellegrini or do the opposite. If David Silva had finished an easy chance on Sunday or if Nasri had not missed an absolute sitter at the death last night we'd still be right in the title race. If both had scored as expected, we'd be the favourites. As Mancini might say – is football.

Now it is truly out of our hands. We need Steven Gerrard to succumb to dehydration from all his crying this week, Mourinho's mind-games to confuse his own team so much they implode and for City to win their final 5 games. Stranger things have happened, but not many. As unlikely as it may seem (and it is unlikely), that scrambled point at home to Sunderland may prove crucial in a few weeks, as it did two seasons ago. Unfortunately, that time we were only up against one team, not two.

Manchester City 3 West Brom 1: Some Thoughts

Job done. Can't ask for more than that at the "business end" of the season.

I hate that phrase.

There was predictably a downbeat approach to the match, not only due to the feeling that the title had slipped away but also due to the ridiculous scheduling over a bank holiday weekend of a game at 8pm on a Monday night.

The day started on a bad note with the news breaking that David Moyes was on the verge of being sacked. Devastating news, but it was good whilst it lasted. As City fans we had always joked that we needed Moyes to do a bit better so that he did just enough to keep his job – hence he needed to win at Everton and he needed to qualify for the Europa League to mess up next season for them too. He has failed on all counts. Still, surely it's the United way that Moyes now gets to choose his successor? Let's hope Ian Holloway's phone is ringing as we speak.
Let's also not forget that United have a proud history of standing by one manager. It turns out they're not any better than the rest of us after all. Who knew?

GIGGS IN!

But back to City. The team had few surprises with the rumour that Silva was fit enough to play one game a week, but Navas, Toure and of course Nastastic were still injured. As per usual, it was a team more than capable of winning, comfortably.
And like Sunderland the week before, a quick start, an early goal and everything looked fine. City's attitude seemed better than the previous home match and the team were well on top. A second soon followed after the ball fell nicely for Aguero, but the sloppiness of recent weeks was still there as shown by West Brom's goal, all resulting from an appalling free-kick routine from City that certainly hadn't perfected on the training ground.

After that though, City were generally dominant. They were extremely dominant in possession and generally comfortable and dangerous in attacking areas, though West Brom were always a threat on the break. After Demichelis became the third Argentinean to score on the night, there was little threat from the away team thereafter, though City wobbled in the minutes after Silva was stretchered off, their focus temporarily gone.

It's just a shame that City saw to see out the match rather than go for more goals, as goal difference could still be a factor at the end of the season, unlikely as that seems. As is often the case, there was a reluctance to shoot but instead the frustrating tactic of trying to walk the ball into the net.

As for the atmosphere, it was better than against Sunderland (it couldn't be any worse) as there was a reaction by some of the crowd to the lethargy of the previous week. It was hardly brilliant, but at least there were occasional attempts by pockets of the crowd to fire things up. Still, for a team still in with a chance of winning the title it was generally poor and whilst the kick-off time will have prevented some people attending, it is rather pathetic of those who have just given up on the season and stopped going. It's a free world though, they can of course do what they want and those that did go can leave when they want (more on that later).

As for the away supporters, they could have come in a taxi etc etc. Their boycott of the game due to exorbitant ticket prices has been well documented and should be applauded. Boycotting is the only way to get things to change in my opinion. Prices are way too high, we all know it, and something needs to be done. Financial Fair Play rules, which result in clubs seeking to squeeze every penny of income they can out of fans, have only made matters worse.

So for such an underwhelming season, it seems barely possible that with three goals last night, City broke the all-time goal-scoring record for a top-level side in all competitions in a season.

More redemption for Martin Demichelis, who has shown his worth over the past couple of months and once more proves that it is best to give players a chance occasionally rather than writing them off after a few months. In the first half he completed 100% of the 26 passes he attempted.

The injury to David Silva however pretty much summed up City's season. I had hoped we could have got a 4th goal and subbed him, but it wasn't to be and another player joins the injury list. My concerns as he was stretchered off was not mainly for City but for the player himself – it would be cruel if he were to miss the World Cup. It's all speculation, but it seems he may be only out for a few weeks, as a scan is carried out. Either way, he surely won't figure for City again this season and without the one player who has made City tick over recent weeks, the job of catching Liverpool has just got even tougher.

And for once, I left early, for which the blame lay squarely in one place – Metrolink, the laughing stock of all transport systems. To be sure of getting home I had to leave as the injury time board went up, all because our wonderful tram operators think it perfectly acceptable to be running a bank holiday service on the night of a football match, leaving me 40 minutes from match-end to get a tram from St. Peters Square (because, just to make things even more fun, Metrolink had also decided not to run any Altrincham trams through Piccadilly for the second match in a row). They are really are a shambles on a daily basis.

And so on to another Super Sunday, where the season could effectively end. It's time to change the habit of a lifetime and root for Chelsea, though I cannot see them winning myself. I am not sure City will either to be honest, but here's to a summer of consolidation and a good crack at it all again next season. Chin(s) up.

(I could have removed that last paragraph – but I didn't. 20/05/14)

An Open Letter To Ed Woodward

Dear Ewar Woowar,

Because I am exasperated and a bit needy I am writing this open letter to you that you will never read, because you don't spend your days trawling United message boards reading about fans slagging you off, but I'm doing it anyway as I consider myself overly-important and a voice for the fans.

Right now United fans are feeling raw. We feel dazed and confused. We feel a sense of freedom also, but there are thoughts swimming round our heads and questions we need answering. I hope you will take the time to answer them and don't have to jet off somewhere on some urgent-but-ultimately-futile transfer business.

My first feeling is one of disappointment. You see, United don't sack managers. Yes there was Wilf McGuinness. Yes, I guess there was Ron Atkinson too. Look, I know 3 of United's last 7 permanent managers have been dismissed within 19 months, but that was different – their positions were untenable. United had to act unlike the United way.

As Ollie Holt said the other day:

Manchester United made the right decision when they sacked David Moyes. But they lost something, too.

They lost a big part of their identity. They lost their sense of separateness. It was a separateness that was built on a lot more than just being English football's pre-eminent force for the last 20 years.

So United have lost what set them apart. Now they are just like all the rest.

Managers will come and go every couple of years .Like they do at Chelsea. Like they do at Manchester City.

When they sacked Moyes, United lost their adherence to permanence and checked into the asylum.

Perhaps if he had stayed for another couple of years, a fans' dream team of Gary Neville and caretaker boss Ryan Giggs would have been able to take charge.

Those two understand instinctively what makes a club like United tick in a way that Moyes never did.

Now may be just too soon for them to take it on a permanent basis but if they are given an opportunity after Moyes' successor has come and gone, maybe the idea of a United dynasty can be revived. The vision, surely, would be a Giggs-Gary Neville spearhead, with Paul Scholes, Nicky Butt and Phil Neville backing them up.

That's the new boot-room. And that could last.
Until then, it's the lucky dip.

OLLIE GETS IT, ED.

Or take Paul Hayward:
There is a Manchester United way, based on attacking, creativity, domination, spirit. Ferguson once said: "I never picked a team without thinking I was going to win the game." The opponent was a dartboard, especially at Old Trafford, where the badge, the history and the will of the crowd were all harnessed to maintain a domineering mindset.

And then there are the rumours. A club of United's size always generate rumours of course, and their global appeal just fans the flames. But can you please confirm the following rumours to be false:
At one team meeting, Giggs lost his patience with Moyes, shouting "this is a waste of time!" before grabbing Robin Van Persie's house keys and storming out of the training ground. He didn't return until the following day, looking dishevelled.
Is Alex Ferguson really helping choose the next manager? When I once worked at Wetherspoons I convinced the manager to put a boiled egg, cabbage and cow brain stew on the menu. I was never allowed anywhere near the kitchen again.
This is the man who recommended Alex McLeish to Aston Villa. The man is clearly taking the ****.

Are the players backing Giggs as the next manager just so they know where he is?
From perusing the media, it appears the Class of 92 have super-powers. What are they?
(I presume Paul Scholes' is invisibility)

Have you got a picture of United's DNA?

Will you just f***ing sign Wesley Sneijder?!

Is it true Toni Kroos had a picture of Neil Webb on his bedroom wall as a nipper?

Was Moyes' biggest mistake was not understanding the United way? Barcelona might style itself as "more than a club", but United are "more than a club than the club that are more than a club" and I think Moyes struggled to grasp this. Gary Neville once commented that United was not a physical entity but more a concept and a state of mind, but I feel he was rather understating the case.

They are of course a plc, but this could easily mean prudence:legends:class.
Privileged, loved, cult.
Poborsky, Law, Cleverley.

United, said Neville, rallied against modern football and all it stood for. They were hipsters before hipsters were invented and they had style and elegance before the sport itself knew the meaning of the words. "More soul than a Motown nightclub," Matt Busby once said of his beloved club.
He knew.
He understood.
He got it.
Will our next manager GET IT? The United way? The DNA?
Under Ferguson, every player understood this, however crap they were. Even Anderson.
Now, the players seem bewildered. Phil Jones looks frightened and confused.
So basically, sort yourself out. We didn't sign up to this. I'm supporting FCUM in the meantime.

An Open Letter To Ed Woodward from A City Fan.

I am writing to express my disgust at your rather impetuous decision to sack David Moyes this week. This is a decision that has saddened and angered me for a number of reasons:

1)   I thought your club gave managers a chance. It's in your DNA and all that. Thus, by removing David Moyes from his post you have ripped the soul from the club and undermined your founding fathers' principles. To make matters worse, you have upset Ollie Holt – he thought you were better than this.

2)   By getting rid of David Moyes, there is now a realistic possibility that United will be managed by someone who knows what he is doing. This worries me.

3)   Thirdly, and this is by far the most important point: a couple of months ago my friends and I grouped together to purchase a banner honouring United's new manager. I have enclosed a picture below.

As you can see, a lot of thought went into the design and a fair bit of money too. Banners are not cheap, as Tufty will tell you (the ****). Anyway, we favoured this particular design because we felt it was a banner that would be relevant for years to come. Safe in the knowledge that United are a class above any other club and that it is part of your soul, your essence, your being, that you give managers time, we went ahead with the purchase. With a six-year contract handed to Mr Moyes, we were confident that he would see this contract out – that's the United way. It thus seemed a safe investment, and we looked forward to upping the number with each passing year.

You can imagine my surprise this morning then when news emerged of David Moyes being close to the sack. At first I dismissed it as spurious media-stirring, but then the news broke that it was all true and the chosen one had gone.

I am, quite frankly, disgusted.

I'll get to the point – you owe me £300. The banner is now worthless, and I hold Manchester United wholly responsible for this. How do you intend to rectify the situation? Would a cheque payable to me be acceptable?

Please let me know of your intentions at the soonest opportunity. I look forward to corresponding with you and rectifying this unfortunate situation. After consultation with my friends I am willing to accept the offer of helping choose your next manager as an alternative form of compensation, or at least a coffee with you Ed to pass on some of my thoughts.

Regards.
Harold Hodgkin
P.S. Would you be interested in taking the banner off our hands to display in your museum?

Crystal Palace 0 Manchester City 2: Some Thoughts
(Champions-Elect Liverpool 0 Chelsea 2)

Oh god, here we go again.

(I wasn't expecting that)

And so Mr Negative himself (me) sat down and prepared himself for the end of season party, the day the title campaign was officially surrendered. A weakened Chelsea team pointed to only one result at Anfield and I didn't think City would show much fight thereafter. That's the spirit eh! The only thing in my favour was being positioned in my lucky spot in my local, from where I had seen City win comfortably away three times this season. It was my last roll of the dice.

Thankfully the players actually involved yesterday thought differently to me. A bedraggled Mourinho did what he does best and we all had a good laugh at the "faces like a slapped arse" on display from the 17,000 ex-Liverpool players in attendance. Kenny Dalglish was my favourite. Suddenly it was BACK IN OUR HANDS and I thought we'd then go and mess everything up at Palace, because that's how my mind works.

How fitting that it was Stevie Geeeee who messed up to hand Chelsea the initiative in the match. I don't really have much against the guy, unlike others, and he is isn't responsible for the love-fest surrounding Merseyside over recent weeks, but his mistake did bring a wry smile.

So onto Part 2 of Super Smashing Sensational Sunday.

No great shocks in the team line–up. Two up front again, Dzeko over Negredo no surprise whatsoever. Milner was in, which was fine as he seems to play better away from home anyway, but the omission of Fernandinho was the nearest thing to a shock.

And then a perfect start. A great header from Dzeko meant the relief of an early goal and from then on, City did the ultimate professional job against a form team managed by a guy with many a point to prove over City. Palace rarely got a sniff at goal, and after Toure's superb second goal (which I bizarrely was convinced was going wide), the second half was a case of seeing the game out and keeping Palace at arm's length, something City did with consummate ease. There was no point going all out for more goals when the three points were the most important thing, especially as our goal difference is easily the best now in the league.

Good performances were scattered through the game. Dzeko played his part and worked hard up front. Yaya was Yaya, Aguero seemed more on the ball than previous games whilst Milner, Garcia, Demichelis and more did their jobs perfectly.

Whatever happens now, yesterday gave us one great gift. The Liverpool love-in is suspended for a few days and instead of proclaiming how they are going to win the league and getting their Champions T-shirts printed (as some already have), instead Liverpool fans are waking up with queasy stomachs and a nerve wracking week ahead. Welcome to our world.

And as was predictable, the shuddering halt in the destiny-inspired Liverpool title-charge was not taken too well by many on the red side of their city. Brendan Rogers had a little cry in the post-match press conference at the horror of Chelsea not letting Liverpool play their natural game, whilst one Liverpool fan phoned 6-0-6 to express his disgust at seeing Ian Rush laughing five minutes before the end of the game. It's what Liverpool fans do best, as we found out after David Silva had the nerve to remove his armband during City's match at Anfield.

And then there was the curious case of Graeme Souness. I occasionally refer to Michael Douglas in Falling Down in my blogs, and yesterday it was Graeme's turn to have a breakdown live on air. We are all used to commentators and pundits spitting their blinkered dummies out when things don't go their team's way, but Souness spat his out so hard it rebounded off a window and knocked a cameraman out. This is a shame really as he has been the best pundit of all over recent years and has always seemed fair to City and other clubs, but yesterday was an embarrassing shambles of a rant that was incomprehensible and quite simply made him look like an idiot. To say Liverpool were unlucky because none of their shots deflected into the goal was bizarre enough, but to then dismiss City's professional performance as not good enough was plainly stupid and would never have been applied to any other team in similar circumstances. The best comment though was claiming City wouldn't have won without Toure in the team. The problem is Graeme, he was in the team, so what point you were trying to make is baffling. I imagine Liverpool wouldn't be anywhere near the top of the table without Suarez, but he is a Liverpool player so that's irrelevant.

Using Graeme's logic, here's some other things we can also deduce:
United wouldn't have won so many trophies if Alex Ferguson wasn't at the helm.
Man wouldn't have landed on the moon if it wasn't for that rocket thing.
One Direction wouldn't actually be that successful if fewer people had bought their records.
Red Rum wouldn't have won as many races if he couldn't run so fast.
Manchester would have a beach if it was on the coast.
If my auntie had balls….

And so to the biggest game of the season, a season-defining 90 minutes conveniently scheduled to ruin my birthday. Everton away is such a tough game that it is clear this title is not back in our grasp just yet. They have injury worries but will always pose us problems. The theory that they will want us to win does not stack up for me as the players will not think like fans and we all know that Everton and Liverpool fans all love each other so will be cheering on their cross-city rivals (sarcasm? Not sure). I'm trying not to think too much about it for now, but the team knows what it has to do and has done it before.

Everton 2 Manchester City 3: Some Thoughts

Breathe in, breathe out. Breathe in, breathe out. Another excruciating 90 minutes saw City show their character in the most important game in years, to take one step closer to the title.

It wasn't the easiest way to start my 40th birthday night out – by the end I had gone straight to 50. Needless to say this won't be much of a match report, as I can't remember everything that happened last night anyway.

The team sheet was of little surprise, though I did wonder if Pellegrini might go for one man upfront. The biggest surprise again was the repeated inclusion of Garcia over Fernandinho. Like Demichelis behind him though, it was a reminder of how much the Spaniard has progressed over recent months. He is no superstar, but he hasn't let the team down.

And so began the game in the strangest of atmospheres. As the impressive Barkley curled a beautiful effort into the back of the net, dreams of title glory seemed so distant. Yet again Everton seemed to be doing a job on us. To answer the question everyone had posed, the home team was certainly not throwing the game. The toffees fought from beginning to end, and the victory was as hard-fought as they come.

A City team of old probably would not have responded after going behind, but as we know this team is different and City responded excellently. A sharp shot from Aguero saw City level in a move that summed up his season – a goal followed by an injury.

Is Aguero worried about the world cup? He goes off a lot as a precaution – well hopefully that was all it is. I doubt he will play any further part in this season though.

Even better was to come though, the thought of going in at half-time inconceivable after Everton's early goal, but it was a sublime header from Dzeko that gave the blues the advantage at the break. The player that frustrates more than any added a 3rd goal in the second half with a simple finish to notch his 10th goal away from home this season in the league. Only Luis Suarez has scored more on the road.

Before that though was perhaps one of the crucial moments of the season, a pivotal save that changed everything. Joe Hart's brilliant save from Naismith kept City ahead and was followed soon after by City's third. How important that save could be.

It had to be with City though that they would make life difficult, and thus Lukaku pulled a goal back and City faced a nervy last 25 minutes, sitting too deep but surviving to the final whistle. That final whistle that came suspiciously late was great to hear. City had completed their first double over Everton (in itself worthy of a trophy) in over 30 years and passed their sternest test.

It's amazing how this season has resembled the title-winning campaign of two seasons ago. Seemingly out of the race, a win over West Brom revitalised things and a scrambled draw at home to Sunderland almost ruined it all whilst a rival's defeat put it back into our hands. It may be a superior goal difference that once more proves decisive. Let's hope the end result is the same, but please please please do it without the stress of last time.

But of course this title race is not over. City need to win two more games to lift the trophy and whilst yesterday's results went our way leaving our two opponents with nothing to play for, they will be no easy touch and City must retain total concentration and do a job.

150 goals this season, the greatest number ever in the top flight. Not bad City, not bad.

Still, if you thought scoring three goals at Everton and winning one of the toughest games of the season with a title on the line was impressive, you thought wrong. Andy Dunn at The Mirror wasn't impressed:

But City – even though they were casual, disorganised and moody for significant parts of the game – would have been rightly derided

had they not navigated this challenge.
That they made such hard work of it might be a reflection of either
their nerves or their over-confidence.
Considering the importance of the stakes, there was an
unfathomable sloppiness about much of this City performance.

And if you thought giving to charity was a GOOD THING, a
NICE GESTURE, especially when a club donates all gate receipts
from a match, then you are wrong again. As Glenn Moore explains
in The Independent:
Manchester City do some valued community work but donating
Under-21 match receipts (est: £10,000) to Stephen Sutton's
Teenage Cancer Trust campaign smacks of a publicity stunt. City
say they are increasing awareness, but Stephen's Story is hardly
unknown. City's daily wage bill: £638,356.

And so it's all about Wednesday now, and the nerves are already
kicking in. Fingers crossed that it is everything we hoped for and
that standards don't slip. Yep, it's a new series of 24.

Manchester City 4 Aston Villa 0: Some Thoughts

Last week I had a wonderful dream. Manchester City were cruising to a league title. They were ten points clear at the top, and another trophy was a matter of time. There were no slip ups, little pressure, no gut-wrenching, nerve-wracking games. It was a procession. Like most of my wonderful dreams, it will probably never happen.

Yes, here we are again. Tomorrow I will be sat at my desk shuffling some paper and suddenly the thought of the Sunday's match will rush quickly through my head and my stomach will clench as if going over the crest of a rollercoaster. That's what happened on Monday and Tuesday and Wednesday and today.

A small part of my brain saw this coming. After the loss to Liverpool, the logical part of my mind rued the missed opportunity and wondered if that defeat was a death knell for our title campaign. Somewhere at the back of that mind though a little voice kept whispering. It kept whispering that this defeat had probably made a title victory more likely, because if City were going to win the league then you could guarantee they would do it via the hardest possible route. Thus, when City went 3-1 up at Goodison Park on Saturday, it was inevitable that Everton would pull a goal back with time to spare and make for a nervy finish, as what's the point of a comfortable win? Where's the fun in that?

That narrative though didn't include Liverpool surrendering a three goal lead at Crystal Palace on Monday. It has given City that little bit of breathing space.

Those nerves returned before last night's match and they were there in abundance at half-time. City had dominated possession as expected in a game they couldn't afford to lose and I dreaded that deadly breakaway goal that I have witnessed so many times down the years.

I was also panicking at the weather which I worried would be a "great leveller" and ruin our plans. I am capable of worrying about anything, basically.

The thing is though that the players do not think like the fans - there is a completely different mind-set at play. We sit there powerless, a bag of nerves, voyeurs watching events unfold over which we have no power. The players are paid big money to deal with situations like this and it has been the City way many times under Pellegrini to show patience and wear down the opposition – and that is precisely what happened.

To be honest, I was a bit disappointed in Aston Villa. I expect any team to try and disrupt City's rhythm and get men behind the ball, but not quite to the extent that Villa did last night, considering that they are safe from relegation and the same applies to the timewasting throughout much of the match. As a fan, a voice inside your head screams constantly – "JUST STOP TRYING VILLA AND LET US WIN, FFS!!"

In the end though it was comfortable, thanks to Villa's one chance not crossing the line, a possible Sliding Doors moment in the match. It could have led to a nervy last 10 minutes, but was instead followed by two further goals.

There's little more to be said about Yaya Toure. As soon as he got the ball I expected a goal, which pretty much says it all.

And what a wonderful way to bring up the 100th league goal of the season. City's goal difference is now the same as the number of goals Manchester United have scored all season (63).

The star of the night though was Pablo Zabaleta. A title triumph for him would be more fitting than for anyone else, especially considering he only started 18 matches the last time City won the league. As the song reminds us, he truly is the sexually-active man.

And with the flood of goals came an atmosphere to saviour. It brought back good memories. I can't speak about anyone else, but I am simply incapable of creating an atmosphere whilst stressed. I think they call it multi-tasking.

City have hogged the headlines elsewhere this week of course, due to Financial Fair Play penalties. Nothing was going to distract from the football for me this week and if we win the league I don't really care what they do. There is also little point me explaining what I think of the regulations as you will all already know what a farce they are and the real reason they have been implemented. What I will say though is that UEFA cannot say where the £50m fine money will go and the figure does not come off the club's balance sheet next season so is little more than a back-hander, which tells you everything you need to know about these rules, and with reports coming out that PSG will receive a smaller fine than City despite making no effort to meet the regulations, despite posting much bigger losses and despite their ridiculous inflated sponsorship deals, it's worth remembering that Michel Platini's son works for PSG, which I am sure had no bearing on UEFA's final decision, no siree. If City's sponsorship deal for the stadium is deemed of unfair market value than City should really tell UEFA where to go, considering United signed a bigger deal just for training kits soon after.

Money is fine in UEFA's/FIFA's/Platini's world of course, especially oil money, if it is used to bribe officials into hosting a World Cup in the middle of a desert and debt is fine too, though the Glazers got their grubby hands on United well before Platini came to power, but then as I said I am telling you nothing new.

The whole deterrent to City is pointless considering they won't be making losses within a year or so, though I do see some good in making clubs self-sufficient, but these rules weren't set up for the good of football but to maintain a status quo. UEFA has paid scant interest in dealing with the real issues in football such as racism, corruption, violence and so on, but with £100m+ in its back pocket for fines, at least we can sleep safe in the knowledge that its top brass can continue to tour the world, feasting on the finest food and the finest wines known to humanity in the shiniest of 5 star hotels.

As for the penalties, the fine and the Champions League squad size restrictions are not the end of the world. Our owner can pay the fine by reaching behind his gold-plated couch. The problem is a limit on wage bills as it could hamper the summer transfer plans.

City have to be cautious about taking UEFA on though. If they refuse the penalties then it goes to an independent panel. I don't know what the penalties could then be, but City need to know what the worse case scenario is. What's more, it's never good to take on your sport's governing body, as it marks your card somewhat. I would hope for a compromise late in the day, then we can all move on.
(though I have heard City expected no problems with UEFA this week, so you do wonder if the club have been stabbed in the back)

Anyway, I'm off to protest against FFP by climbing the Big Wheel. I'll be down at 10pm, point made.

I'd discuss next year's season ticket prices too, but I'll only get even angrier. City will get £96m if they win the league on Sunday – pricing out loyal fans is not only a bad idea prior to a stadium expansion, but totally unnecessary.

And so onto Sunday. So close now, so close. City cannot try and play for a draw and there will no doubt be nervy moments ahead, but their only choice is to be positive and go for goals. Fingers and toes crossed for a wonderful day.

P.S.
I hope no one was inconvenienced by the "large bodies of water" outside the South Stand after the match last night. I'm not sure the stadium announcer needs to warn Mancunians about such matters.

And then the wait until the last match on the Sunday. Days of fretting, of rain, of anxiety, poor appetite, of Brendan Rogers spouting drivel. I just wanted it all to end, one way or the other.

And then it did…..

Manchester City 2 West Ham United 0 & The Parade: Some Thoughts

<u>And relax everyone. Manchester City are the 2013/14 Premier League Champions and double winners. Feels good, right?</u>

The day itself was torture as expected. The morning dragged on and on, the clock seemingly ticking backwards, and I just wanted the match to start. The weather was all over the place and once more I worried as I had in midweek that it would be a "great leveller". As for the team itself, no surprises there, though I half-expected Milner to start. It was a good enough team anyway and at last there was a fully-fit squad to choose from.

In the end, City didn't put us through the wringer quite as much as last time. The news that Liverpool were losing quite early on settled a few nerves as the team pushed forward without reward much like the previous game. And once more the players knew how to hold their nerve when all around them were losing theirs.

What's more, the atmosphere, despite the nerves was good, as it should be. The players went about their business in a professional manner and when you look at the game as a whole, the result was rarely in doubt, though it may not have felt like it at the time. The truth is it could have been more, with the woodwork struck, the keeper making one great save from Nasri, Aguero spurning two good chances and various other shots whistling over the bar. West Ham didn't muster one good chance but got into good positions to do so occasionally.

But of course this is City. After going two goals up their concentration slipped slightly for five minutes or more and news filtered through that Liverpool were now a goal up and a man up as Phil Dowd tried his hardest to help Liverpool. You could sense the nerves kick in around the ground and a subdued atmosphere followed, City fans broken by decades of failure worried that West Ham only needed three goals to ruin everything. Of course, it was never really going to happen, but only on 88 minutes did the crowd deem it say to sing about being champions. A man who tried to on 80 minutes was quickly silenced, the odd death threat slung his way.

So at last full time, and not quite the carnage of last time as City strolled over the line, but it still felt magnificent. Respect also to the West Ham fans who stayed to watch the presentation and a bit of mutual admiration is always heart-warming in this cynical, modern world.

Let's not forget as we look back on what is perhaps City's most successful season that only three weeks ago there were serious questions being asked about Pellegrini's suitability for the job. That says it all really about the modern game and the sense of entitlement that some carry around now.

As I am a sad man, I spent much of the morning retweeting some of the bolder predictions from her majesty's press, none more so than from the depressing Neil Custis, another man who has never quite got over the sacking of Mancini and thus held a grudge against Pellegrini ever since. John Cross held similar views, and of course the utterly pointless Adrian Durham over at Talksport, but it is always this way. There is a breed of journalists who are simply incapable of analysis and cater for the brain-dead and that's just the way it is. But these jibes that have followed Pellegrini around all season have helped show in a way why he was appointed in the first place. He has not reacted, apart from one ill-advised attack on a Swedish referee and had given journalists nothing to feed on, to their obvious frustration. Whilst Mourinho has spent the whole season making a fool of himself as expected, Brendan Rogers has strutted about like the messiah (with new woman in tow) and Arsene Wenger has reverted to type and whinged his way through none months, the holistic Pellegrini has just done his job and eventually the football did all the talking. I'm not only happy for myself and all the other fans today and of course the players, but really happy for the Chilean too. He has deserved these trophies and his European drought is over.

And as the players celebrated on the pitch there was so much to smile about. The English youth players bringing out the trophy, the Toure dance performed by the squad but above all the Pellegrini bumps that will probably result in a summer hip operation, but which showed what high esteem he is held in by his players. I hope he is at the club for a long time.

This is a blog that is big on the media's narratives and you can bet your bottom dollar (whatever that is) that the narrative for City this season will generally be that they should have own the league earlier, you know because the team cost a billion and all that. Never mind breaking the goal-scoring records for the top flight in all competitions, or having a goal difference greater than United have scored all season, nor securing the double or the standard of the football. It could have been better. City were of course hampered by their poor away form at the beginning of the season, and as you will also know, only City are not allowed to have a transition period with a new manager – again because of all the money and that.

So now that the title has been wrapped up and the dust is beginning to settle, it's time to talk about Liverpool. It has to be made clear from the start that much of what I am about to say is not some tirade about their fans, who are numerous and varied like any set of supporters, but more the media-led narrative that developed over the last two months ably led by the club's white-toothed manager. There is no doubt though that there was a general belief among pundits, ex-players and some fans that the title was Liverpool's destiny and somehow fitting for them to win, whilst also believing that they had the support of the nation behind them as they strode for glory. Stevie G was the focal point for the narrative, the Liverpool hero who bleeds red and deserved title glory more than every other player combined, as long as you ignore the fact he once tried to leave the club. The fans were singing about winning the league over a month ago, setting themselves up for the biggest of falls. In the end, they learned something important. Titles go to the team with the most points, the best team, they are earned on the field, and there is no divine right to a title, there is no such thing as destiny and some big flags a #ynwa hashtag at the end of every sentence and bricking rival coaches doesn't change that.

Brendan Rogers certainly believed the hype, acting like a fool for the past month with some dire mind-games that along with the crowing fans certainly proved definitively that the nation was not behind their title charge. The added myth that the team was a massive underdog in the title race, packed as it was with loan players, youth products and cheap signings helped set the tone, despite the hundreds of millions of pounds frittered away on players over recent years and once the title began to slip away the narrative of the fans suddenly changed overnight from "we're gonna win the league" to "we've done brilliantly to come second" so there was nothing to be down about.

Of course they have done brilliantly and Rogers has done a great job, but some impressive tune-changing went on after they lost to Chelsea.

Still, next year is DEFINITELY Liverpool's year.

For the record, Liverpool's financial losses last season were virtually the same as City's, but because they are not in Europe it seems this doesn't matter.

But what a sad way for Alan Hansen to finish his job at Match of the Day. So, so sad.

As for City's summer plans, that all depends on the rumbling arguments over the Financial Fair Play penalty. What many fans and those in the media don't seem to have grasped is that City's arguments do not rest on the fact that they consider the rules unjust (though they probably do), but that they have been stabbed in the back after regular dialogue with UEFA over the past few years and assurances being reneged on. By the end of the day we may know more.

And now to the summer and a few laughs at England, the anticipation of a new fixture list and the Sky premiere of Sky Sports Premier League Years 13/14. Drink it in everyone, drink it in.

The Parade:

As I was sat in a city centre pub on Sunday night thanking Sheikh Mansour for his benevolence, I got an email off a City employee asking if I'd like to watch the parade from the Cityzens bus that would follow the players' bus along the parade route.

I naturally assumed it to be a wind-up, but it turns out it was not. And so last night I had the honour of the most wonderful, surreal night of many a year. It was even worth missing Game of Thrones for – that's how good it was.

But first, British health and safety rules did their best to scupper everything. Despite being stood 6 feet away from the bus, there was a small metal barrier in the way, which of course could not be moved as no one had the required level of training, so instead we had to detour half a mile through 10,000 people to get to the bus, taking half an hour, to get back to where we started. Staggering.

When a child tried to high-five us as we got on the bus, I knew it was going to be a weird night. Then Natalie Pike, Danny Jackson and "Chappers" got on with various City staff and as the bus rolled into the throngs, everything went a bit mental. Seeing everything from the bus, seeing the thousands and thousands of people lining the streets, stretching to the horizon and the sea of blue before me and the flares and the NOISE was one of the most amazing experiences. How many clubs in the world would give their fans such an opportunity?

The players' bus was much closer than I anticipated, and at one point the trophies were passed back to our bus – I was eventually told off for hogging it and told to pass it back to the front bus. Eventually the parade ended, and as we sped through the streets into the back entrance of the Phones4U Arena, I was reminded of the Mike Bassett film where the bus goes the wrong way and ends up on a motorway, as we ducked going through low bridges and past overhanging trees. Sadly we weren't allowed near the players (probably for the best) though the photos I got from the bus are the best I will ever take. And then I was back in the street wandering back to Piccadilly Gardens with the odd vuvuzela siren travelling in the breeze and it all felt like a strange dream and it still does. Thank you City – for everything.

And thank you to all the players, to the owners, to the manager, to the backroom staff, to a wonderful season that saw two trophies, a record number of goals, brilliant football and for me the delights of a legends tour, a parade on a bus and a lot of enjoyable writing. But most of all, thanks to all Manchester United fans for cheering us on to our title triumph – it means a lot.

CHAMPIONS

Manchester City Player Ratings for the 2013/14 Season

After securing a double in the 2013/14 season, I thought it a good time to look back at the squad that made it happen. I haven't listed the likes of Lopes, Huws or Boyata as they haven't really featured enough to merit appraisal, though the future looks bright on that front.

Defence

Joe Hart – 8. There was a point in this season where such a mark seemed the stuff of dreams, but credit to England's Number 1 for getting back on track. You could say "he could have done better there" numerous times since his return from exile, as you could with any keeper, but he has barely put a foot wrong for me in recent months and has his mojo back. Looking at the season as a whole he has done well and I haven't docked him more points as during his shaky spell not all the mistakes were solely his fault, accompanied as they were by mistakes from those in front of him.

Costel Pantilimon – 6. Our Cup keeper won himself a cup medal, performed fine without excelling and proved able back-up, though I still wouldn't be too confident in him having a long stint in the first-team.

Richard Wright – 10. Stunning performance against Al Ain.

Gael Clichy – 7. A player I find hard to judge. In match reports throughout the season you can see me mulling over how good a player he is. He's certainly not made glaring errors and is a consistent performer, but for me is not quite top quality, and underwhelming form early in the season saw him share the left-back berth for the remaining matches in the season. Better defensively than Kolarov but inferior up the field, he has done ok/fine this season, without excelling, but has improved as the season wore on. Just don't ever let him play at right-back again.

Aleksander Kolarov – 7.5. One of the surprise stories of the season was Kolarov's "phoenix from the flames" revival after a public spat with fans in the last home game of the previous season against Norwich. I couldn't see any chance of him staying at the club last summer, but he has dug in, and to quote the man himself, has improved his performances due to increased playing time. Thus the unthinkable has happened and now many consider him our first-choice left-back.

Micah Richards – 4. Most marks lost not due to ineptitude but for being made of glass. Such a crying shame, but his time is probably up at City. A fresh challenge is probably best for both sides.

Pablo Zabaleta – 9. He is the fornicating man. What more can you say? A cult hero, a consistent performer, a warrior – EVERYTHING you want in a player. Superb temperament means such an aggressive player rarely gets into trouble with officials (except after hospital passes from Gareth Barry). Only started 18 league games for City in our previous title-winning campaign, so his rise is more recent than you may think, but since Richard's decline he has stepped in and taken over that berth. Another inspirational Mark Hughes signing.

Vincent Kompany – 7.5. The truth is this has not been Kompany's finest season, but his value to the club is immeasurable, as always. Known as the "glassman" at Hamburg, our captain has had his injury worries once more and has made mistakes too. Michael Cox over at Zonal Marking argues that he always has a mistake in him, and what at first sounds like a ludicrous statement does have an element of truth in it. He has also put in his usual quota of excellent performances, grown in stature alongside Martin Demichelis and his mere presence on the pitch clearly has a positive influence on the team. Despite his troubles, his absence has seen some of our worse defensive performances over the past nine months and a settled partnership in central defence should see him regain total consistency.
Another inspirational Mark Hughes signing.

Martin Demichelis – 8. I was tempted to give him 10 as a two-fingered salute to no one in particular. Costing just a few million pounds and as one of City's lowest earners, you could now feasibly argue he was the signing of last summer. Signed as backup and for his obvious experience, Demichelis immediately got injured then on recovering from that was thrown straight into a game at Stamford Bridge. Injuries have meant he has featured far more than may have been expected. Shaky form to begin with saw him labelled a liability by many if not most football fans, but he has grown and grown with each passing month, was a vital cog in the title run-in and even won player of the month for April. He may lack pace, but his experience and anticipation shines through.

Matija Nastasic – 4. A season wrecked by injury that then contributed to some shaky form meant this was one to forget for the Serbian after such a great campaign the season before. With pain in his knee that seemed to mystify the medical team, he is at last fit as the season ends, and hopefully can start afresh in August and develop further.

Joleon Lescott – 5. Once more, he's top of the league. As expected has had few opportunities this season but has done ok when called upon. His time is up at the club, and he will be remembered as a top-class professional who helped contribute to a trophy-laden few years and he has been worth every penny of his transfer fee.

Midfield

Yaya Toure – 9. I would only give a 10 out for a perfect player having a perfect season, and Yaya is not perfect, but perhaps I should have relaxed the rules on this occasion. My Player of the Year for one of the most complete midfielders in world football. Struggled occasionally against high-tempo teams that packed the midfield, but his season in general was phenomenal, both in goals scored, assists, the free-kicks and his general bossing of many a midfield. Surely the best season of his career? Twenty league goals and 9 assists to boot.

David Silva – 8. Only marked down as he was another player that had his injury woes. When he was fit he was simply on another level to most other players that shared a pitch with him. If only he could shoot. One of the best players to ever wear the shirt, just a joy to watch and a privilege. I LOVE YOU DAVID.

Samir Nasri – 8. An improved season for the Frenchman, though not enough to get him in the French World Cup squad, though I doubt that decision was made on ability alone. Evidence of what an excellent man-manger Pellegrini is, he nurtured Nasri perfectly and the player responded, filling the void in Silva's absence and showing more consistency across the season. He still has his quieter days, but his ability has been there for all to see over the past nine months and his contribution was significant – the stats back this up.

James Milner – 7. Another season where Milner did what you'd expect of him. With a year left on his contract he may want to leave if he can't be guaranteed more playing time. He had his bad days, he had his good days (Bayern Munich away being the best of the lot), but he always gave a disciplined, hard-working performance in a position still not considered to be his best. An excellent squad member to have in any team, he will be 7 or 8 out of 10 every season.

Fernandinho – 8.5. Oh how people laughed as City shelled out £30m for a player who couldn't even get in the Brazil squad in an era when Jo could. In the early weeks of the season, this laughter did not subside as he struggled to develop an effective partnership with Yaya Toure, but thereafter the player has grown week-by-week to become one of City's most effective performers. The end result was a call-up to Brazil's World Cup squad, the only surprise being Pellegrini's favouring of Garcia in the season's closing weeks, but perhaps the long English season had taken its toll on the Brazilian. Either way, whilst Fernandinho is not a natural defensive midfielder, perhaps at last we can move on from Nigel De Jong.

Javi Garcia – 7. Another player who proved that sometimes it is best to give people a chance to develop. A basic player who does what he does effectively, Garcia has grown in stature throughout the season, one small step at a time, to become a useful squad member. As already mentioned, he was entrusted to protect the back four as City won their final five league games to secure the league. Will never dazzle or win awards or even have a song named after him, but at last he has proven he has a role in the squad.

Jesus Navas – 6.5. For me the second biggest disappointment of the season, after Jovetic's disappearance act. Navas has not been a failure, but I feel we haven't seen the best of him yet, as he hasn't used his electric pace to destroy opposing full-backs enough, and thus hasn't been a regular starter. He is great squad player to have though and I am hopeful of seeing much more of what he is about next season.

Stevan Jovetic – 5. A midfielder? Never mind, he's staying here. This was the signing that excited me most of all last summer, but it has been a frustrating year for the young man who struggles to keep his clothes on. Injuries derailed the start of his City career, and he has never recovered. His absence was often not explained fully by Pellegrini, and there were rumours of him being unsettled, but the brief glimpses we have had of him make me believe my excitement was justified. Pellegrini still didn't trust him at the end of the season, but as the cliché goes, I hope that come August he will be like a new signing and a big talent in the coming year.

Scott Sinclair – 0. Who?

Jack Rodwell – 4. Another wasted season and yet I am sure there is a wonderful player in there, but I doubt City fans will ever see that player. More injury problems, little time on the pitch and a frustrating nine months all in all. I've no idea what the future holds for Rodwell, but I dearly hope he can play regular football somewhere.

Attackers

Sergio Aguero – 8. Talking of injuries – is Kun the biggest injury worry of all? Seventeen league goals show that he is as good as ever, but this was a season hampered by seemingly endless niggling injuries. The guy is sheer class, a little piece of dynamite, so we can only pray that other clubs keep their dirty mitts off him and that he can have a fuller season next time around. The number of muscle injuries suffered by City players over the course of the season is a worry though.

Alvaro Negredo – 7.5. It's almost an impossible task to grade a player who had a season of two halves. For the first half, Negredo looked like the buy of the summer (for any team) as he forged a lethal partnership with Sergio Aguero, scoring 23 goals across all competitions in half a season, before injuring his shoulder in a game he didn't need to play in, as City cruised to Wembley in the Capital One Cup. Since then, he has looked a shadow of the player we first saw, the confidence seemingly drained out of him, unless he was still hampered by that shoulder. A fresh start in August will hopefully rekindle the fire.

Edin Dzeko – 7.5. Another rollercoaster ride for Dzeko, who proved his worth once more, and at the business end of the season when it was really needed. Sixteen league goals showed once more what he has to offer though he continued to frustrate at times. Overlooked for much of the first half of the season, he took over from the flagging Negredo to help see City over the finishing line, scoring key goals throughout the final straight, from the opener at Crystal Palace to the crucial brace at Goodison Park. He is the same Edin Dzeko we have always known and mostly loved.

Manager: Manuel Pellegrini – 9. Robbie Savage said today that City should have won the quadruple, whilst only weeks ago a minority were questioning Pellegrini's future, as many journalists did when he was appointed. Back in the realms of reality though, it is fair to say that overseeing a double and a club's most successful season in your debut season in a new country can be considered something of a success, irrespective of resources available. The man oozes class and dignity, the holistic approach our owners crave, and has kept his head and his team's head as those around him floundered or poked him looking for weaknesses. He has made mistakes, of that there is no doubt, and his maths isn't the best, but the trophy haul at the end of the season says it all. The players clearly respect him, the mood around the club is harmonious and he looks like the late, great Dave Allen. He'll do for me.

A Season-End Journalist Q & A:

After an exciting Premiership season, I asked a few football journalists their views on the season just gone, from City, to Suarez to Financial Fair Play and more. This is what Mark Ogden (Daily Telegraph), Oliver Kay (The Times), Simon Mullock (The Mirror), Jonathan Northcroft (The Sunday Times), Nick Miller (football365,com, The Guardian, ESPN and more) and Gary James (Manchester City historian) had to say:

Your brief views of the Premiership season just gone?

Mark Ogden (MO): It had everything really, with the exception of a final day surprise or bit of drama that had people on the edge of their seats.
Obviously, the title hadn't been resolved in City's favour, but it felt
like a formality and Norwich were down bar the counting, so nothing
really happened on the final day which created a memory like Aguero's
goal did a couple of years ago.
But the season had loads of stories, with the best one arguably being
the meltdown at Manchester United. It lasted all season and, when you
are so used to watching a club win and bounce back, it was an interesting new angle to cover.

Oliver Kay (OK): Dramatic, unpredictable and entertaining, with a lot of very good football – much of it from City. It makes such a difference when you have a proper title race. Ultimately, the best team won. They weren't quite flawless, but they were the best all-round team.

Jonathan Northcroft (JN): A 9/10 season in terms of the competitiveness and unpredictability of the competition. But only a

7/10 in terms of quality. Liverpool and Manchester City played some exceptional attacking football at different points of the campaign, but showed sizeable faults – Liverpool defensively, City in their early away form. They were a worthy 1st and 2nd but there was no dominating, truly outstanding side: from 2004-09 English clubs were the best in Europe, dominating the Champions League and to become champions of England required world class standards. You couldn't say that's the case at the moment. Good as Liverpool and City were, Arsenal's 2003-4 side, Chelsea's 2004-6 team and Manchester United from 2007-9 would have won last season's Premier League easily. Great entertainment, twists, turns – and lots of goals in the 2013-14 competition though.

Simon Mullock (SM): It's been the best Premier League season ever – despite lacking the final-day drama of 1995 and 2012. At various times, City, Liverpool, Chelsea and Arsenal all looked unstoppable and to have four teams in the running for so long made it unique in the Sky era. There was a nice contrast between City and Liverpool going on the attack and Chelsea beating them both home and away with disciplined (dour) defence and counter-attack.
In the end, City are champions because they had the best balance of any team in the league. Despite what Richard Scudamore thinks, it was also refreshing to see a title race that didn't involve United.

Nick Miller (NM): I think it's the funniest season I can remember. Liverpool losing it so spectacularly, United not so much imploding but slowly collapsing like a poorly-constructed meringue, Mourinho is always pretty funny, mostly down to how cross he makes people, Kostas Mitroglou, Tim Sherwood. I could go on.

Gary James (GJ): Amazing of course. Thinking about everything except City for a moment it has to be good when so many teams are able to challenge for honours, top four places and also to avoid relegation. When I was a kid in the late 70s Liverpool were fairly dominant, but it still felt like any of about six teams could win the League (teams like Forest & Villa did and City came close) and that's what we now have again to some extent. This year's top 4 all took points off each other and, when you add in rivalries with

London clubs, Everton and United, it's easily possible that teams normally associated to be outside of the top four could sneak into it in future years if results go their way. I said in my Big Book Of City in 2009 that the takeover would open up the so called Big Four and that instead of making it five teams challenging it could easily become six or seven. That's how it feels we're now heading. Thinking about City specifically… What can be better than winning the Premier League again? Twice in three years and when you add into that our other two finishes since 2011 then it's clear we're the most consistent team of recent years. This is our era now!

Did you agree with Suarez winning two player of the year awards,
considering his past indiscretions?

MO: I voted for Yaya Toure in the Football Writers' award, but I can't
argue with Suarez winning either of them.
He has had a brilliant season and I think his past indiscretions are a reason why he actually won both awards.
You cannot fault the guy for turning his career around after the Evra
and Ivanovic incidents. He could easily have gone off the rails, sulked
after not being allowed to leave Liverpool and just played for a move,
but he did the opposite.
If a guy makes a mistake and redeems himself on the pitch as Suarez has
done, then he deserves recognition.

OK: I voted for him for the FWA award – and that was after asking myself if it was "right" to do so. I wouldn't have voted for him in 2011/12, no matter how he performed, because that award is meant to be about "precept and example", not just performance. But because his behaviour has been much improved (if still a long way short of angelic), I was happy to recognise his performances, which were incredibly good for the most part. I know some like to follow the Mourinho argument that these awards should go to a player in a team that wins something, but that's not the idea at all. It's an individual award. With due respect to Toure and some other very good contenders, I thought Suarez was the best individual.

JN: Yes. He's a truly special player. A colleague put it best: other top players are capable of one or two jaw-dropping moments per season. Suarez gives you one or two every game. His 31 goals – a joint PL record for a 38 game campaign – were amassed despite his ban and the fact he doesn't take penalties or, indeed, all Liverpool's free kicks. Amazing.

I'm not a fan of bringing 'indiscretions' into PoTY awards. In an ideal world, maybe a player's character and standards of behaviour could be considered but in the real world players are human beings and flawed – and you could go through a list of the previous PoTY winners making moral cases against them, on the basis of things they've done.

That said, in very serious cases of misbehaviour – like racial abuse – it would be invidious to reward somebody, no matter how well they played. I wouldn't have given Suarez player of the year in 2011-12 but this was 2013-14 and, not only did he play brilliantly, he behaved – and showed improvements in terms of calmness etc, which should also be recognised.

SM: I think everyone deserves a second and even a third chance. Suarez had a fantastic season and has obviously redeemed himself in the eyes of a lot of his peers and members of the Football Writers' Association. But I didn't vote for him because when the going got tough, he reverted to type. When Suarez found himself shackled by both City and Chelsea, his only answer was to start diving in an effort to win penalties and free-kicks and to get opposition players into trouble.

The citation for the FWA award says "by precept and by example" and while I suppose diving is better than biting or racially abusing people, it's still cheating.

The bottom line was that Suarez scored 31 goals – none of them from the penalty spot – after being banned for the first six games of the season, so I can see why he won both awards. But I think there were more deserving players out there.

NM: There's an argument to be made that he shouldn't have even won it based on purely his play given that he disappeared/didn't score in so many big games. Still, he probably deserved it, and that sort of thing should only be judged on play, rather than a moral aspect. Plenty of bad people have won it before, and as a man with a shelf full of Morrissey records I can't really say someone with iffy views on race shouldn't be recognised for their art/sport. Just don't use the 'redemption' word.

GJ: Ignoring his past indiscretions, I still didn't think he deserved the FWA award this year. The PFA award is different because it's voted by the player's peers so I tend to think that they're aware of contributions that I personally am not aware of because I don't play professionally, and although I still disagree with his selection I can't really debate that one. The FWA award is supposed to be about someone's all round contribution and that includes respect, demeanour and many other attributes as well as playing. Past winners like Joe Mercer, Johnny Carey, Stanley Matthews, Tony Book, Bert Trautmann… I could go on, but they won the awards not because they scored a lot of goals or had not been as lacking in discipline as the previous year, they won the award because they were great footballers and superb role-models or ambassadors. We all know that Yaya should have got this, but to be frank Vincent Kompany would also have been in the top three if you were thinking about being a role-model.

Your manager of the year?

MO: Tough one to call. Pellegrini won two trophies in his first season in
English football and did what Mourinho did in his first spell at
Chelsea, Brendan Rodgers took Liverpool from seventh to second and Tony
Pulis did fantastically well at Crystal Palace.
All success stories in their own right, but dealing with different demands and pressures. Steve Bruce has also had a great season at Hull.
But the guy who wins the league is the guy who wins the league,

so you
would have to give it to Pellegrini.

OK: Apologies, but I agree with the LMA — a toss-up between
Rodgers and Pulis. When you're trying to evaluate a manager's
performance, it has to be relative to expectations and resources.
Those two far exceeded expectations, doing things that few (if any)
thought were possible with those teams. Pellegrini? He did roughly
what was expected and demanded with that squad. It's impressive
that he did it in his first season, after a sticky start, with his team
playing some very exciting stuff at times, but you would struggle
to convince me that it is a better managerial performance than what
Rodgers or Pulis did – or, for example, what Pellegrini did with
Villarreal when people were sneering that he couldn't be a top-
class manager because he hadn't got the trophies (in Europe) to
show for it.

JN: Brendan Rodgers. Pulis and Pellegrini did great jobs but what
Rodgers managed – taking a side from seventh to within a game of
being champions – was more special. He improved players, played
great football, developed talent, showed tactical innovation and
handled the weight of expectation and history that's upon
Liverpool.

SM: I'm torn with this one. If it was going to a manager at the top
end of the table, then no doubt Pellegrini should have won it. Title,
Capital One Cup, brilliant attacking football, the way he healed the
squad after Mancini. And the fact that he exudes sheer class. I
don't think there is another manager in the game who would have
waited to shake hands with Liverpool's players after the
disappointment of the defeat at Anfield. He's proved nice guys can
be winners.
The only other candidate for me was Pulis at Crystal Palace.
Taking what was nothing better than a Championship squad to
mid-table was an incredible achievement, whether you like his
style of football or not.
I was surprised by the League Managers Association. Apparently,
Pellegrini wasn't even in the top-four and there were gasps of
disbelief at the annual dinner when the nominations were read out

and his name was missing. There has only been one foreign winner in 21 years – Arsene Wenger – so something isn't right.

NM: Tony Pulis: magician

GJ: Manuel Pellegrini of course. Two trophies in his first season, meaning that he is by far the most successful manager in his first season that either Manchester side have had. All those issues that people said Moyes had – a new club, players used to certain ways, philosophy different etc. – Pellegrini also had. Moyes, apparently, didn't have enough time to buy the right players, well he was appointed before Pellegrini! So, all of this adds up to a great achievement. My gut feel is that all the player & manager awards were voted for before the real end to the season was clear and that at the time people were formulating their ideas of who to vote for Liverpool looked like they'd walk away with the title.

I've seen it mentioned many a time that City should have won this
league more convincingly? Do you agree?

MO: Yes, but they probably would have done had Aguero and Kompany not
missed so many games due to injury.
It makes me laugh when I hear Arsenal fans talking about injuries costing them the title, as though they are the only team to suffer injuries.
It's how you deal with those setbacks and Arsenal fell short again.

OK: I would go further and say that they should have won the past three league titles. This squad is by far the strongest in the Premier League and one of the best in world football – and I wouldn't say that of the teams they were competing with this season or the Manchester United team who beat them to the title in 2013 and 2011 and ran them so close in 2012. City's is a squad that, in my opinion, should be getting 90+ points every season. This season, with a new manager and with Kompany, Silva and Aguero all missing at important times, it was more difficult to get to that level and it was noticeable how much better their record was from mid-

November onwards. With Pellegrini now having got used to his players and to English football, they should be perfectly capable of winning "convincingly" next season, but it's rarely quite so easy in reality unless you're one of those teams that is more than the sum of its parts. I don't think City, for all their quality, have reached that point yet.

JN: Yes and no. Yes in the sense that City are the best side in the country by a bit of a margin. In the last five games of the season we saw that – the squad is bursting with top players and Pellegrini is a very fine manager, so when you look at it that way the title should have come straightforwardly. However this was Pellegrini's first season and new players were bedding in. It was going to take time, so the poor start was understandable. After the first 11 games City were seventh but what came after was a sustained run of champion form. City gained eight points on Liverpool, nine on Chelsea, 11 on Arsenal and 21 on United (or thereabouts – this off the top of my head, check the stats!) That's "convincing".

SM: No. Other managers were given transitional or settling-in periods, so why not Pellegrini? Early-season problems away from home were due to the fact that the team were asked to play a completely different way than under Mancini. High line, both full-backs bombing on, Fernandinho having to cover defensively on his own to enable Toure to get forward. Four defeats in the opening six away games suggest that there were definitely teething problems.
Add to that prolonged absences of Kompany, Silva and, especially Aguero. Only Arsenal had injury problems to the same extent as City – and look what happened to them.

NM: Probably. But I wouldn't waste a huge amount of time arguing the case.

GJ: Not when you consider what happened at the other clubs that expected to challenge AND changed their managers. Liverpool and Arsenal were the two 'steady' clubs who, we were told at one point, right at the start of the season would gain most from the issues that City and Chelsea would face. We were also told that

Moyes' knowledge of the Premier League would give him an advantage, so overall no. Obviously, the squad City have is what most focus on, but that old argument about how much has been spent is a false one because, as we all should know, City were still playing catch up and so how much City paid for players who don't appear often shouldn't really focus minds. Instead the media should focus on starting elevens and, if the maths we heard were correct MUFC's team for the Old Trafford derby that lost to City was more expensive than City's.

This season is comparable with 2011-12 – then Tevez's situation and the African Cup of Nations limited our 1st team during January disrupting our momentum, this time injuries impacted our great run. But we came back strong again when almost everyone was available for selection.

If you have had dealings with Pellegrini, what are your views on him?

MO: Nice guy, decent man, but from a media point of view, massively dull.
The Manchester journalists had dinner with Pellegrini and Txiki Begiristain at Christmas and it was great. Txiki is a character, full of
stories, but Manuel is much more reserved. He is shy, basically, but he
really is a likeable man.
His job was to win trophies for Manchester City, not cultivate the media, so I am not complaining about his approach.
But we do miss Mancini's quotability at times!

OK: The only dealings I've had with him so far have been official press conferences, which are invariably very low-key, lacking much by way of insight. But there's a tendency among journalists to describe Mourinho's press conferences as "box office". Personally I much prefer managers to produce "box office" football than "box office" press conferences.

JN: Huge admiration. His calmness and maturity won City that title. He set the right tone in the run-in, when the heat was on, and he showed great consistency, reassuring the players after the difficult start to keep playing in the same way. In press dealings he's a gent – and not afraid to say what he thinks. I warmed to him when he was asked why he didn't shake Mourinho's hand at Stamford Bridge. "Because I didn't want to," he said. More honesty like that from managers please….

SM: Mancini at City was a hack's dream and a press officer's nightmare because he had an opinion on everything. Pellegrini is very cautious in front of the TV cameras and the dailies don't get much out of him because of that. The Sunday pack are able to speak to him privately in a separate room, away from the cameras, and he does relax a bit more. He's still pretty straight with his answers and won't be led into issues he doesn't want to address. But we do get to see his sense of humour a bit more and he is quite a dry bloke. He hinted that he had a bit of a temper in his younger days and I'd bet it's spectacular when he does lose his rag. But he is a genuinely nice fella with no obvious agendas other than to play great football.

NM: Never had any dealings, but he seems like a man who would be smashing company over a nice glass of red.

GJ: Not really enough to form a strong opinion. But he does feel like a guy who will let his players do the talking. A bit like Tony Book as manager – he's got the knowledge and experience and when allowed to focus on football matters he quietly delivers success.

And if you have had time at the club, has there been a different atmosphere to last season?

MO: Absolutely. It was joy-less last season, everybody had a face on them,
from players to staff and you could tell that it was an unhappy place
and split dressing-room.
It's a much happier place now, Pellegrini has brought calm, but the only danger is that the club is lacking in characters.

Aguero, Yaya and Silva are all great players, genuine world stars, but
they lack the box office status of Tevez or Balotelli or, Suarez or Rooney.

OK: Totally different. It was a volatile atmosphere with Mancini in charge, in dispute with everyone, and with players like Balotelli, Tevez and Adebayor. I know a lot of City fans at the time tended to react to reports of tension by suggesting that either (a) this was normal or (b) it was healthy tension, but no it wasn't normal and, according to pretty much everyone at the club, it wasn't healthy. Although there is a challenge to try to keep the English players involved and happy, it actually feels like a stable club now.
One other thing I'd mention regarding City is that pretty much everyone I know there, across various departments, loves working for the club. They're quite evangelical about it. Far more so than other clubs, in my experience.

JN: Yes. More assurance. More the sense of a grown up and harmonised football club.

SM: Definitely. I really liked Mancini. I know the fans will never forget what he did and I hope the club don't try to airbrush him out because he was exactly what City needed at that time – an absolutely ruthless winner. But the atmosphere towards the end of last season was poisonous. You don't have to be loved to be a successful manager, but you do need to have the trust and respect of the players – and that had gone completely.
I went on the pre-season tour to Hong Kong and the change was unbelievable. The players actually wanted to stop and talk about the new season without being pressed into it by the media team. It's also noticeable that the players praise Pellegrini without being prompted by a question. The common words you hear are "calm" and "respect. The way he handled Hart earlier in the season was a master class in management. Mancini would have stuck the boot in by criticising the player in public; Pellegrini just took him out of the firing line without making a drama of it.

GJ: There's definitely a more positive feel. I also sense that ambitions have rocketed in recent months and that the club really is now becoming established as a power. Before this season we all hoped it would happen and the management were putting the right people and resources in place, but now the success on the field is matched by the success off it. Best thing is that few in the game have yet realised that this is still only the start!

City's Financial Fair Play penalty – fair? A good deterrent?

MO: It's difficult to say really until we know what Uefa have done to the
other clubs.
A £50m fine seems very harsh, but until it is placed in context alongside the other penalties, you can't really judge it.

OK: It's certainly a strong deterrent. But as for whether it is fair, I don't think FFP is geared towards fairness or towards creating the level playing field that Platini and Uefa were talking about when they first raised the concept of "financial fair play" (lower case) in 2008. I dug out an old Platini quote the other day where he said that he wanted FFP to stop those who want to "come into football to make money". Instead, the establishment clubs persuaded Uefa to turn it into something that would stop another Chelsea emerging. It's actually a rule that encourages and allows investors to come into football to make money. I don't like FFP at all. It was meant to be about eradicating financial excesses and inequalities, but instead it has ignored most of them and focused on the one thing that Bayern, Real Madrid, Milan, Manchester United, Arsenal etc were all terrified of, which was big-spending outsiders threatening the elite. I don't particularly sympathise with City over the punishment because they have broken rules. Where I sympathise with them is over this portrayal of them as the bad guys and the establishment clubs as the good. I don't think the case at all.

JN: No. I don't think the FFP rules are being used the way they should be. For me, they were set up to stop clubs over extending themselves and going to the wall – not to curb benefactors and investors. City have owners who want to build for the long term, care about leaving something positive in East Manchester as an area and have kept ticket prices down. What's wrong with that? Other clubs who pass FFP have £1000 per year season tickets, or owe £500m thanks to leveraged buyouts. I'm not sure what 'wrong' FFP – as it's now being used – is trying to right.

SM: I've got no problem with FFP being brought in if it's to prevent clubs going out of business. That's not the case with the regulations as they stand now. Even Platini admitted they have been designed at the behest of powerful clubs like Bayern, Milan and United to protect their position at the top of the game. I'm still yet to hear how attempting to fine a club £50million for allegedly overspending is the best way to promote financial prudence. We don't even know how these decisions are made and we should all be suspicious when there's no transparency. I've got to say, some of my colleagues in the press have written some absolute shite about FFP without challenging its legality or morality. Thankfully, Martin Samuel has produced some great arguments against it – and a few more influential columnists are finally starting to follow his lead.

NM: I'm going to plead the fifth on this one because I don't know enough about it and every time I try to read up on it my head starts to shut down. I think it's the same part of my brain that won't allow me to understand how to play poker.

GJ: If you want something to stop wealthy businessmen investing in potential then yes it's a good deterrent! The real issue is debt and football clubs living beyond their means like Portsmouth, Bradford, Leeds etc. That's what should be tackled. I find it ridiculous that within about 4 miles you have two leading Premier League clubs – one owned by a businessman who has taken millions out of the club to fund his family's life and other interests leaving the club in serious debt, while the other is funded by a businessman who is pumping billions into the club and surrounding area/community which in turn will help the game develop, yet it is the investor who is punished. Ridiculous. Clearly there needs to be safeguards against owners taking money out or putting clubs in serious debt, but investment should not be punished.

What one thing would you change about the modern game?

MO: Not a problem that City have to worry about – or United for that
matter! – but playing the Europa League games on a Thursday night is a
total waste of time.
Get it back to Tuesdays and Wednesdays and people might be interested
in it again.
It just feels like a pointless competition. When City and United played
in it two years ago, I was at Ajax v United and what should have been a
game between two of Europe's most successful and historic clubs felt
like a testimonial because it was shunted onto a Thursday night.

OK: The way that so much is being dictated by ownership. I'm not really referring to City here. I'm referring mostly to the way that clubs have been hawked around to the highest bidder and, in a number of cases, ended up in totally unsuitable hands. City got lucky – and you might well argue that they deserved that break after the previous four decades – but other fans have seen their club being trampled all over, causing the kind of damage that they might never recover from. Leeds, Blackburn, Coventry, Birmingham and Portsmouth, to name but five, have suffered terribly. And with the culture in football right now, where so many clubs seem so desperate to keep the status quo, it might become very hard for those other clubs to recover.

JN: The same thing they all say – diving. I still haven't heard a convincing proposal as to how to do that though.

SM: Drums – in fact, musical instruments of any kind – should be banned from football grounds. I'd also make it a flogging offence

if players wear boots that aren't black. My kids say I'm miserable.
I say I'm a traditionalist.

NM: I'd like to introduce some sort of revenue-sharing provisions
in a similar way to American sports, but I imagine it would be
completely unworkable. Also, get rid of goal music.

GJ: The dominance of the Premier League in terms of money,
attention and the media. Of course, City will benefit from all of
this but we must never forget where we've been and how difficult
it would have been to come back had the gulf been as wide as it is
today. I'd also change seeding in Europe – aimed at protecting the
big clubs. I get why they do it, but it feels that it should be based
more on current merit not your history – the Champions of the
main leagues should be number one seeds and head groups if
seeding is to be used, not in pot 3 or 4.

**What's been the best/most enjoyable single moment in your
job this
season?**

MO: Watching Cristiano Ronaldo score a hat-trick for Portugal
against
Sweden in the World Cup play-off in Stockholm last November.
It was one of those nights when you felt like you had witnessed a
great
at the very top of his game.

OK: As enjoyable as it has been, I would like to think the best
moment is still to come. A World Cup in Brazil, whatever the talk
about travel and logistical chaos, is something to relish. It has been
looming on the horizon all season, but now it finally feels real.

JN: The raw excitement of football never leaves you. For me going
to the Vicente Calderon to watch Atletico Madrid v Chelsea. One
of the great atmospheres in the world game…and about to be
demolished so being there was a privilege.

SM: I did a one-on-one interview with Wayne Rooney and as part of the piece we had to pose for pictures together in front of a huge poster of him celebrating scoring the overhead kick in the derby a few years ago. With a big grin on his face, he nudged me, asked me if I liked the picture and said they'd dug it out especially for me. I told him he shinned it.

NM: I was in the press box for Spurs v City and was about ten feet from Sergio Aguero's thighs. If it wasn't a night game and the sun was out, they would have blocked it out.

GJ: Being able to watch and note another season of success for future use in my next (or next after that) book.

And the worst/least enjoyable moment?

MO: Watching United lose to Olympiakos in Athens, knowing that the next day
would be a nightmare in terms of finding out how long the Glazers would
put up with David Moyes. Not much longer, as it turned out.

OK: Being stuck in the car park at Crewe station for an hour at 3am after getting a lift back from an England match at Wembley. The exit barrier wasn't working and, despite the best efforts of British Transport Police, I couldn't get hold of anyone to sort it out. It wasn't great fun.

JN: Too many hours on the motorway.

SM: Seeing close up how the racial abuse Yaya Toure was subjected to in Moscow really hurt him. I was stood a couple of feet away from him in the mixed zone when he spoke about it and to see this giant man close to tears really hit home.

NM: It's not football but sitting in a freezing living room in England covering the fourth Ashes Test was fairly grim. Particularly when I started to hallucinate due to lack of sleep on day four.

GJ: Seeing how everyone jumps to conclusions when the occasional result goes against us – the Sunderland game is a good example. The mood that followed suggested City were a crisis club once more but in truth everything carried on as before and it turned out to be a point won rather than two lost. I hope we can all exhibit a more stable approach next season.

**Any good news item in football that didn't get the coverage it deserved
during the course of the season?**

MO: Not that I can think of. Football gets so much good press, but people
in the game are quick to moan when it goes negative.
The best stories are those which just happen and not those that are spoon-fed by PRs wanting to tell you how great the latest community
initiative or charity event is.
Just do the good stuff and don't chase the plaudits. Otherwise, people
will think you are doing it for the wrong reasons.

OK: I did like the story of Markus Rosenberg, who left the entire contents of his house to charity when he was released by West Brom. But players do a lot of good work with charitable foundations etc. I think some of them could and probably should promote them more in cases where they want to raise awareness as well as money.

JN: Tens of thousands of selfless acts at grassroots level, never to make the papers.

SM: The Premier League gets a lot of criticism – plenty warranted – but the Christmas Truce Tournament, which sees Academy teams play against clubs from Germany, Belgium and France in Ypres, is a brilliant initiative. It's something I think deserves a lot more coverage.

NM: I think the amount of coverage football gets over the media it's almost impossible for anything to be under-reported. That said, even though it has been well covered, I don't think it's been truly appreciated in England how incredible Atletico's season has been.

GJ: Perhaps instead of the focus on Greg Dyke becoming the new FA boss more time should have been spent on the achievements of David Bernstein's brief period in charge – and that may have helped raise the ridiculous age discrimination policy of the FA (in direct contrast to its own history as well when age was viewed as a positive – both views out of place of course!).

Finally – your tip for the World Cup, and if you like, an outsider tip?

MO: I can't see anybody stopping Brazil in Brazil. And in terms of an outsider, I think England might do better than expected. They will get through the group and then face a decent run to the quarters, so who knows?

OK: I'm split between Brazil, Argentina and Spain. I'll say Brazil, even though I'm well aware it's nothing like the most talented of Brazil teams. Not very original, I know. I didn't want to say Belgium or Colombia as outsiders, because it's too obvious, but the fact is that the draw gives those two a decent chance of getting to the quarter-finals. The same applies to whoever wins Group E – France, Honduras, Switzerland or Ecuador. If France get their act together, they could do quite well. As for England, I can't help going back to my gut feeling when the draw was made, which was that they'll find it tough to get out of the group.

JN: Brazil to win. Chile to shock their group opponents and go on a run.

SM: Belgium to win it, Chile as dark horses.

NM: Tedium alert: Brazil. I think Italy will do better than most expect.

GJ: England and England!

City's Departed Players Since The Takeover of 2008 (stats as of early April 2014).

A lot has happened since the summer of 2008. A lot of players have come and a lot have gone. Here's a look at those that have gone. I haven't mentioned every single player to pass through the Etihad, but those we know best – and that's still a lot of players. The dates generally relate to the year they went off our books, but they're not of great importance.

2009

Richard Dunne. City's multiple Player of The Year signed for Aston Villa in August 2009 for £5m having been edged out of the City team by the arrivals of Kolo Toure and Joleon Lescott. There he remained for four years, before joining the QPR graveyard (as we will see) last summer.

Elano (Blumer). The very talented Brazilian who didn't always bring along a work ethic to match. Elano left City in the summer of 2009 and signed for Galatasaray, where he remained for eighteen months before joining Santos and then Gremio in the summer of 2012, where he remains. He has played 38 times for the club, scoring 11 goals. He no longer makes the national side, but made 50 appearances, scoring 9 goals.

No one will forget that free-kick v Newcastle United.

Danny Mills. Good riddance (sorry, that slipped out). Sadly still punishing us with his punditry skills. I use the word "skills" in the loosest sense possible. Did quite well on Celebrity Masterchef though, I'll give him that. Released into the wild by City in the summer of 2009, never to play again, after previous uninspiring loan periods at the likes of Derby County and Hull City.

Michael Ball. Released on the same day as Danny Mills was Michael Ball. After that he only ever made three more appearances in professional football, for Leicester City.

Glauber (Leandro Honorato Berti). Also leaving City in the summer of 2009 was the infamous Berti. Since then he has appeared at Sao Caetano, Rapid Bucharest and Columbus Crew, unfortunately missing the second half of last year with a cruciate ligament injury.

Daniel Sturridge. The man with the world's worst goal celebration has had a stupendous season – I think everyone knows his career path after he left City. As to why he left, it was never totally clear, but the general consensus is he wanted more money than City were prepared to pay. It didn't seem a huge loss at the time, more so now. With 20 goals in the league this season, the future is bright.

Dietmar Hamann. A liability at City (ha!), another player put out to pasture at the Etihad. As you will know a media career has beckoned for the cricket-loving chain-smoking German, but not before a disastrous spell managing Stockport County. Prior to that he fitted in 12 appearances for MK Dons.

Darius Vassell. In July 2009 Vassell signed for the Turkish side Ankaragücü. Around 3,000 fans turned out and celebrated his arrival. In November of 2010 he spent the last 18 months of his career at Leicester City.

2010

Robinho (Robson de Souza). The player who started it all. The player who brings back memories of that amazing day in 2008 when the new City was born. Robinho was hardly an overwhelming success, but he paved the way for future signings and proved to be a statement of intent by the new owners. Robinho spent the first half of 2010 on loan at Santos, then joined AC Milan for £15m in the summer, where he has remained. He has played 142 games, scoring 32 goals.

Valeri Bojinov. I really thought the Bulgarian would be our Wayne Rooney (without the hair transplants and grannies), but his time at City was wrecked by injuries, and he has struggled since. He initially went to Parma on loan in the summer of 2009 before signing for them permanently the year after. He was often found on the bench though and has since signed for Sporting Lisbon where he also struggled and has been loaned to the likes of Lecce, Vicenza and Verona. In January this year he signed a six-month contract with Levski Sofia, the first time he has played in his home country professionally. Such a waste of a career.

Benjani. The player that City signed after the transfer window had closed, after the Zimbabwean managed to fall asleep in an airport and miss his flight. Twice. Another uninspiring signing to pass through City, the suspicions should have been aroused when it became clear Harry Redknapp was keen to do a deal, though there could be other reasons for that of course, allegedly. At least he scored THAT shouldered goal in THAT derby, and he had a lovely goal celebration, not that it made any sense.

Loaned to Sunderland in 2010, he joined Blackburn Rovers as a free agent in the summer of 2010. He spent a year there, then a year back at Portsmouth, a few months at Chippa United (nope, me neither) and finally Budvest Wits.

2011

Shay Given. One of my favourite keepers was Shay, making 50 appearances for City. In the summer of 2011 he moved on to Aston Villa, City keen to keep Joe Hart, which meant playing him regularly. The fee is thought to be around £3.5m. In the twilight of his career, Shay was on loan at Middlesbrough for a few months until the end of February, before returning to Villa,

Jo (João Alves de Assis Silva). The man who scored a whopping three goals for City can still be found somehow getting into the Brazil team on occasion. Loan spells at Everton and Galatasaray followed, and he has eventually settled at Atletico Minero, scoring 15 goals in his 49 appearances in Brazil. For his national side he has 5 goals in his 15 appearances. That's 9 more appearances than Fernandinho has.

Felipe Caicedo. Another striker who never really flourished at City, he was let go for a ridiculously cheap price of £880,000 to Levante, who promptly sold him on at huge profit to Lokomotiv Moscow. Typical City. The man from Ecuador made 27 appearances for City, scoring 5 goals.

Has scored 15 goals in 47 appearances for Ecuador.

Jerome Boateng. The one that got away. Nothing really went right for Boateng during his stay in Manchester and he didn't appear to settle, but he may now go on to win a swathe of honours with the best club side in world football. Constantly playing him at right-back probably didn't help. Forms a central defence axis for Bayern Munich with Dante, it's hardly the strongest pairing in the world but then they are often protected rather well.

Craig Bellamy. There's nothing I can tell you about Bellamy that you don't already know. And if you don't know, check out his autobiography. A pain in the arse, Bellamy always gave his all for City, scoring 12 goals in 40 appearances. In August 2010 he joined Cardiff on a season-long loan, his boyhood club. A year later he surprisingly signed for Liverpool on a free transfer, before getting a free transfer back to Cardiff in August 2012. Has since scored just the 5 goals in 46 appearances, but has realised his dream of playing for Cardiff in the top division.

Shaun Wright Phillips. Homecomings inevitably disappoint, but it was good to see the prodigal kid back. With City's wealth and the recognition that Shaun wasn't the player he once was, he was sold to QPR in August 2011, where he has sadly rarely shined since. He has made 68 appearances for the Londoners, but has only scored 2 goals.

2012

Stefan Savic. City's scapegoat for a good year or so, for all the criticism it cannot be that surprising that he has moved on and become an established player elsewhere. Considering his father committed suicide months before he joined City in a £6m deal, you can excuse him for failing to settle. In the end it didn't work out and he was part of a rare swap deal, as part of the deal that brought Nastastic to City in August 2012. All the reports from Fiorentina since have been positive, and he has knocked up 50 appearances and two goals for his new team, and 20 appearances for Montenegro, for whom he is a regular.

Nedum Onuoha. Another of the old academy batch who never quite made it, because to be frank he wasn't quite good enough. A very down-to-earth man who dabbled with athletics as a child, he left City in January 2012 to sign for QPR under Mark Hughes, having previously made 32 appearances for Sunderland on loan. Now he's stuck with Harry Redknapp. Poor lad.

Nigel De Jong. Ah, another recipient of pining City fans, separated from their one true love. I never quite worked out why De Jong left, it seemed to be a pay dispute and not entirely of his own volition, but go he did and left a defensive-midfielder gap that hasn't truly been filled since. History was somewhat re-written after he left however, his influence in the title-winning campaign not significant in terms of appearances, but he was rightly a popular figure at City, especially after the witch hunt that followed the Hatem Ben Arfa tackle.

Adam Johnson. The Ian Curtis lookalike promised much but never quite delivered, which remains the case. Moved to Sunderland in August 2012 for £10m, a fee I was happy with. And there he remains, doing fairly well, but nothing more.

Owen Hargreaves. The less said the better. A huge shame for him though, naturally.

Michael Johnson. Likewise, for different reasons. A short loan period at Leicester City never worked out, and that was that.

2013

Mario Balotelli. Ah Mario. The circus has moved on, to AC Milan, where Mario has continued the normal pattern of life. He left City in the January 2013 transfer window, for a fee though to be around £17m. Sometimes brilliant, sometimes anonymous, often in trouble, nothing will ever change for him. The stats stack up though – 29 goals in 48 appearances for Milan. Why always him?

Carlos (Alberto Martínez) Tevez. The man who was always passing through but left a lasting impression, Tevez is of course at Juventus now and doing precisely what you would expect of him – i.e. pretty damn well. Has secured a third league title with three consecutive clubs, he hasn't done bad for himself, all things considered. City could still do with him some of the time, but he was never the type of player to put down roots and his exit had a certain inevitability about it.

At Juventus he has made 39 appearances so far, with 19 goals.

Roque Santa Cruz. Oh dear oh dear. The biggest flop of them all, signing a crock for big money was always going to end in tears, but boy did Mark Hughes want his man. An unsuccessful goal-less loan spell back at Blackburn and a longer loan to Real Betis was followed by a loan spell then permanent transfer to Malaga, where he has done ok, scoring 17 goals in his 70 appearances.

He's so dreamy though.

Gareth Barry. On loan to Everton, but he's not coming back, realistically. A clear success at the Toffees, leading to recriminations as to why we let him go in the first place but this was a decision made for financial reasons above all else, the owners/board not prepared to pay a backup player £150k a week. Fernandinho's form has softened the blow and you would expect Everton to try and sign Barry permanently in the summer on a free transfer. I'm glad he has done well and I am glad he can't play against us. At least now another set of fans can see his worth.

Emmanuel Adebayor. The man who is of course now plying his trade at Tottenham, with City still apparently contributing towards his weekly wage. Having fallen out with yet another manager in Andre Villas Boas, "Manu" has had something of a resurgence under Tim Sherwood, though we all know it won't last. We'll never forget that goal celebration though.

Maicon. I'll be honest, I got a little excited when we signed this guy. It was based mostly on nostalgia, but I hoped he could still prove his worth. In the end it didn't go too well, not helped by injuries. He made just 13 appearances for City before moving to AS Roma on a free transfer last summer.

Kolo Toure. The man with the same weight problems as the rest of us of course joined Liverpool on a free transfer last summer, as part of City's cull of the wage bill. He has hardly wowed the Liverpool fans in his 20 appearances this season, but could be on the way to a title medal with his third club in England. Though hopefully not.

Wayne Bridge. I'll be honest, at the time I thought Bridge was a brilliant signing. There was even the odd whisper from Chelsea fans that he was better than Ashley Cole. Well that didn't go well. Bridge underwhelmed in his 58 appearances for City, and was loaned out during his time at the club to West Ham, Sunderland and Brighton, before making a permanent move to Reading last summer.

You can purchase the 2011/12 & 2012/13 Season Review Books on Amazon.

Missed Goals: Manchester City 2012/13 Season Review

"He did very good things for the club. He stayed there for three years, which is a lot of time. He brought the club to a winning club. Now we are just looking for the next step, the next cycle."

And so another chapter in Manchester City's history came to an end, and another begins. The 2012/13 season was a major disappointment for City, beginning with a second early elimination in Europe, then continuing with the failure to retain their Premiership title, won in such dramatic circumstances in May 2012. By the end of the season, Roberto Mancini's fate was sealed by an FA Cup final defeat to Wigan Athletic, though victory would not have saved a manager known to have lost the support of players, staff and the owners alike.

This book tells the story of another dramatic season for the Citizens, not through match reports alone, but mainly through the stories that shaped the season, from player revolts, Mario Balotelli's antics, through to the media coverage and constant headlines away from the pitch.

Bonus features: Book Reviews, Q & A session with senior football journalists, plus reports on the campaign for cheaper tickets and much, much more.

This Is How It Felt To Be City: Manchester City 2011/12 Season Review

"The thing about obituaries is that it's better to publish them after the subject has died..."

The 2011/12 English Premier League football season provided one of the most thrilling climaxes to a title race in the history of the game. For Manchester City, Sergio Aguero's injury-time winner capped off a roller-coaster season for the club, that culminated in their first top-level title in 44 years. Through the articles written by the author throughout the year, as the club moved from one controversy to another, you can relive the most amazing of seasons, from drug bans, to player strikes, from Derby day drubbings to the key moment in premiership history - there was rarely a dull moment.

Howard Hockin

6846941R00207

Printed in Great Britain
by Amazon.co.uk, Ltd.,
Marston Gate.